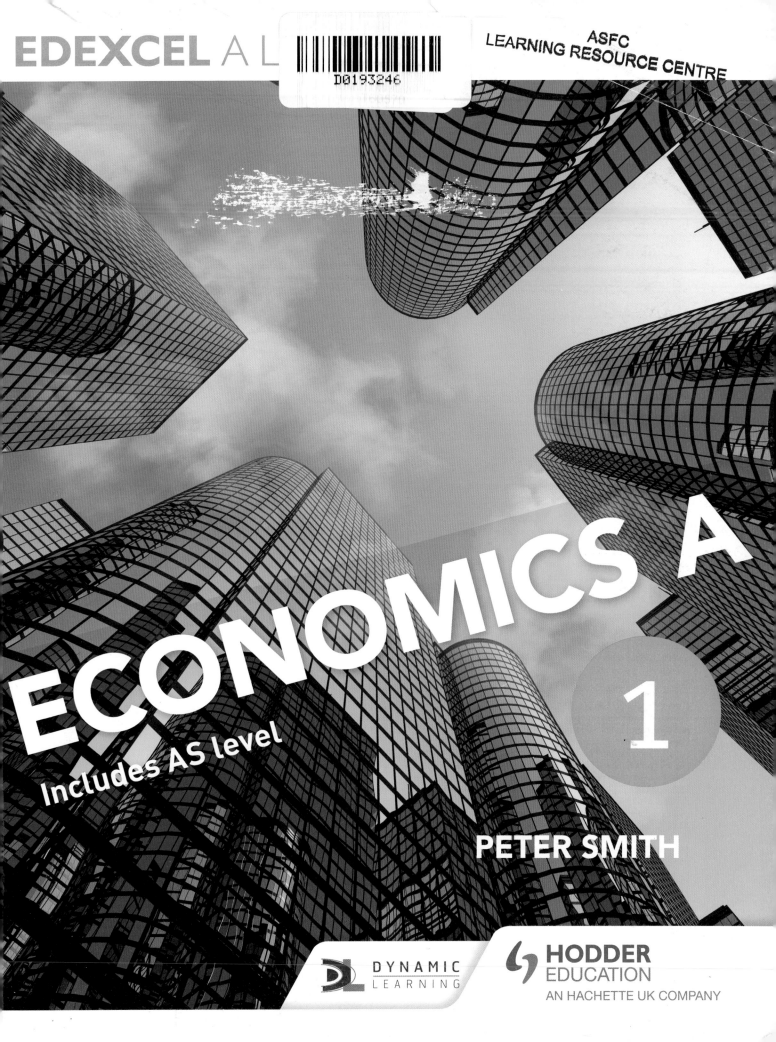

EDEXCEL A L

ECONOMICS A

Includes AS level

1

PETER SMITH

DYNAMIC LEARNING

HODDER
EDUCATION
AN HACHETTE UK COMPANY

Hodder Education, an Hachette UK company, 338 Euston Road, London NW1 3BH

Orders

Bookpoint Ltd, 130 Milton Park, Abingdon, Oxfordshire OX14 4SB
tel: 01235 827827
fax: 01235 400401
e-mail: education@bookpoint.co.uk
Lines are open 9.00 a.m.–5.00 p.m., Monday to Saturday, with a 24-hour message answering
service. You can also order through the Hodder Education website: www.hoddereducation.co.uk

ISBN 978-1-4718-3000-6

Impression number		5	4	3	2	1
Year		2019	2018	2017	2016	2015

In order to ensure that this resource offers high-quality support for the associated Edexcel
qualification, it has been through a review process by the awarding body to confirm that it fully
covers the teaching and learning content of the specification or part of a specification at which
it is aimed, and demonstrates an appropriate balance between the development of subject skills,
knowledge and understanding, in addition to preparation for assessment.

While the publishers have made every attempt to ensure that advice on the qualification and
its assessment is accurate, the official specification and associated assessment guidance materials
are the only authoritative source of information and should always be referred to for definitive
guidance.

Edexcel examiners have not contributed to any sections in this resource relevant to examination
papers for which they have responsibility.

No material from an endorsed resource will be used verbatim in any assessment set by Edexcel.

Endorsement of a resource does not mean that the resource is required to achieve this Edexcel
qualification, nor does it mean that it is the only suitable material available to support the
qualification, and any resource lists produced by the awarding body shall include this and other
appropriate resources.

The publishers would like to thank the following for permission to reproduce photographs:

Cover 3dmentat/Fotolia; **p3** Christopher Dodge/Fotolia; **p6** Fototrm12/Fotolia; **p12** DPA
Picture Alliance/Alamy; **p16** Renate W/Fotolia; **p18** PhotoEdit/Alamy; **p21** KC Hunter/Alamy;
p25 Glowonconcept/Fotolia; **p29** Anjelagr/Fotolia; **p38** Gyula Gyukli/Fotolia; **p42** Costin79/
Fotolia; **p47** DPA Picture Alliance /Alamy; **p48** Antje Lindert-Rottke/Fotolia; **p52** British
Retail Photography/Alamy; **p57** TopFoto; **p60** TopFoto; **p62** Ingram; **p66** Galina Barskaya/
Fotolia; **p69** Kingan/Fotolia; **p74** Sean Gladwell/Fotolia; **p77** Dmitry Naumov/Fotolia;
p80 Riccardo Arata/Fotolia; **p82** BE&W Agencja Fotograficzna Sp. z o.o./Alamy; **p87** David
Pearson/Alamy; **p90** Monkey Business/Fotolia; **p96** JEP News/Alamy; **p100** Pressmaster/
Fotolia; **p102** Nabok Volodymyr/Fotolia; **p114** 06photo/Fotolia; **p120** NLPhotos/Fotolia;
p126 ImageBroker/Alamy; **p129** Keith Morris/Alamy; **p135** Geoffrey Robinson/Alamy;
p139 Agencja Fotograficzna Caro/Alamy; **p145** TopFoto; **p148** RAM/Fotolia; **p153**
think4aphotop/Fotolia; **p157** LianeM/Fotolia; **p163** 67photo/Alamy; **p166** Justin Kase Zninez/
Alamy; **p176** Jake Lyell/Alamy; **p181** Olli Geibel/Alamy; **p184** Robert Stainforth/Alamy;
p187 Desmond Kwande/Stringer; **p192** Bjanka Kadic/Alamy; **p200** Nathan King/Alamy;
p206 AFP/Pool; **p209** Christopher Furlong/Getty

Typeset by Integra Software Services Pvt., Pondicherry, India.
Printed in Italy.

Hachette UK's policy is to use papers that are natural, renewable and recyclable products and
made from wood grown in sustainable forests. The logging and manufacturing processes are
expected to conform to the environmental regulations of the country of origin.

Get the most from this book

This textbook provides an introduction to economics. It has been tailored explicitly to cover the content of the Edexcel specification for AS Economics A and for the first year of the A level course. The book is divided into two parts, each covering one of the themes that make up the Edexcel programme of study.

The text provides the foundation for studying Edexcel Economics A, but you will no doubt wish to keep up to date by referring to additional topical sources of information about economic events. You can do this by reading the serious newspapers, visiting key sites on the internet, and reading such magazines as *Economic Review*.

Special features

Learning objectives
A statement of the intended learning objectives for each chapter.

Key terms
Clear, concise definitions of essential key terms where they first appear and a list at the end of each theme.

Quantitative skills
Worked examples of quantitative skills that you will need to develop.

Extension material
Extension points to stretch your understanding.

Study tips
Short pieces of advice to help you present your ideas effectively and avoid potential pitfalls.

Exercises and practice questions
Exercises to provide active engagement with economic analysis and practice questions at the end of each theme to help you check your knowledge and understanding.

Summaries
Bulleted summaries of each topic that can be used as a revision tool.

Case studies
Case studies to show economic concepts applied to real-world situations.

Contents

Theme 2 The UK economy — performance and policies

Introduction

Prior learning, knowledge and progression

Most students who choose to study AS or A level Economics are meeting economics for the first time, and no prior learning or knowledge of economics is required. The study of economics complements a range of other AS and A level subjects, such as history, geography, business, mathematics and the sciences, and the way of thinking that you will develop as you study economics will help in interpreting issues that you will meet in many of these subjects. Studying economics can provide important employability skills and is a good preparation for those wishing to progress to higher education. If you intend to study economics at university, you may wish to consider studying mathematics as one of your other AS or A level subjects.

Assessment objectives

In common with other economics specifications, Edexcel Economics A entails four assessment objectives. Candidates will therefore be expected to:

- demonstrate knowledge of terms/concepts and theories/models to show an understanding of the behaviour of economic agents and how they are affected by and respond to economic issues
- apply knowledge and understanding to various economic contexts to show how economic agents are affected by and respond to economic issues
- analyse issues within economics, showing an understanding of their impact on economic agents
- evaluate economic arguments and use qualitative and quantitative evidence to support informed judgements relating to economic issues

In the assessment of AS, a greater weighting is given to the first two objectives; in the overall A level, a greater weighting is given to the second two.

Quantitative skills

The assessment of quantitative skills will constitute a minimum of 15% of the overall marks for AS, and 20% for the overall A level award. The skills to be assessed are listed in Appendix 3 of the respective AS and A level specifications on the Edexcel website (see **www.edexcel.com**).

The structure of assessment

AS

The AS in Economics A is assessed by two examinations, one in microeconomics and one in macroeconomics. Each is a written paper lasting 1½ hours, in two sections. Section A is made up of a range of multiple-choice and short-answer questions. Section B contains one data-response question broken down into a number of parts, including a choice of extended open-choice questions. Further details are provided on the Edexcel website.

A level

The A level in Economics A assessment is based on three examinations, one in microeconomics, one in macroeconomics and one synoptic paper. Each written paper lasts 2 hours. The first two papers have three sections. Section A is made up of multiple-choice and short-answer questions. Section B contains one data-response question broken down into a number of parts. Section C has a choice of extended open-response questions — students select one from a choice of two. The synoptic paper consists of two sections. Each section has a data-response question broken down into a number of parts, including a choice of extended open-response questions — students choose one out of two. Further details are provided in the specification, which can be found on the Edexcel website.

Economics in this book

Economics is different from some other subjects in that relatively few students will have studied it before embarking on the AS or A level course. The text therefore begins from the beginning, and provides a thorough foundation in the subject and its applications. By studying this book, you should develop an awareness of the economist's approach to issues and problems, and the economist's way of thinking about the world.

The study of economics also requires a familiarity with recent economic events in the UK and elsewhere, and candidates will be expected to show familiarity with 'recent historical data' — broadly defined as covering the last 7 to 10 years. The following websites will help you to keep up to date with recent trends and events:

- Recent and historical data about the UK economy can be found at the website of the Office for National Statistics (ONS) at: **www.statistics.gov.uk**
- Also helpful is the site of HM Treasury at: **www.hm-treasury.gov.uk**. Especially useful is the Treasury's *Pocket Databank*, which is updated weekly, providing major economic indicators and series for both domestic and international economies: **www.gov.uk/government/statistics/weekly-economic-indicators**
- The Bank of England site is well worth a visit, especially the *Inflation Report* and the Minutes of the Monetary Policy Committee: **www.bankofengland.co.uk**
- The Institute for Fiscal Studies offers an independent view of a range of economic topics: **www.ifs.org.uk**

For information about other countries, visit the following:

- **www.oecd.org**
- **http://europa.eu**
- **www.worldbank.org**
- **www.undp.org**

How to study economics

There are two crucial aspects of studying economics. The first stage is to study the theory, which helps us to explain economic behaviour. However, in studying AS or A level Economics it is equally important to be able to apply the theories and concepts that you meet, and to see just how these relate to the real world.

If you are to become competent at this, it is vital that you get plenty of practice. In part, this means doing the exercises included in this book. However, it also means thinking about how economics helps us to explain news items and data that appear in the newspapers and on the television. Make sure that you practise as much as you can.

In economics, it is important to be able to produce examples of economic phenomena. You will find some examples in this book that help to illustrate ideas and concepts. Do not rely solely on the examples provided here, but be aware of what is going on in the world and find your own examples. Keep a note of these ready for use in essays and exams. This will help to convince the examiners that you have understood economics. It will also help you to understand the theories.

Enjoy economics

Most important of all, I hope that you will enjoy your study of economics. I have always been fascinated by the subject and hope that you will capture something of the excitement and challenge of learning about how markets and the economy operate. I wish you every success with your studies.

Acknowledgements

I would like to express my deep gratitude to Russell Dudley-Smith and Marwan Mikdadi for their careful reading of earlier editions of this book. I would also like to thank the team at Hodder Education, especially Naomi Holdstock, Rachel Furse and Chris Bessant for their efficiency in the production of this book, and also for their support and encouragement.

Many of the data series shown in figures in this book were drawn from the National Statistics website **www.statistics.gov.uk** and contain public sector information licensed under the Open Government Licence v3.0.

Other data were from various sources, including OECD, World Bank, United Nations Development Programme and elsewhere as specified.

While every effort has been made to trace the owners of copyright material, I would like to apologise to any copyright holders whose rights may have unwittingly been infringed.

Peter Smith

THEME 1

INTRODUCTION TO MARKETS AND MARKET FAILURE

The nature of economics

Welcome to economics. Many of you opening this book will be meeting economics for the first time, and you will want to know what is in store for you as you set out to study the subject. This opening chapter sets the scene by introducing you to some key ideas and identifying the scope of economic analysis. As you learn more of the subject, you will find that economics is a way of thinking that broadens your perspective on the world around you.

Learning objectives

This chapter will introduce you to:
→ the nature and scope of economic analysis
→ the role of models and assumptions in economics
→ positive and normative statements
→ the importance of scarcity and choice
→ the concept of opportunity cost
→ the notion of factors of production
→ the distinction between renewable and non-renewable resources and the idea of sustainability
→ the production possibility frontier
→ the concept of the division of labour
→ how specialisation can improve productivity
→ the role of markets and what is meant by a mixed economy
→ alternative ways of coordinating the allocation of resources in society
→ the distinction between microeconomics and macroeconomics

Models and assumptions

Economics sets out to tackle some complex issues concerning what is a very complex real world. In many of the sciences, investigation can proceed by carrying out experiments, testing hypotheses in the laboratory. Experimental economics is a rapidly expanding area in the subject, but although this allows economists to improve their understanding of individual behaviour, there are still many areas of economics where it is not possible to rely on experiments to advance knowledge. An alternative approach is therefore needed.

If economists are to cope with the complexity of the real world, it is essential to simplify reality in some way; otherwise the task would be overwhelming. Economists thus work with **models**. These are simplified versions of reality that are more manageable for analysis, allowing economists to focus on some key aspects of the world.

Key term

model a simplified representation of reality used to provide insight into economic decisions and events

Often this works by allowing them to focus on one thing at a time. A model almost always begins with assumptions that help economists to simplify their questions. These assumptions can then be gradually relaxed so that the effect of each one of them can be observed. In this way, economists can gradually move towards a more complicated version of reality.

Chapter 2 will consider the demand for a good, and the factors that affect how much of a good is demanded by consumers. Trying to analyse all the possible influences on these decisions would be difficult, so it is common to start by exploring how the price of a good affects the quantity demanded, under the assumption that all other influences stay the same. This is a common assumption in economics, which is sometimes expressed by the Latin phrase **ceteris paribus**, meaning 'other things being equal'. Given the complexity of the real world, it is often helpful to focus on one thing at a time.

To evaluate a model, it is not necessary that it be totally realistic. The model's desired objective may help in predicting future behaviour, or in testing empirical evidence collected from the real world. If a model provides insights into how individuals take decisions, or helps to explain economic events, then it has some value, even if it seems remote from reality.

However, it is always important to examine the assumptions that are made, and to ask what happens if these assumptions do not hold.

Positive and normative statements

Economics tries to be objective in analysis. However, some of its subject matter requires careful attention in order to retain an objective distance. In this connection, it is important to be clear about the difference between **positive** and **normative statements**.

In short, a positive statement is about *facts* and in principle is testable. A normative statement is about *what ought to be*. Another way of looking at this is that a statement becomes normative when it involves a *value judgement*.

Suppose the government is considering raising the tax on cigarettes. It may legitimately consult economists to discover what effect a higher tobacco tax will have on the consumption of cigarettes and on government revenues. This would be a *positive* investigation, in that the economists are being asked to use economic analysis to forecast what will happen when the tax is increased.

A very different situation will arise if the government asks whether it *should* raise the tax on cigarettes. This moves the economists beyond positive analysis, because it entails a value judgement — so it is now a *normative* analysis. There are some words that betray normative statements, such as 'should' or 'ought to' — watch for these.

Most of this book is about positive economics. However, you should be aware that positive analysis is often called upon to inform normative judgements. If the aim of a policy is to stop people from smoking (which reflects a normative judgement about what *ought* to happen), then economic analysis may be used to highlight the strengths and weaknesses of those alternatives in a purely positive fashion.

Critics of economics often joke that economists always disagree with one another: for example, it has been said that if you put five economists in a room together, they will come up with at least six conflicting opinions. However, although economists

Key terms

ceteris paribus a Latin phrase meaning 'other things being equal'; it is used in economics when we focus on changes in one variable while holding other influences constant

positive statement a statement about what is (i.e. about facts)

normative statement a statement that involves a value judgement about what *ought to be*

Increasing taxes on tobacco affects consumption of cigarettes and government revenue

may arrive at different value judgements, and thus have differences when it comes to normative issues, there is much greater agreement when it comes to positive analysis. Nonetheless, value judgements do influence economic decision making and policy because different people — and political parties — may have different views about what is desirable for society, even if they agree on how policies may work.

The fundamental economic problem

For any society in the world, the fundamental economic problem faced is that of **scarcity**. You might think that this is obvious for some societies in the less developed world, where poverty and hunger are rife. But it is also true for relatively prosperous economies such as those of Switzerland, the USA and the UK.

It is true in the sense that all societies have *finite resources*, but people have unlimited wants. A big claim? Not really. There is no country in the world in which all wants can be met, and this is clearly true at the global level.

There are some goods that may be regarded as *free goods*. An example might be the earth's atmosphere, which would not normally be regarded as scarce. Goods that are scarce are known as *economic goods*. Most goods fall into this category.

Talking about scarcity in this sense is not the same as talking about *poverty*. Poverty might be seen as an extreme form of scarcity, in which individuals lack the basic necessities of life; whereas even relatively prosperous people face scarcity, because resources are limited.

Scarcity and choice

The key issue that arises from the existence of scarcity is that it forces people to make choices. Each individual must choose which goods and services to consume. In other words, everyone needs to prioritise the consumption of whatever commodities they need or would like to have, as they cannot satisfy all their wants. Similarly, at the national level, governments have to make choices between alternative uses of resources.

It is this need to choose that underlies the subject matter of economics. Economic analysis is all about analysing those choices made by individual people, firms and governments.

Opportunity cost

This raises one of the most important concepts in all of economic analysis — the notion of **opportunity cost**. When an individual chooses to consume one good, she does so at the cost of the item that would have been next in her list of priorities. For example, suppose you are on a strict diet, and at the end of the day you can 'afford' either one chocolate or a piece of cheese. If you choose the cheese, the opportunity cost of the cheese is the chocolate that you could have had instead.

This important notion can be applied in many different contexts, because whenever you make a decision you reject an alternative in favour of your chosen option. You have chosen to read this book — when instead you could be watching television or meeting friends.

The notion of opportunity cost is related to an important tool in economics known as **marginal analysis**. This is based on the idea that people take decisions by considering changes that could be made. For example, in choosing whether to read this book, you may consider if the extra (marginal) benefit you will receive from doing so will exceed the additional benefit you would receive from watching television. Firms may also take decisions in this way, perhaps by checking whether the cost of producing and selling an additional unit of output will exceed the extra (marginal) return they receive from selling it. This approach will become familiar to you as you continue to study economics.

As you move further into studying economics, you will encounter this notion of opportunity cost again and again. For example, firms take decisions about the sort of economic activity in which to engage. A market gardener has to decide whether to plant onions or potatoes; if he decides to grow onions, he has to forgo the opportunity to grow potatoes. From the government's point of view, if it decides to devote more resources to the National Health Service, then it will have fewer resources available for, say, defence. The need to balance the relative merits of alternative choices is challenging, but crucial. Economic analysis helps to explain how such choices are made, and how they could be improved.

Study tip

Opportunity cost is a key concept in economics, and will be important in a variety of contexts. Similarly, marginal analysis is a key part of economic thinking, so make sure that you understand these fully from the outset.

Economic agents

In analysing the process by which choices are made, it is important to be aware of the various economic agents that are responsible for making decisions. In economic analysis, there are three key groups of decision makers: households, firms and government.

- *Households* (and individuals) make choices about their expenditure. In this role, they are consumers who demand goods and services. In order to be able to buy goods, households need income, so they also take decisions about the supply of their labour, which will be discussed in the next section.
- *Firms* exist in order to produce output of goods or services. Firms also make choices, particularly about which goods or services to produce, and the techniques of production to be used. The prices at which they can sell are also important in economic analysis.
- *Government* fulfils several roles in society. It undertakes expenditure, and influences the economy through its taxation and regulation of markets.

Opportunity cost is crucial for each of these economic agents, because they each face constraints on their choices. As soon as they choose one course of action, they forgo the possibility of taking an alternative decision.

Exercise 1.1

Andrew has just started his AS, and has chosen to take economics, mathematics, geography and French. Although he was certain about the first three, it was a close call between French and English. What is Andrew's opportunity cost of choosing French?

Factors of production

People in a society play two quite different roles. On the one hand, they are the consumers, the ultimate beneficiaries of the process of production. On the other, they are a key part of the production process in that they are instrumental in producing goods and services.

More generally, it is clear that both *human resources* and *physical resources* are required as part of the production process. These productive resources are known as the **factors of production**.

The most obvious human resource is labour. Labour is a key input into production. Of course, there are many different types of labour, encompassing different skill

Key term

factors of production resources used in the production process; inputs into production, particularly including labour, capital, land and entrepreneurship

levels and working in different ways. *Entrepreneurship* is another key human resource. An entrepreneur is someone who organises production and identifies projects to be undertaken, often bearing the risk of the activity. *Management* might also be classified as a key human resource. *Natural resources* are also inputs into the production process. In particular, all economic activities require some use of land, and most use some raw materials.

There are also *produced resources* — inputs that are the product of a manufacturing process. For example, machines are used in the production process; they are resources manufactured for the purpose of producing other goods. These inputs are referred to as capital, which may include things like factory buildings and transport equipment as well as plant and machinery.

The way in which these inputs are combined in order to produce output is another key part of the allocation of resources. Firms need to take decisions about the mix of inputs used in order to produce their output. Such decisions are required in whatever form of economic activity a firm is engaged.

Renewable and non-renewable resources

An important distinction is between **renewable resources** such as forests, and **non-renewable resources** such as oil or coal.

In the case of renewable resources, there have been many debates in recent years about the dangers of depleting such resources at too rapid a rate to allow replacement. One example of this has been the stocks of some fish such as cod, where it has been

Key terms

renewable resources
natural resources that can be replenished, such as forests that can be replanted, or solar energy that does not get used up

non-renewable resources
natural resources that once used cannot be replenished, such as coal or oil

Factors of production — labour (workers), capital (buildings) and land

argued that overfishing may lead to the extinction of the species. Similar arguments have been applied to other resources such as the rainforests. This has highlighted the importance of sustainable development, which has been defined as 'development which meets the needs of the present without compromising the ability of future generations to meet their own needs' (Brundtland Commission, 1987). Applying this to the case of cod fishing, for example, sustainable fishing would be seen in terms of not catching so many cod that the overall population becomes unsustainable.

For non-renewable resources, reserves are finite — by definition — so concern has arisen over their possible exhaustion. Attention has tended to focus on oil, which is much in demand, especially given rapidly rising car ownership. This has led to a search for renewable sources of energy, which would also contribute to sustainability. One economic issue here is whether the prices of resources such as oil will rise as reserves are depleted. This could then have the effect of giving incentives to firms to develop alternative sources of energy. It could also mean that some reserves of oil that are currently uneconomic may become viable. This is one example of how prices can be seen to guide resource allocation.

Exercise 1.2

Classify each of the following as human, natural (renewable or non-renewable) or produced resources:

a timber

b services of a window cleaner

c natural gas

d solar energy

e a combine harvester

f a computer programmer who sets up a company to market his software

g a computer

By now you should be getting some idea of the subject matter of economics. The American economist Paul Samuelson (who won the Nobel Prize for Economic Sciences in 1970) identified three key questions that economics sets out to investigate:

1 *What?* What goods and services should be produced in a society from its scarce resources? In other words, how should resources be allocated among producing Blu-ray players, potatoes, banking services and so on?

2 *How?* How should the productive resources of the economy be used to produce these various goods and services?

3 *For whom?* Having produced a range of goods and services, how should these be allocated among the population for consumption?

Exercise 1.3

With which of Samuelson's three questions (what, how, for whom) would you associate the following?

a A firm chooses to switch from producing DVDs in order to increase its output of Blu-ray discs.

b The government reduces the highest rate of income tax.

c Faced with increased labour costs, a firm introduces labour-saving machinery.

d There is an increase in social security benefits.

e The owner of a fish-and-chip shop decides to close down and take a job in a local factory.

Summary

- Positive statements are about what is, whereas normative statements are about what ought to be.
- The fundamental problem faced by any society is scarcity, because resources are finite but wants are unlimited. As a result, choices need to be made.
- Each choice has an opportunity cost — the value of the next-best alternative forgone.
- Decisions need to be coordinated within a society, either by market forces or by state intervention, or by a mixture of the two.
- The amount of output produced in a period depends on the inputs of factors of production.
- The rate at which renewable resources are used needs to be seen in the light of the notion of sustainability.
- Economics deals with the questions of what should be produced, how it should be produced, and for whom.

The production possibility frontier

Key term

production possibility frontier (PPF) a curve showing the maximum combinations of goods or services that can be produced in a given period with available resources

Economists rely heavily on diagrams to help in their analysis. In exploring the notion of opportunity cost, a helpful diagram is the **production possibility frontier (PPF)**. This shows the maximum combinations of goods that can be produced with a given set of resources.

First consider a simple example. In an earlier exercise, Andrew was studying for his AS. Suppose now that he has got behind with his homework. He has limited time available, and has five economics questions to answer and five maths exercises. An economics question takes the same time to answer as a maths exercise.

Quantitative skills 1.1

Drawing and interpreting graphs

An important quantitative skill is to be able to draw and interpret graphs. The diagram showing the production possibility frontier is a good example to introduce this skill.

Figure 1.1 shows the options that Andrew faces. He can devote all of his efforts to maths, and leave the economics for another day. He will then be at point *A* in the figure, choosing to do 5 maths exercises (which you read off as the value on the vertical axis), but no economics exercises (reading zero on the horizontal axis).

Alternatively, he can do all the economics exercises and no maths, and be at point *B*. The line joining these two extreme points shows the intermediate possibilities. For example, at *C* he does 2 economics exercises and 3 maths problems — again you read off the values from the two axes.

The line shows the maximum combinations that Andrew can tackle — which is why it is sometimes called a 'frontier'. There is no way he can manage to be beyond the frontier (for example, at point *D*), as to do 3 maths exercises and 4 economics ones would need more time than he has available. However,

he could end up inside the frontier, at a point such as *E*. This could happen if he gives up, and squanders his time by watching television; that would be an inefficient use of his resources — at least in terms of tackling his homework.

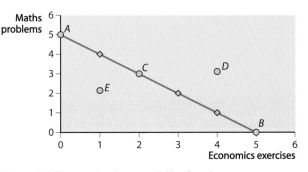

Figure 1.1 The production possibility frontier

As Andrew moves down the line from left to right, he is spending more time on economics and less on maths. The opportunity cost of tackling an additional economics question is an additional maths exercise forgone. One way of expressing this is that Andrew faces a trade-off between the time spent on economics and on maths.

What are the options? Suppose he knows that in the time available he can tackle either all of the maths and none of the economics, or all of the economics and none of the maths. Alternatively, he can try to keep both teachers happy by doing some of each.

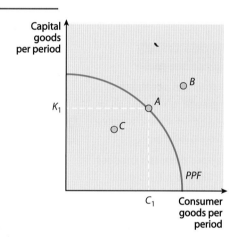

Figure 1.2 shows how the *PPF* provides information about opportunity cost. Suppose we have a farmer with 10 hectares of land who is choosing between growing potatoes and onions. The *PPF* shows the combinations of the two crops that could be produced. For example, if the farmer produces 300 tonnes of onions on part of the land, then 180 tonnes of potatoes could be produced from the remaining land. In order to increase production of potatoes by 70 tonnes from 180 to 250, 50 tonnes of onions must be given up. Thus, the opportunity cost of 70 extra tonnes of potatoes is seen to be 50 tonnes of onions.

Figure 1.2 Opportunity cost and the PPF

Consumption and investment

To move from thinking about an individual to thinking about an economy as a whole, it is first necessary to simplify reality. Assume an economy that produces just two types of good: capital goods and consumer goods. Consumer goods are for present use, whereas the capital goods are to be used to increase the future capacity of the economy — in other words, for investment.

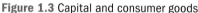

Figure 1.3 illustrates society's options in a particular period. Given the resources available, society can produce any combination of capital and consumer goods along the *PPF* line. Thus, point A represents one possible combination of outputs, in which the economy produces C_1 consumer goods and K_1 capital goods. (Economists often use K to denote capital — because they normally use C to denote consumption.)

Figure 1.3 Capital and consumer goods

As with the simpler example, if society were to move to the right along the *PPF*, it would produce more consumer goods — but at the expense of capital goods. Thus, it can be seen that the opportunity cost of producing consumer goods is forgone opportunities to produce capital goods. Notice that this time the *PPF* has been drawn as a curve instead of a straight line. This is because not all factors of production are equally suited to the production of both sorts of good. When the economy is well balanced, as at A, the factors can be allocated to the uses for which they are best equipped. However, as the economy moves towards complete specialisation in one of the types of good, factors are no longer being best used, and the opportunity cost changes. For example, if nearly all of the workers are engaged in producing consumer goods, it becomes more difficult to produce still more of these, whereas those workers producing machinery find they have too few resources with which to work. In other words, the more consumer goods are being produced, the higher is their opportunity cost.

It is now possible to interpret points B and C. Point B is unobtainable given present resources, so the economy cannot produce that combination of goods. This applies to any point outside the *PPF*. On the other hand, at point C society is not using its resources efficiently. In this position there is *unemployment* of some resources in the economy. By making better use of the resources available, the economy can move towards the frontier, reducing unemployment in the process. However, at any point on the frontier, production is undertaken efficiently in the sense that all resources are being fully utilised.

Economic growth or decline

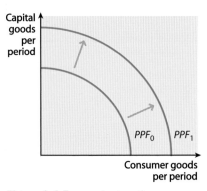

Figure 1.4 Economic growth

Figure 1.3 focused on a single period. However, if the economy is producing capital goods, then in the following period its capacity to produce should increase, as it will have more resources available for production. How can this be shown on the diagram? An expansion in the available inputs suggests that in the next period the economy should be able to produce more of both goods. This is shown in Figure 1.4.

In the initial period the production possibility frontier is at PPF_0. However, in the following period the increased availability of resources enables greater production, and the frontier moves to PPF_1. This is a process of **potential economic growth**, an expansion of the economy's productive capacity through the increased availability of inputs. If the economy were to go into decline, such that less output could be produced, the frontier would shift inwards.

Notice that the decision to produce more capital goods today means that fewer consumer goods will be produced today. People must choose between 'more jam today' or 'more jam tomorrow'.

Key terms

potential economic growth an expansion in the productive capacity of the economy

gross domestic product (GDP) a measure of the economic activity carried out in an economy over a period

Total output in an economy

Remember that the *PPF* is a model: a much simplified version of reality. In a real economy, many different goods and services are produced by a wide range of different factors of production — but it is not possible to draw diagrams to show all of them.

The total output of an economy like the UK is measured by its **gross domestic product (GDP)**.

By calculating the *average* level of GDP per person in a country, it is possible to derive a measure of the average amount of resources per person — or average income per head.

Summary

- The production possibility frontier shows the maximum combinations of goods or services that can be produced in a period by a given set of resources.
- At any point on the frontier, society is making full use of all resources.
- At any point inside the frontier, there is unemployment of some resources.
- Points beyond the frontier are unobtainable.
- In a simple society producing two goods (consumer goods and capital goods), the choice is between consumption and investment for the future.
- As society increases its stock of capital goods, the productive capacity of the economy increases, and the production possibility frontier moves outwards: this may be termed 'economic growth'.

Megan has been cast away on a desert island, and has to survive by spending her time either fishing or climbing trees to get coconuts. The *PPF* in Figure 1.5 shows the maximum combinations of fish and coconuts that she can gather during a day. Which of the points *A* to *E* represents each of the following?

a a situation where Megan spends all her time fishing

b an unobtainable position

c a day when Megan goes for a balanced diet — a mixture of coconuts and fish

d a day when Megan does not fancy fish, and spends all day collecting coconuts

e a day when Megan spends some of the time trying to attract the attention of a passing ship

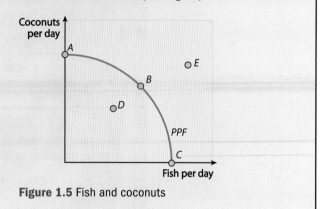

Figure 1.5 Fish and coconuts

Specialisation

How many workers does it take to make a pin? The eighteenth-century economist Adam Smith figured that 10 was about the right number. He argued that when a worker was producing pins on his own, carrying out all the various stages involved in the production process, the maximum number of pins that could be produced in one day was 20 — given the technology of his day, of course. This would imply that 10 workers could produce about 200 pins if they worked in the same way as the lone worker. However, if the pin production process were broken into 10 separate stages, with one worker specialising in each stage, the maximum production for a day's work would be a staggering 48,000. This is known as **division of labour**.

The division of labour is effective because individual workers become skilled at performing specialised tasks. By focusing on a particular stage, they can become highly adept, and thus more efficient, at carrying out that task. In any case, people are not all the same, so some are better at certain activities. Furthermore, this specialisation is more efficient because workers do not spend time moving from one activity to another. Specialisation may also enable firms to operate on a larger scale of production. You will see later that this may be advantageous.

This can be seen in practice in many businesses today, where there is considerable specialisation of functions. Workers are hired for particular tasks and activities. You do not see Wayne Rooney pulling on the goalkeeper's jersey at half time because he fancies a change. Earlier in the chapter, it was argued that 'labour' is considered a factor of production. This idea can be developed further by arguing that there are different types of labour, having different skills and functions.

Specialisation therefore means that workers can focus on the tasks that they perform well and hence become more productive. Training can be provided more cost-effectively when it can be focused on specific tasks that workers need to perform. Furthermore, working as a team allows more overall output to be produced. However, it is possible to take specialisation too far. A worker who spends all his time on a narrow and repetitive task may find that it becomes tedious or that he becomes bored and careless. Over-specialisation may also mean that a team of workers becomes inflexible: if a worker specialising in a key part of the production process becomes ill, it may be difficult to find cover.

Key term

division of labour
a process whereby the production procedure is broken down into a sequence of stages, and workers are assigned to a particular stage

Employees at a car factory. Each worker specialises in a particular task, creating an efficient assembly line

Although we refer to the division of labour, we can extend these arguments to consider specialisation among firms. For example, consider car manufacturing. The process of mass producing cars does not all take place within a single firm. One firm may specialise in producing tyres; another may produce windscreens; another may focus on assembling the final product. Here again, specialisation enables efficiency gains to be made.

Specialisation also takes place among nations, simply because some countries are better equipped to produce some products than others. For example, it would not make sense for the UK to go into commercial production of pineapples or mangoes. There are other countries with climatic conditions that are much more suitable for producing these products. On the other hand, most Formula 1 racing teams have their headquarters in the UK, and there are benefits from this specialisation.

Summary

- Adam Smith introduced the notion of division of labour.
- This suggests that workers can become more productive by specialising in stages of the production process.
- This enables more output to be produced.
- There may be limits to specialisation, as performing repetitive tasks may become tedious and induce errors.

Key term

market a set of arrangements that allows transactions to take place

Markets

You will find that in economics the term **market** is used frequently, so it is important to be absolutely clear about what is meant by it.

A market need not be a physical location (although it could be — you might regard the local farmers' market as an example of 'a set of arrangements that allows transactions to take place'). With the growth of the internet, everyone is becoming accustomed to ways of buying and selling that do not involve direct physical contact between buyer and seller, so the notion of an abstract market should not be too alien a concept.

In relation to a particular product, a market brings together potential buyers and sellers. This will be explored in the coming chapters.

Markets are important in the process of resource allocation, with prices acting as a key signal to potential buyers and sellers. If a firm finds that it cannot sell its output at the price it has chosen, this is a signal about the way that buyers perceive the product. Price is one way that firms find out about consumers and their willingness to pay for a particular product. This will be explored more carefully in Chapter 5.

Money and exchange

Imagine a world without money. It is lunchtime, and you fancy a banana. In your bag you have an apple. Perhaps you can find someone with a banana who fancies an apple? But the only person with a banana available fancies an ice cream. The problem with such a *barter economy* is that you need to find someone who wants what you have and who has what you want — a *double coincidence of wants*. If this problem were to be faced by a whole economic system, undertaking transactions would be so inefficient as to be impossible. Hence the importance of *money* as a *medium of exchange*.

In order to fulfil this role, money must be something that is acceptable to both buyers and sellers. Nobody would accept money in payment for goods or services if they did not trust that they could proceed to use money for further transactions. Money must thus also act as a *store of value*: it must be possible to use it for future transactions. This quality of money means that it can be used as one way of storing wealth for future purchases.

Money also allows the value of goods, services and other assets to be compared — it provides a *unit of account*. In this sense, prices of goods reflect the value that society places on them, and must be expressed in money terms. So money is also a *measure of value*.

A further role for money is that it acts as a *standard of deferred payment*. For example, a firm may wish to agree a contract for the future delivery of a good, or may wish to hire a worker to be paid at the end of the month. Such contracts are typically agreed in terms of a money value.

All of these *functions of money* are important to the smooth operation of markets, and are crucial if prices are to fulfil their role in allocating resources within society. This will become apparent as you learn more about economics.

The coordination problem

With so many different individuals and organisations (consumers, firms, governments) all taking decisions, a major question is how it all comes together. How are all these separate decisions coordinated so that the overall allocation of resources in a society is coherent? In other words, how can it be ensured that firms produce the commodities that consumers wish to consume? And how can the distribution of these products be organised? These are some of the basic questions that economics sets out to answer.

Market economy

Key terms

market economy an economy in which market forces are allowed to guide the allocation of resources

command economy an economy in which decisions on resource allocation are guided by the state

mixed economy an economy in which resources are allocated partly through price signals and partly on the basis of intervention by the state

A **market economy** is one in which market forces are allowed to guide the allocation of resources within a society. Prices play a key role in this sort of system, providing signals and incentives to producers and consumers. Adam Smith argued that in such a system resources would be allocated effectively through the operation of an 'invisible hand'. This guides firms to produce the goods and services that consumers wish to consume.

Karl Marx argued that in a capitalist society in which there is private ownership of productive resources, the owners of capital would exploit their position at the expense of labour, eventually resulting in revolution. Although this did not transpire in the way that Marx expected, there was a move in some countries away from private ownership of capital and towards state control of resource allocation through central planning.

Command economy

A **command economy** is thus one in which the government undertakes the coordination role, planning and directing the allocation of resources. Given the complexity of modern economies, reliance on central planning poses enormous logistical problems. In order to achieve a satisfactory allocation of resources across the economy, the government needs to make decisions on thousands of individual matters.

One example of this emerges from the experience of central planning in Russia after the revolution in 1917. Factories were given production targets to fit in with the overall plan for the development of the economy. These targets then had to be met by the factory managers, who faced strong incentives to meet those targets. Factories producing nails were given two sorts of target. Some factories were given a target to produce a certain number of nails, whereas others were given targets in weight terms. The former responded by producing large numbers of very small nails; the latter produced a very small number of very big nails. Neither was what the planners had in mind!

Micromanagement on this sort of scale proved costly to implement administratively. The collapse of the Soviet bloc in the 1990s largely discredited this approach, although a small number of countries (such as North Korea and Cuba) continue to stick with central planning. China has moved away from pure central planning by beginning to allow prices to be used as signals.

Mixed economy

Another influential economist was Friedrich von Hayek, who came from what became known as the neo-Austrian School. He saw that in the period after the Second World War, there was a move towards more intervention in the economy by governments which perceived that markets were not working effectively. For example, John Maynard Keynes had argued for a more active government in times of high unemployment, such as occurred in many countries in the inter-war period. Hayek argued that such intervention would be damaging, because governments are faced with imperfect information. Markets would be more effective because they rely on people responding to signals and incentives.

Today, most economies operate a **mixed economy** system, in which market forces are complemented by some state intervention. It has been argued that any such state intervention should be *market-friendly*: in other words, when governments do intervene in the economy, they should do so in a way that helps markets to work, rather than trying to have the government replace market forces. In such an economy, the government plays a minimal role by setting the framework in which markets can operate: for example, by securing property rights.

Incentives

Another important concept that is at the heart of economic analysis is the notion that individuals respond to *incentives*. The coordination problem is handled in different forms of economy through the operation of different forms of incentive that influence decision making. In a market economy, prices and profits provide incentives, whereas in a centrally planned economy these incentives are replaced by state directives.

Microeconomics and macroeconomics

The discussion so far has focused sometimes on individual decisions, and sometimes on the decisions of governments, or of 'society' as a whole. Economic thinking is applied in different ways, depending on whether the focus is on the decisions taken by individual agents in the economy or on the interaction between economic variables at the level of the whole economy:

- **Microeconomics** deals with individual decisions taken by households or firms, or in particular markets.
- **Macroeconomics** examines the interactions between economic variables at the level of the aggregate economy.

In some ways the division between the two types of analysis is artificial. The same sort of economic reasoning is applied in both types, but the focus is different.

Exercise 1.5

Think about the following, and see whether you think each represents a microeconomic or macroeconomic phenomenon:

a the overall level of prices in an economy

b the price of ice cream

c the overall rate of unemployment in the UK

d the unemployment rate among catering workers in Aberdeen

f the average wage paid to construction workers in Southampton

Summary

- Decisions about resource allocation need to be coordinated within a society.
- This may happen by allowing markets to guide decisions, through direct intervention by the state, or through a combination of the two in a mixed economy.
- Microeconomics deals with individual decisions made by consumers and producers, whereas macroeconomics analyses the interactions between economic variables in the aggregate — but both use similar ways of thinking.

Case study 1.1

Plantains or tobacco?

Jacob is a subsistence farmer who lives in Nangare, a village in the west of Uganda. He lives in a mud hut and owns two sheep, two chickens and one mattress for his household of ten people. He farms a small piece of land, on which he grows plantains (a staple food crop in Uganda, related to the banana) and some tobacco. One of the key decisions that Jacob faces is how to allocate his land between plantains and tobacco. If he chooses to plant more tobacco in his field, he faces a cost, as growing more tobacco means growing fewer plantains.

A number of factors are likely to influence this decision. For example, the prices of plantains and tobacco may be important, and it may be that the costs involved in growing the two crops are different. Or it may be that some parts of the land are more suitable for growing one of the crops.

There may also be other crops that could be grown on the land. All of these factors could affect Jacob's decisions.

Plantains or tobacco? How will Jacob allocate his land?

Follow-up questions

a With reference to Jacob's choice between growing plantains and tobacco, explain the concept of **opportunity cost**.

b Draw a possible **production possibility frontier** to illustrate Jacob's choice of producing plantains and tobacco.

c Identify a point on the diagram that you drew for part (b) to illustrate a situation in which:

   i Jacob uses his land to produce only plantains

   ii Jacob uses his land to produce a combination of plantains and tobacco

   iii Jacob does not use all of the land available, but produces a combination of the two crops

2 The nature of demand

The demand and supply model is perhaps the most famous of all pieces of economic analysis; it is also one of the most useful. It has many applications that help explain the way markets work in the real world. It is thus central to understanding economics. This chapter introduces the 'demand' side of the model. Chapter 3 will introduce supply.

Learning objectives

After studying this chapter, you should:
→ be aware of the assumptions of rational economic decision making
→ be familiar with the notion of the demand for a good or service
→ be aware of the relationship between the demand for a good and its price
→ be familiar with the demand curve and the law of demand
→ understand the distinction between a movement along the demand curve and a shift in its position
→ be aware of the distinction between normal and inferior goods
→ understand the other influences that affect the position of the demand curve
→ understand the concept of elasticity measures and appreciate their importance and applications

Decision making

Before trying to analyse the way in which economic agents take decisions, it is important to make assumptions about what it is that they are aiming to achieve. This is the case for consumers and for firms.

Consider an individual consumer, taking a decision about which products to consume. What motivates that decision? A simple assumption is that the individual wants to gain as much satisfaction as possible from the combination of products that are consumed. Economists refer to satisfaction in this context as *utility*, so the assumption that is made is that rational consumers set out to maximise their utility.

The corresponding assumption for firms is that they aim to make as much profit as possible: in other words, they aim to maximise profits.

Will this always be the case? Not necessarily. Later, we will explore situations in which consumers or firms may choose to pursue other objectives, and analyse how this affects the economic analysis of behaviour.

Demand

Consider an individual consumer. Think of yourself, and a product that you consume regularly. What factors influence your **demand** for that product? Put another way, what factors influence how much of the product you choose to buy?

When thinking about the factors that influence your demand for your chosen product, common sense will probably mean that you focus on a range of different points. You may think about why you enjoy consuming the product. You may focus on how much it will cost to buy the product, and whether you can afford it. You may decide that you have consumed a product so much that you are ready for a change; or perhaps you will decide to try something advertised on television, or being bought by a friend.

Whatever the influences you come up with, they can probably be categorised under four headings that ultimately determine your demand for a good. First, the *price of the good* is an important influence on your demand for it, and will affect the quantity of it that you choose to buy. Second, the *price of other goods* may be significant. Third, your *income* will determine how much of the good you can afford to purchase. Finally, almost any other factors that you may have thought of can be listed as part of your *preferences*.

This reasoning is based on the assumption that consumers act rationally, by seeking to take decisions that will produce the best result possible given the constraints that they face. This provides the basis for the economic analysis of demand. A lot of economic analysis begins in this way, by constructing a model rooted in how we expect rational people or firms to behave.

Individual and market demand

A similar line of argument may apply if we think in terms of the demand for a particular product — say, Blu-ray discs. The market for Blu-ray discs can thus be seen as bringing together all the potential buyers (and sellers) of the product, and market demand can be analysed in terms of the factors that influence all potential buyers of that good or service. In other words, market demand can be seen as the total quantity of a good or service that all potential buyers would choose to buy at any given price. The same four factors that influence your own individual decision to buy will also influence the total market demand for a product. In addition, the number of potential buyers in the market will clearly influence the size of total demand at any price.

Demand and the price of a good

Assume for the moment that the influences mentioned above, other than the price of the good, are held constant, so that the focus is only on the extent to which the price of a good influences the demand for it. This common sort of assumption in economics was introduced in Chapter 1, using the Latin phrase 'ceteris paribus'. Given the complexity of the real world, it is often helpful to focus on one thing at a time.

For an individual, the utility that you gain from consuming a product is likely to decline the more of it you consume. You may gain lots of utility from the first chocolate bar that you eat, but the 10th bar will add less satisfaction. In other words, the additional utility that you receive from a good is likely to decline as you consume more of it. This is referred to as **diminishing marginal utility**, and suggests that you will place a lower value on a product, the more of it you have already consumed. This being so, the price that you would pay for relatively large amounts of a product would be correspondingly low.

How is the demand for Blu-ray discs influenced by their price in the market as a whole? Other things being equal (ceteris paribus), you would expect the demand for Blu-ray discs to be higher when the price is low and lower when the price is high. In other words, you would expect an inverse relationship between the price and the quantity demanded. This is such a strong phenomenon that it is referred to as the **law of demand**.

If you were to compile a list that showed how many Blu-ray discs would be bought at any possible price and plot these on a diagram, this would be called the **demand curve**. Figure 2.1 shows what this might look like. As it is an inverse relationship, the demand curve slopes downwards. Notice that this need not be a straight line: its shape depends on how consumers react at different prices.

Key terms

law of demand a law that states that there is an inverse relationship between quantity demanded and the price of a good or service, ceteris paribus

demand curve a graph showing how much of a good will be demanded by consumers at any given price

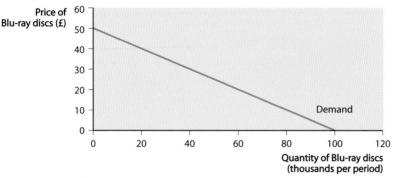

Figure 2.1 A demand curve for Blu-ray discs

Quantitative skills 2.1

Reading a graph

An important skill is to be able to read off numerical values from a graph such as Figure 2.1. If you wanted to see what the quantity demanded would be at a particular price, you would select the price on the vertical axis, and then read off the value on the horizontal axis at that price. For example, in this figure, if price were to be set at £40, the quantity demanded would be 20,000 per period. However, if the price were only £20, the demand would be higher, at 60,000.

Exercise 2.1

Table 2.1 shows how the demand for oojits varies with their price. Draw the demand curve.

Table 2.1 The demand for oojits

Price (£)	100	90	80	70	60	50	40	30	20
Quantity	0	3	7	15	25	40	60	85	120

Extension material

An analysis of why the demand curve should be downward sloping would reveal that there are two important forces at work. At a higher price, a consumer buying a Blu-ray disc has less income left over. This is referred to as the *real income effect* of a price increase. In addition, if the price of Blu-ray discs goes up, consumers may find other goods more attractive and choose to buy something else instead of Blu-ray discs. This is referred to as the *substitution effect* of a price increase.

As the price of a good changes, a movement along the demand curve can be observed as consumers adjust their buying pattern in response to the price change.

Notice that the demand curve has been drawn under the ceteris paribus assumption. In other words, it was assumed that all other influences on demand were held constant in order to focus on the relationship between demand and price. There are two important implications of this procedure.

First, the price drawn on the vertical axis of a diagram such as Figure 2.1 is the *relative* price — it is the price of Blu-ray discs under the assumption that all other prices are constant.

Second, if any of the other influences on demand change, you would expect to see a shift of the whole demand curve. It is very important to distinguish between factors that induce a *movement along* a curve, and factors that induce a *shift of* a curve. This applies not only in the case of the demand curve — there are many other instances where this is important.

The two panels of Figure 2.2 show this difference. In panel (a), the demand curve has shifted to the right because of a change in one of the factors that influence demand. In panel (b), the price of Blu-ray discs falls from P_0 to P_1, inducing a movement along the demand curve as demand expands from Q_0 to Q_1.

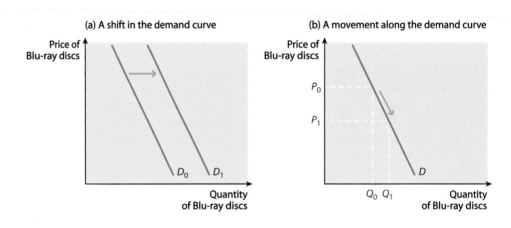

Figure 2.2 A shift in the demand curve and a movement along it

Snob effects

It is sometimes argued that for some goods a 'snob effect' may lead to the demand curve sloping upwards. The argument is that some people may value certain goods more highly simply because their price is high, especially if they know that other people will observe them consuming these goods; an example might be Rolex watches. In other words, people gain value from having other people notice that they are rich enough to afford to consume a particular good. This *conspicuous consumption* effect was first pointed out by Thorstein Veblen at the end of the nineteenth century. Indeed, it is sometimes known as the *Veblen effect*.

However, although there may be some individual consumers who react to price in this way, there is no evidence to suggest that there are whole markets that display an upward-sloping demand curve for this reason. In other words, most consumers would react normally to the price of such goods.

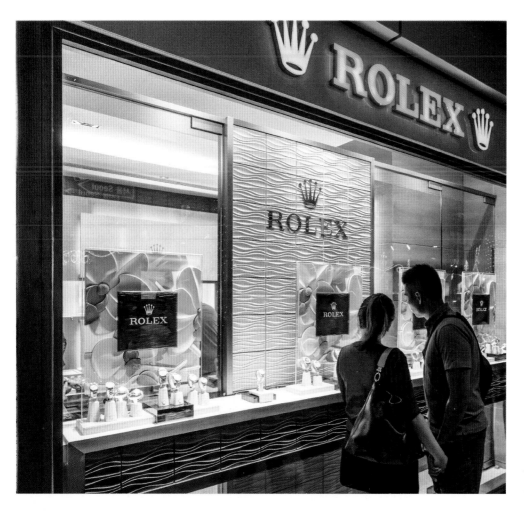

Rolex watches may benefit from the conspicuous consumption effect

Demand and consumer incomes

The second influence on demand is consumer incomes. For a **normal good**, an increase in consumer incomes will, ceteris paribus, lead to an increase in the quantity demanded at any given price. Foreign holidays are an example of a normal good because, as people's incomes rise, they will tend to demand more foreign holidays at any given price.

Figure 2.3 illustrates this. D_0 here represents the initial demand curve for foreign holidays. An increase in consumers' incomes causes demand to be higher at any given price, and the demand curve shifts to the right — to D_1.

However, demand does not always respond in this way. For example, think about bus journeys. As incomes rise in a society, more people can afford to have a car, or to use taxis. This means that, as incomes rise, the demand for bus journeys may tend to fall. Such goods are known as **inferior goods**.

This time an increase in consumers' incomes in Figure 2.4 causes the demand curve to shift to the left, from its initial position at D_0, to D_1 where less is demanded at any given price.

The relationship between quantity demanded and income (QDI) can be shown more directly on a diagram. Panel (a) of Figure 2.5 shows how this would look for a normal good. The income–demand curve is upward sloping, showing that the quantity demanded is higher when consumer incomes are higher. In contrast, the income–demand curve for an inferior good, shown in panel (b) of the diagram, slopes downwards, indicating that the quantity demanded will be lower when consumer incomes are relatively high.

Key terms

normal good one where the quantity demanded increases in response to an increase in consumer incomes

inferior good one where the quantity demanded decreases in response to an increase in consumer incomes

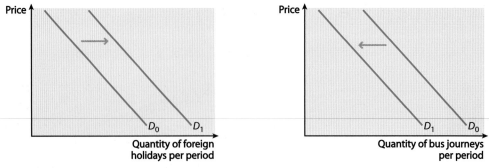

Figure 2.3 A shift in the demand curve following an increase in consumer incomes (a normal good)

Figure 2.4 A shift in the demand curve following an increase in consumer incomes (an inferior good)

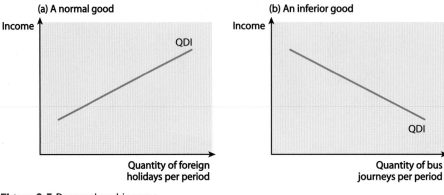

Figure 2.5 Demand and income

Exercise 2.2

Identify each of the following products as being either a normal good or an inferior good:

a digital camera   **b** magazine   **c** potatoes

d bicycle   **e** fine wine   **f** cheap wine

Extension material

Remember that a consumer's response to a change in the price of a good is made up of a substitution effect and a real income effect (see the extension material on page 19). The substitution effect always acts in the opposite direction to the price change: in other words, an increase in the price of a good always induces a switch *away* from the good towards other goods. However, it can now be seen that the real income effect may operate in either direction, depending on whether it is a normal good or an inferior good that is being considered.

Suppose there is a good that is very inferior. A fall in the price of a good induces a substitution effect towards the good, but the real income effect works in the opposite direction. The fall in price is equivalent to a rise in real income, so consumers will consume less of the good. If this effect is really strong, it could overwhelm the substitution effect, and the fall in price could induce a *fall* in the quantity demanded: in other words, for such a good the demand curve could be upward sloping.

Such goods are known as *Giffen goods*, after Sir Robert Giffen, who pointed out that this could happen. However, in spite of stories about the reaction of demand to a rise in the price of potatoes during the great Irish potato famine, there have been no authenticated sightings of Giffen goods. The notion remains a theoretical curiosity.

Demand and the price of other goods

The demand for a good may respond to changes in the price of other related goods, of which there are two main types. On the one hand, two goods may be **substitutes** for each other. For example, consider two different (but similar) breakfast cereals. If there is an increase in the price of one of the cereals, consumers may switch their consumption to the other, as the two are likely to be close substitutes for each other. Not all consumers will switch, of course — some may be deeply committed to one particular brand — but some of them are certainly likely to change over.

On the other hand, there may also be goods that are **complements** — for example, products that are consumed jointly, such as breakfast cereals and milk, or cars and petrol. Here a fall in the price of one good may lead to an increase in demand for *both* products.

Whether goods are substitutes or complements determines how the demand for one good responds to a change in the price of another. Figure 2.6 shows the demand curves (per period) for two goods that are substitutes — tea and coffee. If there is an increase in the price of tea from P_0 to P_1 in panel (a), more consumers will switch to coffee and the demand curve in panel (b) will shift to the right — say, from D_{c0} to D_{c1}.

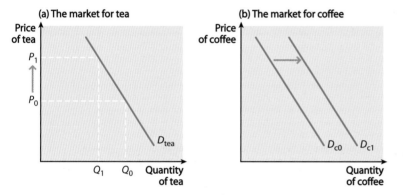

Figure 2.6 A shift in the demand curve following an increase in the price of a substitute good

For complements the situation is the reverse: in Figure 2.7 an increase in the price of tea from P_0 to P_1 in panel (a) causes the demand curve for milk to shift leftwards, from D_{m0} to D_{m1}.

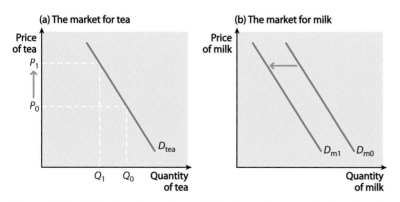

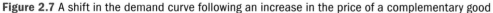

Figure 2.7 A shift in the demand curve following an increase in the price of a complementary good

Demand, consumer preferences and other influences

The discussion has shown how the demand for a good is influenced by the price of the good, the price of other goods and consumer incomes. It was stated earlier that almost everything else that determines demand for a good can be represented as 'consumer preferences'. In particular, this refers to whether you like or dislike a good. There may be many things that influence whether you like or dislike a product. In part it simply depends on your own personal inclinations — some people like dark chocolate, others prefer milk chocolate. However, firms may try to influence your preferences through advertising, and sometimes they succeed. Or you might be one of those people who get so irritated by television advertising that you compile a blacklist of products that you will never buy! Even this is an influence on your demand.

In some cases your preferences may be swayed by other people's demand — again, this may be positive or negative. Fashions may influence demand, but some people like to buck (or lead) the trend.

You may also see a movement of the demand curve if there is a sudden surge in the popularity of a good — or, indeed, a sudden collapse in demand.

Exercise 2.3

Sketch some demand curves for the following situations, and think about how you would expect the demand curve to change (if at all):

a the demand for chocolate following a campaign highlighting the dangers of obesity

b the demand for oranges following an increase in the price of apples

c the demand for oranges following a decrease in the price of oranges

d the demand for Blu-ray discs following a decrease in the price of Blu-ray players

e the demand for private transport following an increase in consumer incomes

f the demand for public transport following an increase in consumer incomes

The above discussion has covered most of the factors that influence the demand for a good. However, in some cases it is necessary to take a time element into account. Not all of the goods bought are consumed instantly. In some cases, consumption is spread over long periods of time. Indeed, there may be instances where goods are not bought for consumption at all, but are seen by the buyer as an investment, perhaps for resale at a later date. In these circumstances, expectations about future price changes may be relevant. For example, people may buy fine wine or works of art in the expectation that prices will rise in the future. There may also be goods whose prices are expected to fall in the future. This has been common with many high-tech products; initially a newly launched product may sell at a high price, but as production levels rise, costs may fall, and prices too. People may therefore delay purchase in the expectation of future price reductions.

Summary

- A market is a set of arrangements that enables transactions to take place.
- The market demand for a good depends on the price of the good, the price of other goods, consumers' incomes and preferences, and the number of potential consumers.
- The demand curve shows the relationship between demand for a product and its price, ceteris paribus.
- The demand curve is downward sloping, as the relationship between demand and price is an inverse one.
- A change in price induces a movement along the demand curve, whereas a change in the other determinants of demand induces a shift in the demand curve.
- When the demand for a good rises as consumer incomes rise, that good is referred to as a normal good; when demand falls as income rises, the good is referred to as an inferior good.
- A good or service may be related to other goods by being either a substitute or a complement.
- For some products, demand may be related to expected future prices.

Case study 2.1

Smoothies and Cola

A few years ago, growing concerns about obesity in the British population led the government to launch a campaign to encourage healthier eating. Part of this campaign aimed to encourage people to consume more fruit and vegetables, which was reinforced by the 'five-a-day' slogan, the idea being that five portions per day of fruit and vegetables were an essential part of a balanced diet.

Firms selling food products naturally tried to take advantage of the campaign by emphasising in their advertising that their products contributed in some way to the five-a-day. Smoothies were one such product advertised in this way as helping people to meet their five-a-day quota. One result was that sales of cola and other soft drinks were affected, with people keen to switch to smoothies as a healthier alternative. Whether it is true that they are healthier is another matter, and some people argued that the sugar content of smoothies was in fact much higher than that of some other fizzy drinks...but that's another story.

Smoothies — part of your five-a-day?

Follow-up questions

a Consider the factors that influence demand. Which of these explains the increase in demand for smoothies following the campaign?

b What effect would the campaign have on the demand curve for smoothies and fizzy drinks such as cola?

c Would you see smoothies and fizzy soft drinks as being substitutes or complements? Explain your answer.

Elasticity: the sensitivity of demand

Both the demand for and the supply of a good or service can be expected to depend on its price as well as other factors. It is often interesting to know just how sensitive demand and/or supply will be to a change in either price or one of the other determinants — for example, in predicting how market equilibrium will change in response to a change in the market environment. The sensitivity of demand to a change in one of its determining factors can be measured by its **elasticity**.

> **Key term**
>
> **elasticity** a measure of the sensitivity of one variable to changes in another variable

Key term

price elasticity of demand (*PED*) a measure of the sensitivity of quantity demanded to a change in the price of a good or service. It is measured as:

$$\frac{\% \text{ change in quantity demanded}}{\% \text{ change in price}}$$

The price elasticity of demand

The most common elasticity measure is the **price elasticity of demand (*PED*)**. This measures the sensitivity of the quantity demanded of a good or service to a change in its price.

The elasticity is defined as the percentage change in quantity demanded divided by the percentage change in the price. There are two important things to notice about this. First, because the demand curve is downward sloping, the elasticity will always be negative. This is because the changes in price and quantity are always in the opposite direction. Economists often ignore the minus sign when discussing the *PED*. Second, you should try to calculate the elasticity only for a relatively small change in price, as it becomes unreliable for very large changes.

When the demand is highly price sensitive, the percentage change in quantity demanded following a price change will be large relative to the percentage change in price. In this case, *PED* will take on a value that is greater than 1 (ignoring the minus sign). For example, suppose that a 2% change in price leads to a 5% change in quantity demanded; the elasticity is then −5 divided by 2 = −2.5. When the price elasticity is greater than 1, demand is referred to as being **relatively elastic**.

When demand is not very sensitive to price, the percentage change in quantity demanded will be smaller than the original percentage change in price, and the elasticity will then be less than 1. For example, if a 2% change in price leads to a 1% change in quantity demanded, then the value of the elasticity will be −1 divided by 2 = −0.5. In this case, demand is referred to as being **relatively inelastic**.

We define the percentage change in price as $100 \times \Delta P/P$ (where Δ means 'change in' and P stands for price). Similarly, the percentage change in quantity demanded is $100 \times \Delta Q/Q$. Then the formula for the elasticity is:

$$PED = \frac{100 \times \Delta Q/Q}{100 \times \Delta P/P}$$

This phenomenon is true for any straight-line demand curve: in other words, demand is price elastic at higher prices and inelastic at lower prices. At the halfway point the elasticity is exactly −1, and demand is referred to as **unitary elastic**.

Why should this happen? The key is to remember that elasticity is defined in terms of the percentage changes in price and quantity. Thus, when price is relatively high, a 1p change in price is a small percentage change, and the percentage change in quantity is relatively large — because when price is relatively high, the initial quantity is relatively low. The reverse is the case when price is relatively low. Notice that the *PED* is infinity when quantity is zero, and zero when price is zero. Figure 2.9 shows how the elasticity of demand varies along a straight-line demand curve.

Key terms

relatively elastic a term used when the price elasticity of demand is greater than 1 but less than infinity

relatively inelastic a term used when the price elasticity of demand is less than 1 but greater than zero

unitary elastic a term used when the price elasticity of demand is equal to 1

Calculating an elasticity

Figure 2.8 shows a demand curve for pencils. When the price of a pencil is 40p, the quantity demanded will be 20. If the price falls to 35p, the quantity demanded will rise to 30. The percentage change in quantity is $100 \times 10/20 = 50$ and the percentage change in price is $100 \times -5/40 = -12.5$. Thus, the elasticity can be calculated as $(50/-12.5) = -4$. At this price, demand is highly price elastic.

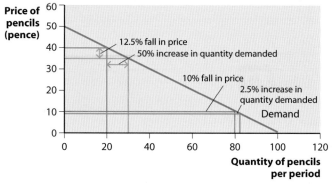

Figure 2.8 A demand curve for pencils

At a lower price, the result is quite different. Suppose that price is initially 10p, at which price the quantity demanded is 80. If the price falls to 9p, demand increases to 82. The percentage change in quantity is now $100 \times 2/80 = 2.5$, and the percentage change in price is $100 \times -1/10 = -10$, so the elasticity is calculated as $2.5/-10 = -0.25$, and demand is now price inelastic.

Extension material

An alternative way of looking at this is to notice that, because the demand curve is drawn as a straight line, the ratio of the change in quantity to the change in price ($\Delta Q/\Delta P$) is always the same. (In fact, this is the slope of the demand curve.)

However, the ratio of the level of quantity to price varies along the demand curve. When price is relatively high, quantity is relatively low, so P/Q is high and elasticity is high. Conversely, when price is low, quantity is high and P/Q is low.

An example

A study by the Institute for Fiscal Studies for the UK found that the price elasticity of demand for wine was −1.69. This means that demand for wine is elastic. If the price of wine were to increase by 10% (ceteris paribus), there would be a fall of 16.9% in the quantity of wine demanded.

The price elasticity of demand and total revenue

One reason why firms may have an interest in the price elasticity of demand is that, if they are considering changing their prices, they will be eager to know the extent to which demand will be affected. For example, they may want to know how a change in price will affect their total revenue. As it happens, there is a consistent relationship between the price elasticity of demand and total revenue.

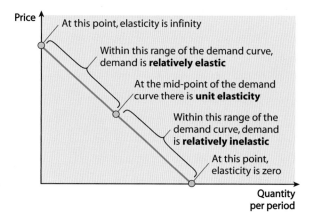

Figure 2.9 The price elasticity of demand varies along a straight line

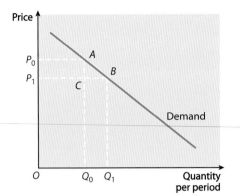

Price

P_0

P_1

A

B

C

Demand

O Q_0 Q_1 Quantity per period

Figure 2.10 Demand and total revenue

Total revenue is given by price multiplied by quantity. In Figure 2.10, if price is at P_0, quantity demanded is at Q_0 and total revenue is given by the area of the rectangle OP_0AQ_0. If price falls to P_1 the quantity demanded rises to Q_1, and you can see that total revenue has increased, as it is now given by the area OP_1BQ_1. This is larger than at price P_0, because in moving from P_0 to P_1 the area P_1P_0AC is lost, but the area Q_0CBQ_1 is gained, and the latter is the larger. As you move down the demand curve, total revenue at first increases like this, but then decreases — try sketching this for yourself to check that it is so.

Quantitative skills 2.3

Elasticity and total revenue

Quantitative skills 2.2 showed how to calculate the price elasticity of demand at different points along a demand curve for pencils. When the price of a pencil fell from 40p to 35p, the quantity demanded rose from 20 to 30, and elasticity was calculated to be −4.

Total revenue before and after the price change can be calculated. Total revenue is equal to price multiplied by quantity, so at the original price revenue was 40 × 20 = 800. At the new lower price, total revenue was 35 × 30 = 1050. We can therefore see that when the price elasticity of demand is elastic, a fall in price leads to a rise in revenue.

When the price of a pencil fell from 10p to 9p, and quantity demanded rose from 80 to 82, demand was inelastic (−0.25). At the original price, revenue was 10 × 80 = 800, and at the lower price it was 9 × 82 = 738. This time, total revenue has fallen with a fall in price and inelastic demand.

In the case of a straight-line demand curve the relationship is illustrated in Figure 2.11. Remember that demand is price elastic when price is relatively high. This is the range of the demand curve in which total revenue rises as price falls. This makes sense, as in this range the quantity demanded is sensitive to a change in price and increases by more (in percentage terms) than the price falls. This implies that, as you move to the right in this segment, total revenue rises. The increase in quantity sold more than compensates for the fall in price. However, when the mid-point is reached and demand becomes unit elastic, total revenue stops rising — it is at its maximum at this point. The remaining part of the curve is inelastic: that is, the increase in quantity demanded is no longer sufficient to compensate for the decrease in price, and total revenue falls. Table 2.2 summarises the situation.

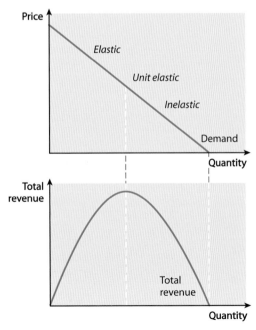

Price

Elastic

Unit elastic

Inelastic

Demand

Quantity

Total revenue

Total revenue

Quantity

Figure 2.11 Elasticity and total revenue

Table 2.2 Total revenue, elasticity and a price change

Price elasticity of demand	For a price increase, total revenue...	For a price decrease, total revenue...
Elastic	falls	rises
Unit elastic	does not change	does not change
Inelastic	rises	falls

Thus, if a firm is aware of the price elasticity of demand for its product, it can anticipate consumer response to its price changes, which may be a powerful strategic tool.

One very important point must be made here. If the price elasticity of demand varies along a straight-line demand curve, such a curve cannot be referred to as either elastic or inelastic. To do so is to confuse the elasticity with the slope of the demand curve. It is not only the steepness of the demand curve that determines the elasticity, but also the point on the curve at which the elasticity is measured.

Two extreme cases of the *PED* should also be mentioned. Demand may sometimes be totally insensitive to price, so that the same quantity will be demanded whatever price is set for it. In such a situation, demand is said to be *perfectly inelastic*. The demand curve in this case is vertical — as in D_i in Figure 2.12. In this situation, the numerical value of the price elasticity is zero, as quantity demanded does not change in response to a change in the price of the good.

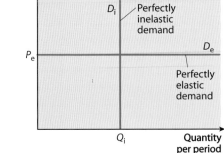

The other extreme is shown on the same figure, where D_e is a horizontal demand curve and demand is *perfectly elastic*. The numerical value of the elasticity here is infinity. Consumers demand an unlimited quantity of the good at price P_e. No firm has any incentive to lower price below this level, but if price were to rise above P_e, demand would fall to zero.

Figure 2.12 Perfectly elastic and inelastic demand

Influences on the price elasticity of demand

A number of important influences on the price elasticity of demand can now be identified. The most important is the *availability of substitutes* for the good or service under consideration. For example, think about the demand for cauliflower. Cauliflower and broccoli are often seen as being very similar, so if the price of cauliflower is high one week, people might quite readily switch to broccoli. The demand for cauliflower can be said to be price sensitive (relatively elastic), as consumers can readily substitute an alternative product. On the other hand, if the price of all vegetables rises, demand will not change very much, as there are no substitutes for vegetables in the diet. Thus, goods that have close substitutes available will tend to exhibit relatively elastic demand, whereas the demand for goods for which there are no substitutes will tend to be more inelastic.

Associated with this is the question of whether an individual regards a good or service as a *necessity* or as a *luxury* item. If a good is a necessity, then demand for it will tend to be inelastic, whereas if a good is regarded as a luxury, consumers will tend to be more price sensitive. This is closely related to the question of substitutes, as by labelling a good as a necessity one is essentially saying that there are no substitutes for it.

A third influence on the *PED* is the *relative share of the good or service in overall expenditure*. You may tend not to notice small changes in the price of an inexpensive item that is a small part of overall expenditure, such as salt or sugar. This tends to mean that demand for that good is relatively inelastic. On the other hand, an item that figures large in the household budget will be seen very differently, and consumers will tend to be much more sensitive to price when a significant proportion of their income is involved.

Finally, the *time period* under consideration may be important. Consumers may respond more strongly to a price change in the long run than in the short run. An increase in the price of petrol may have limited effects in the short

Cauliflower and broccoli are easily substituted, so demand will be elastic

run; however, in the long run, consumers may buy smaller cars or switch to diesel. Thus, the elasticity of demand tends to be more elastic in the long run than in the short run. Habit or commitment to a certain pattern of consumption may dictate the short-run pattern of consumption, but people do eventually adjust to price changes.

Study tip

Be ready to identify the four key influences on the *PED*:
- the availability of close substitutes for the good
- whether the good is perceived as a necessity
- the proportion of income or expenditure devoted to the good
- the time period over which elasticity is considered

Summary

- The price elasticity of demand (*PED*) measures the sensitivity of the quantity of a good demanded to a change in its price.
- As there is an inverse relationship between quantity demanded and price, the price elasticity of demand is always negative.
- Where consumers are sensitive to a change in price, the percentage change in quantity demanded will exceed the percentage change in price. The elasticity of demand then takes on a value that is numerically greater than 1, and demand is said to be relatively elastic.
- Where consumers are not very sensitive to a change in price, the percentage change in quantity demanded will be smaller than the percentage change in price. Elasticity of demand then takes on a value that is numerically smaller than 1, and demand is said to be relatively inelastic.
- When demand is elastic, a fall (rise) in price leads to a rise (fall) in total revenue.
- When demand is inelastic, a fall (rise) in price leads to a fall (rise) in total revenue.
- The size of the price elasticity of demand is influenced by the availability of substitutes for a good, the relative share of expenditure on the good in the consumer's budget and the time that consumers have to adjust.

Exercise 2.4

Examine Table 2.3, which shows the demand for a particular red wine at different prices.

a Draw the demand curve.

b Calculate the price elasticity of demand when the initial price is £8.

c Calculate the price elasticity of demand when the initial price is £6.

d Calculate the price elasticity of demand when the initial price is £4.

Table 2.3 Demand for Château Econ

Price (£)	10	8	6	4	2
Quantity demanded (bottles per week)	20	40	60	80	100

Key term

income elasticity of demand (*YED*) a measure of the sensitivity of quantity demanded to a change in consumer incomes

The income elasticity of demand

Elasticity is a measure of the sensitivity of a variable to changes in another variable. In the same way as the price elasticity of demand is determined, an elasticity measure can be calculated for any other influence on demand or supply. **Income elasticity of demand (*YED*)** is therefore defined as:

$$YED = \frac{\%\ \text{change in quantity demanded}}{\%\ \text{change in consumer income}}$$

Unlike the price elasticity of demand, the income elasticity of demand may be either positive or negative. Remember the distinction between normal and inferior goods? For normal goods the quantity demanded will increase as consumer income rises, whereas for inferior goods the quantity demanded will tend to fall as income rises. Thus, for normal goods the *YED* will be positive, whereas for inferior goods it will be negative.

For normal goods, the size of the elasticity indicates the extent to which a good is regarded as a necessity. A **luxury good** is one with a *YED* greater than 1, as the quantity demanded tends to rise more than proportionately with income, whereas a good with a low *YED* is regarded as a **necessity**.

Suppose you discover that the *YED* for cheese is 0.2. How do you interpret this number? If consumer incomes were to increase by 10%, the demand for cheese would increase by $10 \times 0.2 = 2\%$. This example of a normal good may be helpful information for cheese sellers, if they know that consumer incomes are rising over time. Notice that this value of the *YED* implies that cheese is a necessity, as demand is income inelastic.

In some cases the *YED* may be very strongly positive. For example, suppose that the *YED* for smart phones is +2. This implies that the quantity demanded of such phones will increase by 20% for every 10% increase in incomes. An increase in income is encouraging people to devote more of their incomes to this product, which increases its share in total expenditure. Such goods are referred to as luxury goods.

On the other hand, if the *YED* for coach travel is −0.3, that means that a 10% increase in consumer incomes will lead to a 3% fall in the demand for coach travel — perhaps because more people are travelling by car. In this instance, coach travel would be regarded as an inferior good.

When interpreting the *YED* in this way, notice that not all consumers will view goods in the same way. A good that is regarded as a luxury by some people (such as a second car) might be viewed differently by wealthy households.

Cross-price elasticity of demand

Another useful measure is the **cross-price elasticity of demand (XED)**. This is helpful in revealing the interrelationships between goods. Again, this measure may be either positive or negative, depending on the relationship between the goods. It is defined as:

$$XED = \frac{\% \text{ change in quantity demanded of good X}}{\% \text{ change in price of good Y}}$$

If the *XED* is seen to be positive, it means that an increase in the price of good Y leads to an increase in the quantity demanded of good X. For example, an increase in the price of apples may lead to an increase in the demand for pears. Here apples and pears are regarded as substitutes for each other; if one becomes relatively more expensive, consumers will switch to the other. A high value for the *XED* indicates that two goods are very close substitutes. This information may be useful in helping a firm to identify its close competitors.

On the other hand, if an increase in the price of one good leads to a fall in the quantity demanded of another good, this suggests that they are likely to be complements. The *XED* in this case will be negative. An example of such a relationship would be that between coffee and sugar, which tend to be consumed together. If the *XED* were seen to be zero, this would indicate that the goods concerned were unrelated — neither substitutes nor complements.

Does this notion of the cross-price elasticity of demand have any relevance in the real world? One part of government policy that you will meet later in your study of economics is competition policy. The Competition and Markets Authority has the responsibility of safeguarding consumer interests by ensuring that firms do not exploit excessive market power. An important part of their investigations entails an evaluation of whether firms face competition in their markets. The cross-price elasticity of demand can reveal whether two products are regarded as substitutes for each other. If they are shown to be, then this implies that the firms do face competition. This is an important application of this concept, as it can affect the judgement of whether a firm is in a position to exploit its market position.

Examples

A study by the Institute for Fiscal Studies using data for the UK found that the cross-price elasticity of demand for wine with respect to a change in the price of beer was −0.60, whereas the cross-price elasticity with respect to the price of spirits was +0.77. The negative cross-price elasticity with beer suggests that wine and beer are complements: a 10% increase in the price of beer would lead to a 6% fall in the quantity demanded of wine. In contrast, the cross-price elasticity of demand for wine with respect to the price of spirits is positive, suggesting that wine and spirits are substitutes. An increase in the price of spirits leads to an increase in the quantity demanded of wine.

Summary

- The income elasticity of demand (*YED*) measures the sensitivity of quantity demanded to a change in consumer incomes. It serves to distinguish between normal, luxury and inferior goods.
- The cross-price elasticity of demand (*XED*) measures the sensitivity of the quantity demanded of one good or service to a change in the price of some other good or service. It can serve to distinguish between substitutes and complements.

Using elasticities

The various elasticity measures can be useful to firms and to the government as part of their decision making. For example, suppose you are responsible for choosing the price to charge for a product sold by your firm. The *PED* will be informative about how buyers of the good are likely to respond to a price change. If you know they will be sensitive to a price increase, you might hesitate about raising price because this would affect revenues. Furthermore, the *YED* will help to forecast changing demand if real incomes are increasing, or if the economy is heading into a recession. The *XED* helps in anticipating changes in demand if the prices of other products are changing.

From the government perspective, imposing an indirect tax will raise the price and lead to a fall in demand, so knowing the *PED* helps to forecast the tax revenues expected. This is explored in Chapter 8. Introducing a subsidy would reduce the selling price of a good, and knowing the *PED* allows the government to assess the impact of such a move.

Case study 2.2

Bicycles

If you had visited Shanghai in the early 1990s, one thing that would have struck you is that the roads were dominated by bicycles. Cars were relatively few in number, and in busy streets in the city centre, cars had to thread their way through the mass of bicycles.

Now, things are different. True, there are still many more bicycles on the streets than you would find in the UK, but they have their own part of the road. This still causes mayhem at junctions, when cars need to turn across the cycle tracks, but things are more orderly. The number of cars has increased significantly.

In the period since the early 1990s, China's economy has gone through a period of rapid economic growth and transformation. As part of this process, real incomes have risen, and many households have become much better off, especially in the urban areas where much of the change has been concentrated.

Follow-up questions

a What reasons might help to explain the change in the pattern of traffic between cars and bicycles in China over the period described in the passage?

b What would you expect to be the nature of the income elasticity of demand for bicycles in China?

c What would you expect to be the nature of the income elasticity of demand for cars in China?

The nature of supply

The previous chapter introduced you to the demand curve. The other key component of the demand and supply model is, of course, supply. For any market transaction, there are two parties, buyers and sellers. The question this chapter considers is what determines the quantity that sellers wish to supply to the market.

Learning objectives

After studying this chapter, you should:
→ be familiar with the notion of the supply of a good or service
→ be aware of the relationship between the supply of a good and its price in a competitive market
→ understand what is meant by the supply curve and the factors that influence its shape and position
→ be able to distinguish between shifts of the supply curve and movements along it
→ be aware of the effect of taxes and subsidies on the supply curve
→ understand what is meant by the price elasticity of supply

Supply

Key terms

supply the quantity of a good or service that firms choose to sell at any possible price in a given period

firm an organisation that brings together factors of production in order to produce output

In discussing demand, the focus of attention was on consumers, and on their willingness to pay for goods and services. In thinking about **supply**, attention switches to firms, as it is firms that take decisions about how much output to supply to the market. It is important at the outset to be clear about what is meant by a 'firm'. A **firm** exists to organise production: it brings together various factors of production, and organises the production process in order to produce output.

There are various forms that the organisation of a firm can take. A firm could be a *sole proprietor*: probably a small business, such as a newsagent, where the owner of the firm also runs the firm. A firm could be in the form of a *partnership* — for example, a dental practice in which profits (and debts) are shared between the partners in the business. Larger firms may be organised as private or public *joint stock companies*, owned by shareholders. The difference between private and public joint stock companies is that the shares of a public joint stock company are traded on the stock exchange, whereas this is not the case with a private company.

In order to analyse how firms decide how much of a product to supply, it is necessary to make an assumption about what it is that firms are trying to achieve. Assume that they aim to maximise their profits, where 'profits' are defined as the difference between a firm's total revenue and its total costs.

As discussed in Chapter 2, the demand curve shows a relationship between quantity demanded and the price of a good or service. A similar relationship between the quantity supplied by firms and the price of a good can be identified in relation to the behaviour of firms in a **competitive market** — that is, a market in which individual firms cannot influence the price of the good or service that they are selling, because of competition from other firms.

As with the demand curve, there is a distinction between the supply curve of an individual firm, and the supply curve for a *market*. The individual supply curve shows the amount that an individual firm is prepared to supply at any given price. The market supply curve shows the total amount of a product that firms wish to supply at any given price.

In such a market it may well be supposed that firms will be prepared to supply more goods at a high price than at a lower one (ceteris paribus), as this will increase their profits. The **supply curve** illustrates how much the firms in a market will supply at any given price, as shown in Figure 3.1. As firms are expected to supply more goods at a high price than at a lower price, the supply curve will be upward sloping, reflecting this positive relationship between quantity and price.

Key terms

competitive market a market in which individual firms cannot influence the price of the good or service they are selling, because of competition from other firms

supply curve a graph showing the quantity supplied at any given price

Quantitative skills 3.1

Interpreting lines on a graph

Be clear about why the upward-sloping nature of the supply curve reflects the fact that firms are willing to supply more output at a higher price, whereas the downward-sloping nature of the demand curve reflects the way that consumers are willing to purchase more of a good when the price is relatively low. This is bound up with the way in which we interpret the supply (or demand) curve. In Figure 3.1, think about how firms behave when the price is relatively low — that is, when you pick a price low down on the vertical axis. The quantity that firms are willing to supply is read off from the supply curve — and is relatively low. However, if you read off the quantity from a higher price level, the quantity is also higher. You need to become accustomed to interpreting lines and curves on a diagram in this way. The shape of the line (or curve) shows the extent to which firms respond at different prices.

A movement along the supply curve

A change in the price of a good will induce firms to change their supply decision. For example, consider Figure 3.2. Suppose that initially the price of the good is at P_0. Firms will choose to supply the quantity Q_0 of the good. If the price then falls to P_1, firms will find it less profitable to supply the good, and will reduce their supply, causing a movement along the supply curve to a new quantity at Q_1.

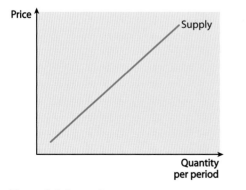

Figure 3.1 A supply curve

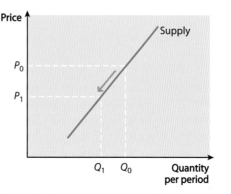

Figure 3.2 A movement along the supply curve

Exercise 3.1

The following table shows how the supply of oojits varies with their price. Draw the supply curve.

Table 3.1 The supply of oojits

Price (£)	100	90	80	70	60	50	40	30	20	10
Quantity	98	95	91	86	80	70	60	50	35	18

Notice that the focus of the supply curve is on the relationship between quantity supplied and the price of a good in a given period, ceteris paribus — that is, holding other things constant. As with the demand curve, there are other factors affecting the quantity supplied. These other influences on supply will determine the position of the supply curve: if any of them changes, the supply curve can be expected to shift.

What influences supply?

Study tip

Be sure that you are familiar with the various factors that can influence the quantity that firms will be prepared to supply to the market at any given price.

We can identify five important influences on the quantity that firms will be prepared to supply to the market at any given price:

- production costs
- the technology of production
- taxes and subsidies
- the price of related goods
- firms' expectations about future prices

Costs and technology

If firms are aiming to maximise profits, an important influence on their supply decision will be the costs of production that they face. Chapter 1 explained that in order to produce output, firms need to use inputs of the factors of production — labour, capital, land, etc. If the cost of those inputs increases, firms will in general be expected to supply less output at any given price. The effect of this is shown in Figure 3.3, where an increase in production costs induces firms to supply less output at each price. The curve shifts from its initial position at S_0 to a new position at S_1. For example, suppose the original price was £10 per unit; before the increase in costs, firms would have been prepared to supply 100 units of the product to the market. An increase in costs of £6 per unit that shifted the supply curve from S_0 to S_1 would mean that, at the same price, firms would now supply only 50 units of the good. Notice that the vertical distance between S_0 and S_1 is the amount of the change in cost per unit.

In contrast, if a new technology of production is introduced, which means that firms can produce more cost-effectively, this could have the opposite effect, shifting the supply curve to the right. This is shown in Figure 3.4, where improved technology induces firms to supply more output at any given price, and the supply curve shifts from its initial position at S_0 to a new position at S_1. Thus, if firms in the initial situation were supplying 50 units with the price at £10 per unit, then a fall in costs of £6 per unit would induce firms to increase supply to 100 units (if the price remained at £10).

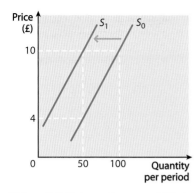

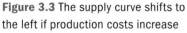

Figure 3.3 The supply curve shifts to the left if production costs increase

Figure 3.4 The supply curve shifts to the right if production costs fall

Taxes and subsidies

Suppose the government imposes a sales tax such as value added tax (VAT) on a good or service. The price paid by consumers will be higher than the revenue received by firms, as the tax has to be paid to the government. This means that firms will (ceteris paribus) be prepared to supply less output at any given market price. Again, the supply curve shifts to the left. This is shown in panel (a) of Figure 3.5, which assumes a fixed per unit tax. Such a tax is known as a specific tax, and will be discussed in more detail in Chapter 5. The supply curve shifts, as firms supply less at any given market price. On the other hand, if the government pays firms a subsidy to produce a particular good, this will reduce their costs, and induce them to supply more output at any given price. The supply curve will then shift to the right, as shown in panel (b).

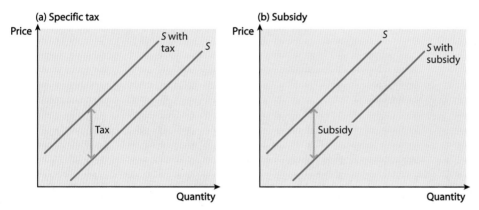

Figure 3.5 The effects of taxes and subsidies on supply

Prices of other goods

It was shown earlier that from the consumers' perspective, two goods may be substitutes for each other, such that if the price of one good increases, consumers may be induced to switch their consumption to substitute goods. Similarly, there may be substitution on the supply side. A firm may face a situation in which there are alternative uses to which its factors of production may be put: in other words, it may be able to choose between producing a range of different products. A rise in the price of a good raises its profitability, and therefore may encourage a firm to switch production from other goods. This may happen even if there are high switching costs, provided the increase in price is sufficiently large. For example, a change in relative prices of potatoes and organic swedes might encourage a farmer to stop planting potatoes and grow organic swedes instead.

In other circumstances, a firm may produce a range of goods jointly. Perhaps one good is a by-product of the production process of another. An increase in the price of one of the goods may mean that the firm will produce more of both goods. This notion of joint supply is similar to the situation on the demand side where consumers regard two goods as complements.

Expected prices

Because production takes time, firms often take decisions about how much to supply on the basis of expected future prices. Indeed, if their product is one that can be stored, there may be times when a firm will decide to allow stocks of a product to build up in anticipation of a higher price in the future, perhaps by holding back some of its production from current sales. In some economic activities, expectations about future prices are crucial in taking supply decisions because of the length of time needed in order to increase output. For example, a firm producing palm oil, rubber or wine needs to be aware that newly planted trees or vines need several years to mature before they are able to yield their product.

Market power

In some markets, firms may be able to use market power in order to influence the supply of a commodity. For example, think about the oil industry. Here, the oil-exporting nations work together as a **cartel** to influence the quantity supplied. One motivation for this is to influence price and hence the profits of the members of the cartel.

Key term

cartel an agreement between firms in a market on price and output with the intention of maximising their joint profits

Wine producers have to take supply decisions based on expected future prices

Movements along and shifts of the supply curve: a reminder

As with the demand curve, it is important to remember that there is a distinction between *movements along* the supply curve and *shifts of* the supply curve. If there is a change in the market price, this induces a movement along the supply curve. After all, the supply curve is designed to reveal how firms will react to a change in the price of the good. For example, in Figure 3.6, if the price is initially at P_0 firms will be prepared to supply the quantity Q_0, but if the price then increases to P_1 this will induce a movement along the supply curve as firms increase supply to Q_1.

In contrast, as seen in the previous section, a change in any of the other influences on supply will induce a shift of the whole supply curve, as this affects the firm's willingness to supply at any given price.

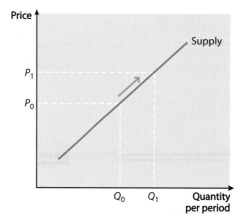

Figure 3.6 A movement along a supply curve in response to a price change

Exercise 3.2

For each of the following, decide whether the demand curve or the supply curve will move, and in which direction:

a Consumers are convinced by arguments about the benefits of organic vegetables.

b A new process is developed that reduces the amount of inputs that firms need in order to produce bicycles.

c There is a severe frost in Brazil that affects the coffee crop.

d The government increases the rate of value added tax.

e Real incomes rise.

f The price of tea falls: what happens in the market for coffee?

g The price of sugar falls: what happens in the market for coffee?

Summary

- Other things being equal, firms in a competitive market can be expected to supply more output at a higher price.
- The supply curve traces out this positive relationship between price and quantity supplied.
- Changes in the costs of production, technology, taxes and subsidies or the prices of related goods may induce shifts of the supply curve, with firms being prepared to sell more (or less) output at any given price.
- Expectations about future prices may affect current supply decisions.

Price elasticity of supply

In the previous chapter, the concept of elasticity was introduced as a way of measuring the sensitivity of quantity demanded to any of the components that affect demand. As elasticity is a measure of sensitivity, its use need not be confined to influences on demand, but can also be turned to evaluating the sensitivity of quantity *supplied* to a change in its determinants — price in particular.

Study tip

As with the discussion of demand, it is important to be clear about the difference between a shift of the supply curve and a movement along it. Again, the convention is adopted to use an *extension* (or *contraction*) of supply for a movement along the supply curve, and to use an *increase* (or *decrease*) to denote a shift of the curve. It is also helpful to distinguish between those factors that affect the position of the supply curve and those that affect the position of the demand curve. The factors that affect the position of the supply curve are:

- production costs
- the technology of production
- taxes and subsidies
- the price of related goods
- firms' expectations about future prices

Key term

price elasticity of supply (**PES**) a measure of the sensitivity of quantity supplied of a good or service to a change in the price of that good or service

It has been argued that the supply curve is likely to be upward sloping, so the price elasticity of supply can be expected to be positive. In other words, an increase in the market price will induce firms to supply more output to the market. The **price elasticity of supply (PES)** is defined as:

$$PES = \frac{\% \text{ change in the quantity supplied}}{\% \text{ change in price}}$$

Quantitative skills 3.2

Calculating the elasticity of supply

Suppose that the price of a good increases from £10 to £12, and that in response, firms increase the quantity supplied from 2,000 units to 2,200 units. What is the price elasticity of supply?

To find out, we need first to calculate the percentage changes in price and quantity. Price has changed by $100 \times 2/10 = 20\%$; the quantity supplied has changed by $100 \times 200/2,000 = 10\%$. The price elasticity of supply is therefore $10/20 = 0.5$.

The interpretation of the elasticity of supply is straightforward. If the *PES* is 0.8, an increase in price of 10% will encourage firms to supply 8% more. As with the *PED*, if the elasticity is greater than 1, supply is referred to as being relatively elastic, whereas if the value is between 0 and 1, supply is considered relatively inelastic. Unit elasticity occurs when the *PES* is exactly 1, so that a 10% increase in price induces a 10% increase in quantity supplied.

The value of the price elasticity of supply will depend on how able and willing firms are to respond to a change in price. If a firm is currently running below full capacity, then it may be able to respond quickly to an increase in price. Similarly, if the firm is holding stockpiles of goods ready to be sold, then it may be able to respond quickly to an increase in the selling price of the good. On the other hand, if the firm needs to pay overtime to its workers, or to rent new buildings or hire additional machinery in order to expand production, then the increase in costs may not justify responding to the increase in price. The willingness of the firm to expand output may also depend on whether the firm expects the change in price to be permanent or temporary.

The short run and the long run

An issue that arises in many areas of economic analysis is the importance of time. For example, economic agents often need time to adjust to a changing market environment. A higher price may induce firms to want to supply more of a good, but how quickly will they change? A firm may choose to wait in order to see whether a change is permanent or temporary. Even if a firm wants to change immediately, it may take time to adjust, especially if it needs to obtain new machinery or other equipment in order to expand, or if it needs to hire more skilled labour. This provides the important distinction between the short run and the long run.

It is thus important to realise that it may be more feasible for firms to change their supply decision in the long run than in the short run. For example, if firms are operating close to the capacity of their existing plant and machinery, they may be unable to respond to an increase in price, at least in the short run. So here again, supply can be expected to be more elastic in the long run than in the short run.

Figure 3.7 illustrates this. In the short run, firms may be able to respond to an increase in price only in a limited way, and so supply may be relatively inelastic, as shown by S_s in the figure. An important issue here is whether the nature of the good is such that it is possible for firms to hold stocks of the good, which might allow them to expand sales in the short run even if it takes time to expand production. The extent to which goods can be stored in this way will reflect the nature of the good concerned: for example, depending on whether or not the good is perishable, or costly to store.

However, firms can become more flexible in the long run by installing new machinery or building new factories, so supply can then become more elastic, moving to S_l. When analysing the theory of the firm, economists define the short run and the long run in this way, seeing the short run as a period in which the firm is not able to vary its inputs of all factors of production, and the long run as the period in which this becomes possible. In particular, it is often supposed that capital inputs are relatively difficult to vary in the short run, whereas firms may be more able to vary the amount of labour input.

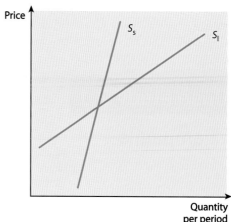

Figure 3.7 Short- and long-run supply

Two special cases

There are two limiting cases of supply elasticity. For some reason, supply may be fixed such that, no matter how much price increases, firms will not be able to supply any more. For example, it could be that a certain amount of fish is available in a market, and however high the price goes, no more can be obtained. Equally, if the fishermen know that the fish they do not sell today cannot be stored for another day, they have an incentive to sell, however low the price goes. In these cases, supply is perfectly inelastic. At the other extreme is perfectly elastic supply, where firms would be prepared to supply any amount of the good at the going price.

These two possibilities are shown in Figure 3.8. Here S_i represents a perfectly inelastic supply curve: firms will supply Q_i whatever the price, perhaps because that is the amount available for sale. Supply here is vertical. At the opposite extreme, if supply is perfectly elastic then firms are prepared to supply any amount at the price P_e, and the supply curve is given by the horizontal line S_e.

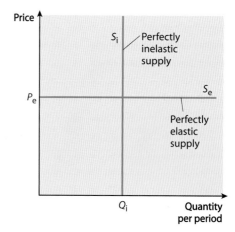

Figure 3.8 Perfectly elastic and inelastic supply

Exercise 3.3

Imagine the following scenario. You are considering a pricing strategy for a bus company. The economy is heading into recession, and the company is running at a loss. Your local rail service provider has announced an increase in rail fares. How (if at all) do you use the following information concerning the elasticity of bus travel with respect to various variables to inform your decision on price? Do you raise or lower price?

- price elasticity of demand   −1.58
- income elasticity of demand   −2.43
- cross-price elasticity of demand with respect to rail fares   +2.21
- your price elasticity of supply   +1.15

Summary

- The price elasticity of supply (*PES*) measures the sensitivity of the quantity supplied to a change in the price of a good or service.
- The price elasticity of supply can be expected to be greater in the long run than in the short run, as firms have more flexibility to adjust their production decisions in the long run.

Case study 3.1

Champagne

The market for champagne has been changing in recent years. Champagne has always commanded a premium price compared with other sparkling wines because of its reputation and status as the wine for celebrations of all kinds. Christmas is one such focus for drinking champagne, and major events such as the millennium celebrations cause blips in demand, with no party being complete without a few bottles of champagne. However, the increased availability of good-quality alternatives to champagne at competitive prices has affected champagne producers. It has even been known for some English sparkling wines to fare well at blind tastings compared with some champagnes. Nonetheless champagne production has remained profitable as consumer incomes have risen. Mechanisation of some parts of the production process has benefited producers.

There are strict rules governing the production of champagne. Indeed, champagne can only be called by that name if it comes from a particular designated area in France, and this has effectively limited the amount that can be produced. In early 2008, it was announced that consideration was being given to expanding the area that could be recognised as

producing champagne. The proposal was accepted, and the first vines should be planted in 2015. This will not affect the market for some period, as it takes time for newly planted vines to produce grapes that can be used to make wine — it is unlikely that any champagne from the expanded region will come to market before 2021.

More affordable alternatives have affected the market for champagne

Follow-up questions

a From the passage, identify factors that would be expected to affect the demand curve for champagne.

b From the passage, identify factors that would be expected to affect the supply curve for champagne.

Rice

In 2007/08, sudden and unexpected food prices hit the headlines. There were riots on the streets of cities in many countries around the world, with protestors demonstrating against massive increases in the prices of some staple foods, especially wheat and rice.

The increases affected some countries especially severely. In much of southeast Asia, rice is a staple commodity, forming a part of most people's daily diet. For some countries, such as the Philippines, much of the rice consumed has to be imported, so the price rises caused particular difficulties. The demonstrators wanted governments to intervene to control the prices and protect the poor.

It was reported that in some countries, poor households were coping with the price rises by changing their eating habits, by consuming less meat, or by finding other ways of cutting down. The United Nations called for worldwide action to prevent hunger and malnutrition from spreading.

Follow-up questions

a Would you expect the demand for rice to be price elastic or inelastic?

b Explain your answer to part (a), referring to the passage to provide evidence to support your explanation.

c Do you think that government intervention to control prices would be an effective answer to the problem?

Fish

Imagine a remote island in the South Seas. Some of the islanders own canoes which they use to go fishing, selling their catch on the beach when they return each day. Some islanders only go fishing occasionally, as they find it more worthwhile to spend their time on other activities. The island has no electricity, so there is no way of storing the fish that are caught — if they are not consumed on the day of the catch, they must be thrown away.

The market for fish on the island is limited by the size of the population. Fortunately for the fishermen, the islanders enjoy fish, and regard it as an important part of their diet, although they also grow vegetables and raise goats and chickens. Fruit and coconuts are also abundant.

Follow-up questions

a What would you expect to be the nature of the price elasticity of supply in the short run (that is, on any given day)?

b Suppose that, on one particular day, fishing conditions are so good that all fishermen return with record catches. How would this affect the price of fish?

c How might the situation in (b) affect the supply of fish on the following day?

d How would you expect the supply of fish to be affected by the invention of a new style of canoe that makes it easier to catch fish?

e How would the market be affected if this new-style canoe also enabled fish to be traded with a neighbouring island?

How markets work: price determination

The previous chapters introduced the notions of demand and supply, and it is now time to bring these two curves together in order to meet the key concept of market equilibrium. The model can then be further developed to see how it provides insights into how markets operate. Indeed, it is time to take a wider view of the process of resource allocation within society. An important question is whether markets can be relied on to guide this process, or whether there are times when markets will fail. This chapter begins to address this by examining how prices can act as market signals to guide resource allocation. In this discussion, some new tools will be needed in order to identify what constitutes an efficient allocation of resources.

Learning objectives

After studying this chapter, you should:
→ understand the notion of equilibrium and its relevance in the demand and supply model
→ be aware of what is meant by comparative static analysis
→ have an overview of how the price mechanism works to allocate resources
→ be able to see how prices provide incentives to producers
→ understand the meaning and significance of consumer surplus
→ understand the meaning and significance of producer surplus
→ be aware of the effects of the entry and exit of firms into and out of a market
→ understand the concept of allocative efficiency
→ be familiar with the way in which resources are allocated in a free market economy

Market equilibrium

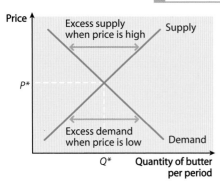

Figure 4.1 Bringing demand and supply together

Chapters 2 and 3 have described the components of the demand and supply model. It only remains to bring them together, for this is how the power of the model can be appreciated. Figure 4.1 shows the demand for and supply of butter.

Suppose that the price were to be set relatively high (above $P\star$). At such a price, firms wish to supply lots of butter to the market. However, consumers are not very keen on butter at such a high price, so demand is not strong. Firms now have a problem: they find that their stocks of butter are building up. What has happened is that the price has been set at a level that exceeds the value that most consumers place on butter, so they will not buy it. There is *excess supply*. The only thing that the firms can do is to reduce the price in order to clear their stocks.

Suppose they now set their price relatively low (below $P\star$). Now it is the consumers who have a problem, because they would like to buy more butter at the low price than firms are prepared to supply. There is *excess demand*. Some consumers may offer to pay more than the going price in order to obtain their butter supplies, and firms realise that they can raise the price.

How will it all end? When the price settles at $P\star$ in Figure 4.1, there is a balance in the market between the quantity that consumers wish to demand and the quantity that firms wish to supply, namely $Q\star$. This is the **market equilibrium**. In a free market the price can be expected to converge on this equilibrium level, through movements along both demand and supply curves.

Key term

market equilibrium a situation that occurs in a market when the price is such that the quantity that consumers wish to buy is exactly balanced by the quantity that firms wish to supply

Quantitative skills 4.1

Identifying and interpreting an intersection on a graph

You will meet many diagrams in economics where there are upward- and downward-sloping lines that intersect at some point. Such intersection points are almost always significant. In the case of demand and supply, the downward-sloping line represents demand, and the upward-sloping line shows supply. Only at the point where the two lines meet are the decisions of consumers and firms mutually consistent. In other words, consumers are choosing to demand exactly the quantity that firms are willing to supply. The important question to explore is the mechanism that will lead to this equilibrium point. This in turn depends upon the incentives facing economic agents if the starting point is away from the intersection point.

Exercise 4.1

Identify the equilibrium market price if demand and supply are as in Figure 4.2.

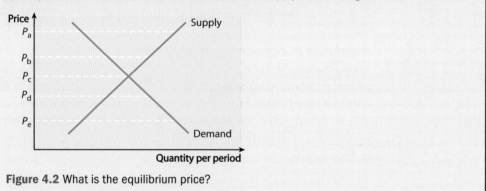

Figure 4.2 What is the equilibrium price?

Summary

- Bringing demand and supply together, you can identify the market equilibrium.
- The equilibrium price is the unique point at which the quantity demanded by consumers is just balanced by the quantity that firms wish to supply.
- In a free market, natural forces can be expected to encourage prices to adjust to the equilibrium level.

Comparative statics

In order to make good use of the demand and supply model, it is necessary to introduce another of the economist's key tools — **comparative static analysis**. You have seen the way in which a market moves towards equilibrium between demand and supply through price adjustments and movements along the demand and supply curves. This is called static analysis, in the sense that a ceteris paribus assumption is imposed by holding constant the factors that influence demand and supply, and focusing on the way in which the market reaches equilibrium.

In the next stage, one of these background factors is changed, and the effect of this change on the market equilibrium is then analysed. In other words, beginning with a market in equilibrium, one of the factors affecting either demand or supply is altered, and the new market equilibrium is then studied. In this way, two equilibrium positions — before and after — will be compared. This approach is known as comparative static analysis.

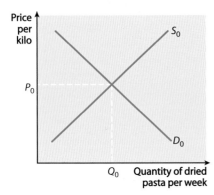

Figure 4.3 A market for dried pasta

A market for dried pasta

Begin with a simple market for dried pasta, a basic staple foodstuff obtainable in any supermarket. Figure 4.3 shows the market in equilibrium. D_0 represents the demand curve in this initial situation, and S_0 is the supply curve. The market is in equilibrium with the price at P_0, and the quantity being traded is Q_0. It is equilibrium in the sense that pasta producers are supplying just the amount of pasta that consumers wish to buy at that price. This is the 'before' position. Some experiments will now be carried out with this market by disturbing the equilibrium.

A change in consumer preferences

Suppose that a study is published highlighting the health benefits of eating pasta, backed up with an advertising campaign. The effect of this is likely to be an increase in the demand for pasta at any given price. In other words, this change in consumer preferences will shift the demand curve to the right, as shown in Figure 4.4.

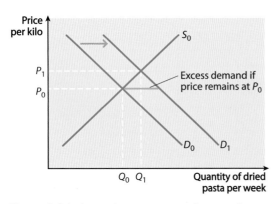
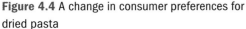

Figure 4.4 A change in consumer preferences for dried pasta

The market now adjusts to a new equilibrium, with a new price P_1 and a new quantity traded at Q_1. In this case, both price and quantity have increased as a result of the change in preferences. There has been a movement along the supply curve.

A change in the price of a substitute

A second possibility is that there is a fall in the price of fresh pasta. This is likely to be a close substitute for dried pasta, so the probable result is that some former consumers of dried pasta will switch their allegiance to the fresh variety. This time the demand curve for dried pasta shifts in the opposite direction, as can be seen in Figure 4.5. Here the starting point is the original position, with market equilibrium at price P_0 and a quantity traded Q_0. After the shift in the demand curve from D_0 to D_2, the market settles again with a price of P_2 and a quantity traded of Q_2. Both price and quantity traded are now lower than in the original position.

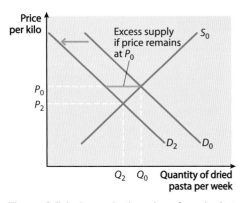

Figure 4.5 A change in the price of a substitute for dried pasta

Improvements in technology are just one factor affecting the market for dried pasta

An improvement in pasta technology

Next, suppose that a new pasta-making machine is produced, enabling dried pasta makers to produce at a lower cost than before. This advancement reduces firms' costs, and consequently they are prepared to supply more dried pasta at any given price. The starting point is the same initial position, but now it is the supply curve that shifts — to the right. This is shown in Figure 4.6.

Again, comparative static analysis can be undertaken. The new market equilibrium is at price P_3, which is lower than the original equilibrium, but the quantity traded is higher at Q_3.

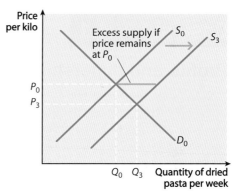

Figure 4.6 New pasta-making technology

An increase in labour costs

Finally, suppose that pasta producers face an increase in their labour costs. Perhaps the Pasta Workers' Union has negotiated higher wages, or the pasta producers have become subject to stricter health and safety legislation, which raises their production costs. Figure 4.7 starts as usual with equilibrium at price P_0 and quantity Q_0.

The increase in production costs means that pasta producers are prepared to supply less dried pasta at any given price, so the supply curve shifts to the left — to S_4. This takes the market to a new equilibrium at a higher price than before (P_4), but with a lower quantity traded (Q_4).

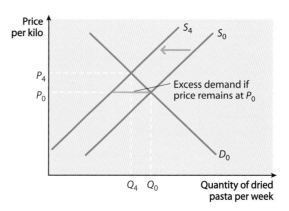

Figure 4.7 An increase in labour costs

Study tip

Economists use diagrams a lot to analyse how equilibrium is affected by external changes — in this case, a change in market conditions that induces a shift in the demand curve. Remember that practice makes perfect, so watch in the news for examples of events that are likely to affect a market, and sketch demand and supply curves to analyse what is expected to happen next. For example, in February 2013 there was outrage in the media when horse-meat was found in burgers and ready meals. What effect would this have on the market?

Summary

- Comparative static analysis enables you to analyse the way in which markets respond to external shocks, by comparing market equilibrium before and after a shock.
- All you need to do is to figure out whether the shock affects demand or supply, and in which direction.
- The size and direction of the shifts of the demand and supply curves determine the overall effect on equilibrium price and quantity traded.

Exercise 4.2

For each of the following market situations, sketch a demand and supply diagram, and undertake a comparative static analysis to see what happens to the equilibrium price and quantity. Explain your answers.

a An increase in consumer incomes affects the demand for bus travel.

b New regulations on environmental pollution force a firm making paint to increase outlay on reducing its emission of toxic fumes.

c A firm of accountants brings in new, faster computers, which have the effect of reducing the firm's costs.

d An outbreak of bird flu causes consumers of chicken to buy burgers instead. (What is the effect on both markets?)

Case study 4.1

Profits and superships

In August 2001, the *Financial Times* reported that ship-owners were facing serious problems. Shipping rates (the prices that ship-owners charge for carrying freight) had fallen drastically in the second quarter of 2001. For example, on the Europe–Asia route, rates fell by 8% eastbound and 6% westbound, causing the ship-owners' profits to be squeezed. Below are some relevant facts and issues:

1 New 'superships', having been ordered a few years earlier, were coming into service with enhanced capacity for transporting freight.

2 A worldwide economic slowdown was taking place; Japan was in lengthy recession and the US economy was also slowing, affecting the growth of world trade.

3 Fuel prices were falling.

4 The structure of the industry is fragmented, with ship-owners watching each other's orders for new ships.

5 New ships take a long time to build.

6 Shipping lines face high fixed costs with slender margins.

Shipping rates fell drastically in 2001

Follow-up questions

Assume that this is a competitive market. (This will allow you to draw supply and demand curves for the market.) There is some evidence for this, as shipping lines face 'slender margins' (see 6). This suggests that the firms face competition from each other, and are unable to use market power to increase profit margins.

a How would you expect the demand and supply curves to move in response to the first three factors mentioned (i.e. 1, 2 and 3)? Sketch a diagram for yourself.

b Why should the shipping lines undertake a large-scale expansion at a time of falling or stagnant demand?

Prices and resource allocation

The coordination problem

As Chapter 1 indicated, all societies face the fundamental economic problem of scarcity. Because there are unlimited wants but finite resources, it is necessary to take decisions on which goods and services should be produced, how they should be produced and for whom they should be produced. For an economy the size of the UK, there is thus an immense coordination problem. Another way of looking at this is to ask how consumers can express their preferences between alternative goods so that producers can produce the best mix of goods and services.

Some alternative possibilities for handling this problem will now be considered. In a completely free market economy, market forces are allowed to allocate resources. At the other extreme, in a centrally planned economy the state plans and directs resources into a range of uses. In between there is the mixed economy. In order to evaluate these alternatives, it is necessary to explore how each of them operates. In a free market economy, prices play the key role; this is sometimes referred to as the laissez-faire approach to resource allocation.

Consumer surplus

Think a little more carefully about what the demand curve represents. Figure 4.8 shows the demand curve for laptop computers. Suppose that the price is set at $P^\star$ and quantity demanded is thus $Q^\star$. $P^\star$ can be seen as the value that the last customer places on a laptop. In other words, if the price were even slightly above $P^\star$, there would be one consumer who would choose not to buy: this individual will be referred to as the *marginal consumer*.

To that marginal consumer, $P^\star$ represents the satisfaction derived from consuming this good — it is the price that just reflects the consumer's benefit from a laptop, as it is the price that just induces her to buy.

In most markets, all consumers face the same prices for goods and services. This leads to an important concept in economic analysis. $P^\star$ may represent the value of laptops to the marginal consumer, but what about all the other consumers who are also buying laptops at $P^\star$? They would all be willing to pay a higher price for a laptop. Indeed, consumer A in Figure 4.8 would pay a very high price indeed, and thus values a laptop much more highly than $P^\star$. When consumer A pays $P^\star$ for a laptop, he gets a great deal, as he values the good so much more highly — as represented by the vertical green line on Figure 4.8. Consumer B also gains a surplus above her willingness to pay (the blue line).

If all these surplus values are added up, they sum to the total surplus that society gains from consuming laptops. This is known as the **consumer surplus**, represented by the shaded triangle in Figure 4.9. It can be interpreted as the welfare that society gains from consuming the good, over and above the price that has to be paid for it.

Indeed, thinking of the society as a whole, we can think of the price $P^\star$ as the benefit that society gains from consuming the last unit of the good. This will be known as the **marginal social benefit (MSB)** derived from consuming the good. The same argument could be made about any point along the demand curve, so the curve itself can be interpreted as the marginal social benefit to be derived from consuming laptop computers.

> ### Key terms
>
> **consumer surplus** the value that consumers gain from consuming a good or service over and above the price paid
>
> **marginal social benefit (MSB)** the additional benefit that society gains from consuming an extra unit of a good

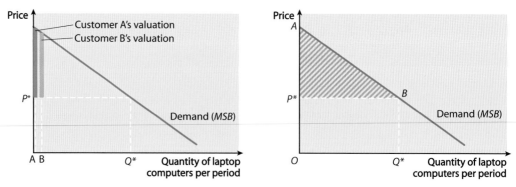

Figure 4.8 Price as a marginal social benefit   **Figure 4.9** Consumer surplus

> ## Quantitative skills 4.2
>
> ## Interpreting areas on a graph
>
> In using diagrams like Figure 4.9, it is important to be able to interpret *areas* on the graph as well as lines and positions. In this case, the area of interest is the total amount of consumer surplus. The area under the demand curve up to the quantity sold (*Q**) represents the total value of the good that is sold. In total, consumers spend an amount on this which is the price multiplied by the quantity sold, namely *P** multiplied by *Q**. In Figure 4.9 this is the area of the rectangle *OP*BQ**. The surplus is then the shaded triangle *P*AB*.

Producer surplus

Parallel to the notion of consumer surplus is the concept of **producer surplus**. Think about the nature of the supply curve: it reveals how much output firms are prepared to supply at any given price in a competitive market. Figure 4.10 depicts a supply curve. Assume the price is at *P★* and that all units are sold at that price. *P★* represents the value to firms of the marginal unit sold. In other words, if the price had been set slightly below *P★*, the last unit would not have been supplied, as firms would not have found this profitable.

Notice that the threshold at which a firm will decide it is not profitable to supply is the point at which the price received by the firm reaches the cost to the firm of producing the last unit of the good. The supply curve shows that, in the range of prices between point *A* and *P★*, firms would have been willing to supply positive amounts of this good or service. So at *P★*, they would gain a surplus value on all units of the good supplied below *Q★*. The total area is shown in Figure 4.11 — it is the area above the supply curve and below *P★*, shown as the shaded triangle.

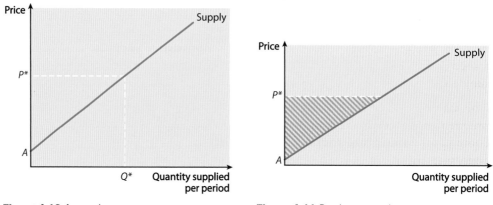

Figure 4.10 A supply curve   **Figure 4.11** Producer surplus

One way of defining this producer surplus is as the surplus earned by firms over and above the minimum that would have kept them in the market. It is the *raison d'être* of firms.

Extension material

The notions of producer and consumer surplus are important when we come to think about the total welfare that economic agents receive from their economic activities. For consumers, the consumer surplus represents the surplus that they receive over and above what they are willing to pay for a good or service. For firms, the producer surplus represents the surplus that they receive over and

above their costs of production. There is thus a sense in which we interpret the sum of these two surpluses as being the net welfare that society as a whole gains from the production and consumption of this good or service. It could be argued that efficient resource allocation is achieved when this is maximised.

Summary

- The demand curve shows the valuation that consumers place on a good, reflecting the satisfaction they gain from consuming it.
- Consumer surplus represents the benefit that consumers gain from consuming a product over and above the price they pay for that product.
- Producer surplus represents the benefit gained by firms over and above the price at which they would have been prepared to supply a product.

Prices and preferences

How can consumers signal their preferences to producers? Demand and supply analysis provides the clue. Consumer and producer surplus can be shown on the same diagram. Figure 4.12 shows a market in equilibrium, with price at $P\star$ and quantity traded at $Q\star$. The green shaded area shows consumer surplus, while the pink area represents producer surplus.

Figure 4.13 shows the demand and supply for laptop computers. These have become popular goods in recent years. That is to say, over time there has been a rightward shift in the demand curve — in the figure, from D_0 to D_1. This simply means that consumers are placing a higher value on these goods; they are prepared to demand more at any given price. The result, as you know from comparative static analysis, is that the market will move to a new equilibrium, with price rising from P_0 to P_1 and quantity traded increasing from Q_0 to Q_1: there is a movement along the supply curve.

The shift in the demand curve is an expression of consumers' preferences; it embodies the fact that they value laptop computers more highly now than before. The price that consumers are willing to pay represents their valuation of laptop computers.

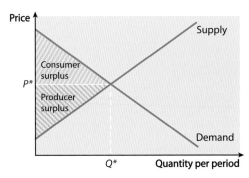

Figure 4.12 Consumer and producer surplus

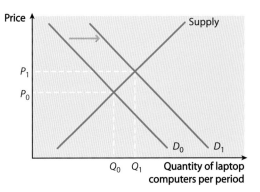

Figure 4.13 The market for laptop computers

Consumer demand for laptops has risen over the last few years

Prices as signals and incentives

From the producers' perspective, the question is how they receive signals from consumers about their changing preferences. Price is the key. Figure 4.13 showed how an increase in demand for laptop computers leads to an increase in the equilibrium market price. The shift in the demand curve leads to an increase in the equilibrium price, which encourages producers to supply more computers — there is a movement along the supply curve. This is really saying that producers find it profitable to expand their output of laptop computers at that higher price. The price level is thus a signal to producers about consumer preferences.

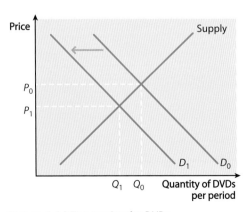

Figure 4.14 The market for DVDs

Notice that the price signal works equally well when there is a decrease in the demand for a good or service. Figure 4.14, for example, shows the market for DVDs. With the growth of Blu-rays, streaming video and music, there has been a fall in the demand for DVDs, so the demand for them has shifted to the left — consumers are demanding fewer DVDs at any price. Thus, the demand curve shifts from D_0 to D_1. Producers of DVDs are beginning to find that they cannot sell as many DVDs at the original price as before, so they have to reduce their price to avoid an increase in their unsold stocks. They have less incentive to produce DVDs, and will supply less. There is a movement along the supply curve to a lower equilibrium price at P_1, and a lower quantity traded at Q_1. The rise of Blu-ray discs reinforced this trend.

Thus, you can see how existing producers in a market receive signals from consumers in the form of changes in the equilibrium price, and respond to these signals by adjusting their output levels. Notice that the threshold at which a firm will decide it is not profitable to supply is the point at which the price received by the firm reaches the cost to the firm of producing the last unit of the good. If the price is higher than the cost of an extra unit, the firm will make a profit by producing it. The cost of producing an additional unit of a good is known by economists as the **marginal cost**. In a competitive market, the supply curve reflects that marginal cost.

Notice that the price signal works both ways. Firms receive signals from consumers about changing preferences, but in similar fashion, prices act as a rationing device if firms are unable to supply the goods that consumers want to buy. For example, suppose there is a poor harvest of coffee because of weather conditions in Brazil. The equilibrium price will rise, and consumers will find themselves rationed.

Entry and exit of firms

The discussion so far has focused on the reactions of existing firms in a market to changes in consumer preferences. However, this is only part of the picture. Think back to Figure 4.13, where there was an increase in demand for laptop computers following a change in consumer preferences. The equilibrium price rose, and existing firms expanded the quantity supplied in response. Those firms are now earning a higher producer surplus than before. Other firms not currently in the market will be attracted by these surpluses, perceiving this to be a profitable market in which to operate.

If firms are free to enter the market, they will do so. This in turn will tend to shift the supply curve to the right, as there will then be more firms prepared to supply. As a result, the equilibrium market price will tend to drift down again, until the market reaches a position in which there is no further incentive for new firms to enter the market. This will occur when the rate of return for firms in the laptop market is no better than in other markets.

Figure 4.15 illustrates this situation. The original increase in demand leads, as before, to a new equilibrium with a higher price P_1. As new firms join the market in quest of producer surplus, the supply curve shifts to the right to S_2, pushing the price back down to P_0, but with the quantity traded now up at Q_2.

If the original movement in demand is in the opposite direction, as it was for DVDs in Figure 4.14, a similar long-run adjustment takes place. As the market price falls, some firms in the market may decide that they no longer wish to remain in production, and will exit from the market altogether. This will shift the supply curve to the left in Figure 4.16 (to S_2) until only firms that continue to find it profitable will remain in the market. In the final position, price is back to P_0 and quantity traded has fallen to Q_2.

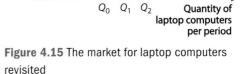

Figure 4.15 The market for laptop computers revisited

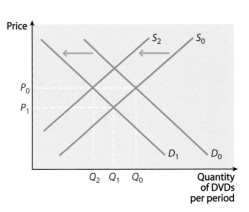

Figure 4.16 The market for DVDs

Summary

- If market forces are to allocate resources effectively, consumers need to be able to express their preferences for goods and services in such a way that producers can respond.
- Consumers express their preferences through prices, as prices will adjust to equilibrium levels following a change in consumer demand.
- Producers have an incentive to respond to changes in prices. In the short run this occurs through output adjustments of existing firms (movements along the supply curve), but in the long run firms will enter the market (or exit from it) until there are no further incentives for entry or exit.

Aspects of efficiency

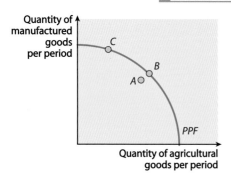

Figure 4.17 Efficiency in production

In tackling the fundamental economic problem of scarcity, a society needs to find a way of using its limited resources as effectively as possible. In normal parlance it might be natural to refer to this as a quest for efficiency. From an economist's point of view there are two key aspects of efficiency, both of which are important in evaluating whether markets in an economy are working effectively.

Chapter 1 introduced one of these aspects in relation to the production possibility frontier (*PPF*). Figure 4.17 shows a country's production possibility frontier. One of the choices to be made in allocating resources in this country is between producing agricultural or manufactured goods.

In Chapter 1 it was seen that at a production point such as *A* the economy would not be using its resources fully, since by moving to a point on the *PPF* it would be possible to produce more of both types of good. For example, if production took place at point *B*, then more of both agricultural and manufactured goods could be produced, so that society would be better off than at *A*.

A similar claim could be made for any point along the *PPF*: it is more efficient to be at a point on the frontier than at some point within it. However, if you compare point *B* with point *C*, you will notice that the economy produces more manufactured goods at *C* than at *B* — but only at the expense of producing fewer agricultural goods.

This draws attention to the trade-off between the production of the two sorts of goods. It is difficult to judge whether society is better off at *B* or at *C* without knowing more about the preferences of consumers.

This discussion highlights the two aspects of efficiency. On the one hand, there is the question of whether society is operating on the *PPF*, and thus using its resources effectively. On the other hand, there is the question of whether society is producing the balance of goods that consumers wish to consume. This aspect of efficiency is known as **allocative efficiency**.

Allocative efficiency

Allocative efficiency is about whether an economy allocates its resources in such a way as to produce a balance of goods and services that matches consumer preferences. In a complex modern economy, it is clearly difficult to identify such an ideal result. How can an appropriate balance of goods and services be identified?

Take the market for an individual product, such as the market for laptop computers that was considered earlier in the chapter. It was argued then that in the long run, the market could be expected to arrive at an equilibrium price and quantity at which there was no incentive for firms either to enter the market or to exit from it. Figure 4.18 will remind you of the market situation.

The sequence of events in the diagram shows that, from an initial equilibrium with price at P_0 and quantity traded at Q_0, there was an increase in demand, with the demand curve shifting to D_1. In response, existing firms expanded their supply, moving up the supply curve. However, the lure of the producer surplus (abnormal profits) that was being made by these firms then attracted more firms into the market, such that the supply curve shifted to S_2, a process that brought the price back down to the original level of P_0.

Now think about that price from the point of view of a firm. P_0 is at a level where there is no further incentive to attract new firms, but no firm wishes to leave the market. In other words, no surplus is being made on that marginal unit, and the marginal firm is just breaking even on it. The price in this context would seem to be just covering the marginal cost of production.

However, it was also argued that from the consumers' point of view any point along the demand curve could be regarded as the satisfaction received from consuming an additional unit of a good or service. We can regard this as the *marginal social benefit* from consuming the good.

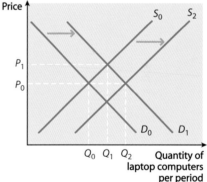

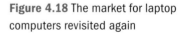

Figure 4.18 The market for laptop computers revisited again

Where is all this leading? Putting together the arguments, it would seem that market forces can carry a market to a position in which, from the firms' point of view, the price is equal to marginal cost, and from the consumers' point of view, the price is equal to marginal benefit.

This is an important result. Suppose that the marginal benefit from consuming a good were higher than the marginal cost to society of producing it. It could then be argued that society would be better off producing more of the good because, by increasing production, more could be added to benefits than to costs. Equally, if the marginal cost were above the marginal benefit from consuming a good, society would be producing too much of the good and would benefit from producing less. The best possible position is thus where marginal benefit is equal to marginal cost — in other words, where *price is set equal to marginal cost.*

If all markets in an economy operated in this way, resources would be used so effectively that no reallocation of resources could generate an overall improvement.

Allocative efficiency would be attained. The key question is whether the market mechanism will work sufficiently well to ensure that this happens — or whether it will fail. In other words, are there conditions that could arise in a market, in which price would not be set at marginal cost?

Exercise 4.4

Consider Figure 4.19, which shows a production possibility frontier (*PPF*) for an economy that produces consumer goods and investment goods.

Identify each of the following (Hint: in some cases more than one answer is possible):

a a point of productive inefficiency

b a point of productive efficiency

c a point of allocative efficiency

d an unattainable point (Hint: think about what would need to happen for society to reach such a point)

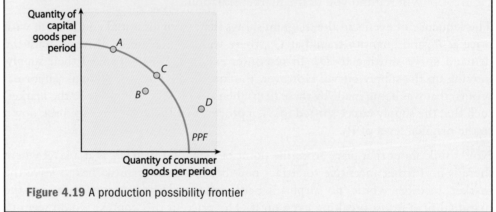

Figure 4.19 A production possibility frontier

The working of a market economy

The previous section showed that the price mechanism allows a society to allocate its resources effectively if firms respond to changes in prices. Consumers express changes in their preferences by their decisions to buy (or not to buy) at the going price, which leads to a change in the equilibrium price. Firms thus respond to changes in consumer demand, given the incentive of profitability, which is related to price. In the short run, existing firms adjust their output levels along the supply curve. In the long run, firms enter into markets (or exit from them) in response to the relative profitability of the various economic activities that take place in the economy. But how does this work out in practice in a 'real-life' economy?

Opportunity cost

One way of viewing this system is through the notion of opportunity cost, introduced in Chapter 1. For example, in choosing to be active in the market for DVDs, a firm faces an opportunity cost. If it uses its resources to produce DVDs, it is not using those resources to produce something else. There may come a point at which the cost of producing DVDs becomes too high, if the profitability of other goods is so much higher than that for DVDs because of changes in the pattern of consumer demand. When the firm finds that it is not covering its opportunity costs, it will transfer production away from the DVD market.

The government's role

The government's role in a free economy is relatively limited, but nonetheless important. A basic framework of *property rights* is essential, together with a basic legal framework. However, the state does not intervene in the production process directly. Secure property rights are significant, as this assures the incentives for the owners of capital.

Within such a system, consumers try to maximise the satisfaction (utility) they gain from consuming a range of products, and firms seek to maximise their profits by responding to consumer demand through the medium of price signals. This goes back to Adam Smith's notion of the invisible hand, which was introduced in Chapter 1.

It is worth noting that Adam Smith also sounded a word of warning. He felt that there were too many factors that interfered with the free market system, such as over-protectionism and restrictions on trade. At the same time, he was not utterly convinced that a free market economy would be wholly effective, noting also that firms might at times collude to prevent the free operation of the market mechanism:

> *People of the same trade seldom meet together, even for merriment and diversion, but the conversation ends in a conspiracy against the public, or in some contrivance to raise prices...*

> (Adam Smith, *The Wealth of Nations*, Vol. I)

Adam Smith was not convinced that a free market economy would be wholly effective

So there may be situations in which consumer interests need to be protected, if there is some sort of market failure that prevents the best outcome from being achieved. This will be explored in Chapters 6 and 7.

Summary

- A society needs to find a way of using its limited resources as efficiently as possible.
- Allocative efficiency occurs when firms produce an appropriate bundle of goods and services, given consumer preferences.
- An individual market exhibits aspects of allocative efficiency when the marginal benefit received by society from consuming a good or service matches the marginal cost of producing it — that is, when price is equal to marginal cost.
- Free markets do not always lead to the best possible allocation of resources: there may be market failure.

How markets work: the price mechanism in action

In the previous chapters, you have seen how the demand and supply model can be used in order to analyse market situations. It is now time to begin to apply this model in a variety of circumstances to see how it provides insights into how different markets operate. You will encounter demand and supply in a wide variety of contexts, and begin to glimpse some of the ways in which the model can help to explain how the economic world works. You will also see how government intervention in the form of indirect taxation and subsidies can affect markets.

Learning objectives

After studying this chapter, you should be able to:
➡ apply demand and supply analysis in a variety of different market situations
➡ analyse the effect of taxes and subsidies in a market, using demand and supply analysis
➡ evaluate the extent to which a sales tax is borne by buyers and sellers
➡ use demand and supply analysis to interpret economic events in the real world
➡ be aware that consumers may not always act rationally

The examples of demand and supply discussed so far were consumer goods of some sort — Blu-ray discs, butter, pencils and so on. However, it would be wrong to think that demand and supply analysis is of relevance only in that sort of market. So this chapter broadens the horizons, looking beyond consumer goods markets.

Agricultural markets

The markets for agricultural produce have some interesting characteristics that can be analysed with the demand and supply model. One particular characteristic of many such markets is that the supply side of the market can be strongly affected by weather and climate, sometimes in random or unpredictable ways. This can create conditions in which it is difficult to forecast market outcomes in advance. In particular, this means that prices can vary quite widely from year to year, making conditions in agricultural markets difficult to predict. For some commodities, attempts can be made to stabilise prices by storing surplus produce in good years to sell in bad years.

Exercise 5.1

In April 2003 southeast Asia was suffering from an outbreak of the SARS virus which had spread around the region. On 20 April one of the main wholesale fruit and vegetable markets in Singapore, at Pasir Panjang, had to be closed when workers were found to have been infected. Sketch a demand and supply diagram to predict how the retail market for vegetables was affected.

Commodity markets

Another category of market that is of particular interest is the one for commodities. This encompasses markets for various types of raw material used in the production process of many manufacturing industries. Prices in these markets too can be volatile, but this time the volatility arises from the demand side of the market.

Figure 5.1 shows the market for bauxite, a commodity used as a raw material in the production of aluminium. Many countries experience fluctuations in the overall level of economic activity over time. There are periods of boom and periods of recession. The demand for aluminium (and hence for bauxite) tends to vary with these cycles of activity. D_{av} here represents the average position of the demand curve for bauxite. At the peak of the cycle demand is high and the price rises to P_{peak}, but at the trough of the cycle prices fall to P_{trough}. The quantity traded does not vary very much. This is because the figure has been drawn showing supply to be relatively inelastic, so the main burden of adjustment to market equilibrium takes place through the price level.

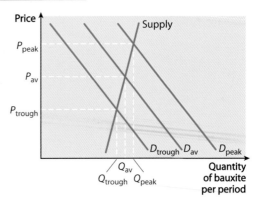

Figure 5.1 The market for bauxite

Such markets are sometimes complicated by the existence of futures markets, in which commodities can be bought in the present period for delivery at a future date at prices agreed now. This adds a speculative element to the demand.

Exercise 5.2

The *Financial Times* in March 1998 reported that the Jamaican bauxite industry was experiencing a combination of record output and falling revenues. It seems that capacity in the industry was rising, and improved labour relations were increasing productivity. However, there was considerable uncertainty in the market, with weak demand for aluminium, following the Asian financial crisis. On the basis of this information, sketch a demand and supply diagram to show the market situation. From your diagram, would you expect price to increase or decrease? How about quantity?

A commodity market that has been much discussed in recent years is the market for oil. This is seen as being especially significant for the global economy because oil is so important for the functioning of other markets, especially transport. The market for oil is inevitably a global one. All countries use oil, but oil reserves are concentrated in only some countries. The price of oil over time has followed something of an erratic path, as you can see in Figure 5.2.

The Organisation of Petroleum Exporting Countries (OPEC) has played an influential role in the way that prices have evolved over time, but other factors have also been important. OPEC is an organisation that operates as a producer **cartel**. A cartel is an agreement between firms in a market on price and output with the intention of maximising their joint profits. Although such agreements are illegal in countries such as the UK and the USA, OPEC is an agreement between nation producers, so is less easy to regulate. Cartel agreements can interfere with the free working of the price mechanism.

Although the market for oil may not be a freely operating competitive market, demand and supply analysis can still help in the interpretation of how it has evolved over time. Before the first so-called 'oil-price crisis' of 1973–74, the price of oil

> **Key term**
>
> **cartel** an agreement between firms in a market on price and output with the intention of maximising their joint profits

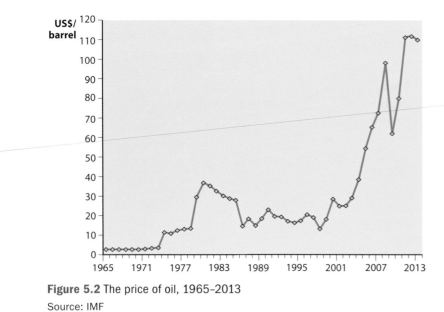

Figure 5.2 The price of oil, 1965–2013

Source: IMF

had been stable over a long period. Two events occurred in the early 1970s that affected the supply side of the oil market. One was the Yom Kippur War (1973), which interrupted the supply of oil from the Middle East. The second was a decision by OPEC to restrict supply. With demand being relatively inelastic, the disruption to supply resulted in a substantial increase in the price of oil.

Demand was inelastic in the short run because consumers had become accustomed to relatively low prices, and could not adjust demand quickly. For example, in the UK many houses were heated through oil-fired central heating. In addition, cars of the day were relatively fuel-inefficient. As time went by, new houses were no longer built with oil-fired heating, and cars became more efficient in their use of petrol. In other words, demand was less inelastic in the longer term.

You can see, therefore, that the first major oil price increase was supply driven. This was also the case for the second crisis, which took place in 1979–80 when OPEC again decided to reduce supply. Looking at Figure 5.2, the sudden fall in oil prices in the mid-1980s was also the result of an oil supply shock, when Saudi Arabia increased its supply of oil, leading to a fall in the price of oil.

The rises in the price of oil in the early 2000s arose in a rather different way. There were again some supply-side influences, such as the Iraq War. However, there were also effects on the demand side, particularly with the rapid economic growth that was taking place in China. You may find it helpful to sketch some demand and supply diagrams to analyse the effects of these changes in the oil market for yourself.

The destruction of oil wells during the Iraq War disrupted the supply of oil in the early 2000s

The housing market

Everyone needs somewhere to live, and housing makes up a large part of the household budget. This makes the housing market particularly important in any economy. Here too, demand and supply can be used to explain how the market operates.

The housing market is not in fact a single market, as there are different segments that may operate in quite different ways. There are the owner-occupier market and the private and public rental sectors. Of course, these segments interact in some ways, but they may be influenced by different factors.

The owner-occupier housing market often features in the news. The purchase of a house is the largest single transaction that most people will make in their lifetimes, and is normally funded through borrowing (apart from the occasional lottery win!). The demand for houses to buy is thus influenced partly by the cost of borrowing — in other words, the interest rate. Later chapters of this book will cover the way in which interest rates are used as a policy instrument to stabilise the overall economy. In the early part of the twenty-first century, interest rates have been relatively low by historical standards, and this has encouraged borrowing, which has fed into the demand for houses, pushing the demand curve to the right.

At the same time, the supply of houses has been expanding only slowly — at least in some regions. Building takes time, of course, but also there have been environmental concerns, and the resulting regulation has limited the growth of the housing stock by restricting the amount of new stock being built.

Figure 5.3 sketches how this might be seen in terms of demand and supply. Demand increases rapidly, but supply expands relatively slowly. The result is an increase in the equilibrium price, from P_0 to P_1, with only a modest expansion of supply, from Q_0 to Q_1. The late 1990s and the early 2000s did indeed see a rapid increase in house prices, and there was much speculation that they were rising too rapidly to be sustainable. This proved to be the case and house prices fell between 2007 and 2009 with the onset of recession and the financial crisis. There was a mild recovery in 2010 but this was followed by a period of stagnation. The significant role of housing in everyone's lives makes this an important issue.

Demand and supply may help to explain why house prices have been rising. However, there are other factors to be considered before arriving at a complete explanation of the market.

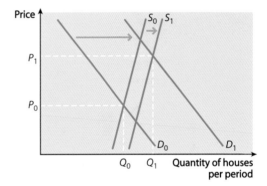

Figure 5.3 The market for houses for owner occupation

The foreign exchange market

When you take your holidays in Spain you need to buy euros. Equally, when German tourists come to visit London they need to buy pounds. If there is buying going on, then there must be a market — remember from Chapter 1 that a market is a set of arrangements that enable transactions to be undertaken. So here is another sort of market to be considered. The exchange rate is the price at which two currencies exchange, and it can be analysed using demand and supply.

Exchange
rate
(€ per £)

Supply

e*

Demand

Quantity of pounds
per period

Figure 5.4 The market for pounds sterling

Consider the market for pounds, and focus on the exchange rate between pounds and euros, as shown in Figure 5.4. Think first of all about what gives rise to a demand for pounds. It is not just German tourists who need pounds to spend on holiday: anyone holding euros who wants to buy British goods needs pounds in order to pay for them. So the demand for pounds comes from people in the euro area who want to buy British goods or services — or assets. When the exchange rate for the pound in euros is high, potential buyers of British goods get relatively few pounds per euro so the demand will be relatively low, whereas if the euros per pound rate is relatively low, they get more for their money. Hence the demand curve is expected to be downward sloping.

Foreign exchange as a derived demand

One point to notice from this is that the foreign exchange market is an example of a *derived demand*, in the sense that people want pounds not for their own sake, but for the goods or services that they can buy. This notion of a derived demand is explored more fully in Chapter 5 of Book 2, as it is important in explaining the demand for labour. One way of viewing the exchange rate is as a means by which to learn about the international competitiveness of British exports. When the exchange rate is high, British goods are less competitive in Europe, ceteris paribus. Notice the ceteris paribus assumption there. This is important, because the exchange rate is not the only determinant of the competitiveness of British goods: it also depends on the relative price levels in the UK and Europe.

What about the supply of pounds? Pounds are supplied by UK residents wanting euros to buy goods or services from Europe. From this angle, when the euros per pound rate is high, UK residents get more euros for their pounds, and therefore will tend to supply more pounds.

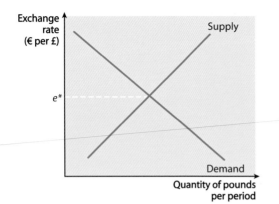

Pounds are traded for euros on the foreign exchange market

If the exchange market is in equilibrium, the exchange rate will tend to e★, where the demand for pounds is matched by the supply.

▌The stock market

Another important financial market is the stock market. Firms that want to raise funds for investing in new machinery or other projects can do so by issuing 'stocks', which are then sold on the stock market. People wanting a good return on their savings may then purchase stocks and shares in the hope of receiving good dividends (sharing in the profits of the firm), or capital gains as the value of the firm (hopefully) rises with success.

Although it may sound as if the stock market is a quite different sort of market, it too can be analysed by using demand and supply analysis. The demand for stocks comes from savers looking for a return, so the strength of demand will depend on their expectations of the future success of the firm, and future movements in the price of the stock, which will affect the capital gain. The supply of stocks will depend on firms' expectations of the future demand for the product, which will determine whether or not they are keen to invest in new capital goods.

The interaction of demand and supply will thus determine the price of the stock in the market. However, notice how important expectations are on both sides of the market. This suggests that there will be substantial uncertainty surrounding market conditions. One result of this is that there could be some instability in the positions of both demand and supply, especially where people react strongly to news about the markets. If people suddenly come to believe that stock prices are about to tumble, perhaps because of gloomy forecasts about the economy, then demand is likely to fall as savers move their funds to alternative financial assets. Demand and supply analysis then predicts that prices will fall — all because people expect this to happen. In other words, the stock market could be characterised by self-fulfilling expectations.

Financial markets

Chapter 1 highlighted the importance of money in enabling exchange to take place through the operation of markets. This implies that people have a *demand for money*. This demand for money is associated with the functions of money set out on page 13 — as a medium of exchange, a store of value, a unit of account and a standard of deferred payment. If there is a demand for money, then perhaps there should also be a market for money?

The demand for and supply of money

We can think of the demand for money depending on a number of factors — in particular, upon the number of transactions that people wish to undertake — which probably depends upon income. But is there a price of money? The price of money can be viewed in terms of opportunity cost. When people choose to hold money, they incur an opportunity cost, which can be seen as the next best alternative to holding money. For example, instead of holding money, you could decide to purchase a financial asset that would provide a rate of return, represented by the rate of interest. This rate of interest can thus be interpreted as the price of holding money.

How about the supply of money? This will be discussed much later in the course, but for now, it can be assumed that the supply of money is determined by the Bank of England, and it can be assumed that this money supply will not depend upon the rate of interest. Figure 5.5 illustrates the market for money. The demand for money is shown to be downward sloping, as the higher the rate of interest, the greater the return that is sacrificed by holding money, so the smaller will be the demand for money. The supply of money does not depend upon the rate of interest (by assumption), so is shown as a vertical line. The market is in equilibrium when the rate of interest is at $r^\star$, the level at which the demand and supply of money are equal.

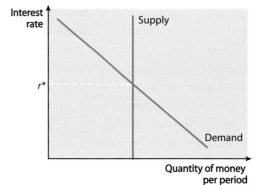

Figure 5.5 The market for money

Indirect taxes and subsidies

One final application of the demand and supply model is to analyse the effect on a market of the imposition of **indirect taxes** and subsidies.

In the UK, value added tax (VAT) is the most prominent example of an indirect tax, although other levies, such as excise duties on alcohol and tobacco, are also indirect taxes. An indirect tax is paid by the seller, so it affects the supply curve for a product.

Figure 5.6 illustrates the case of a fixed-rate, or specific, tax — a tax that is set at a constant amount per pack of cigarettes. Without the tax, the market equilibrium is at the intersection of demand and supply, with price P_0 and quantity traded Q_0. The effect of the tax is to reduce the quantity that firms are prepared to supply at

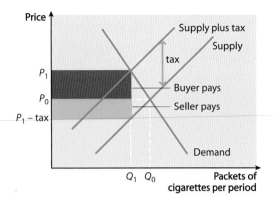

Price

P_1
P_0
$P_1 -$ tax

Supply plus tax
Supply
tax
Buyer pays
Seller pays
Demand

Q_1 Q_0 Packets of
cigarettes per period

Figure 5.6 The effects of an indirect tax on cigarettes

any given price; to put it another way, for any given quantity of cigarettes, firms need to receive the amount of the tax over and above the price at which they would have been prepared to supply that quantity. The effect is thus to move the supply curve upwards by the amount of the tax, as shown in the figure. A new equilibrium is reached with a higher price at P_1 and a lower quantity traded at Q_1.

An important question is: who bears the burden of the tax? If you look at the diagram, you will see that the price difference between the with- and without-tax situations (i.e. $P_1 - P_0$) is less than the amount of the tax, which is the vertical distance between the with- and without-tax supply curves. So, although the seller (producer) may be responsible for the mechanics of paying the tax, part of the tax is effectively passed on to the buyer (consumer) in the form of the higher price. So the **incidence of the tax** falls partly upon the seller, but in Figure 5.6 most of the tax is borne by the buyer.

The price elasticity of demand determines the incidence of the tax. If demand were perfectly inelastic, sellers would be able to pass the whole burden of the tax on to buyers (consumer) through an increase in price equal to the value of the tax, knowing that this would not affect demand. However, if demand were perfectly elastic, sellers would not be able to raise the price at all, so they would have to bear the entire burden of the tax.

If the tax is not a constant amount, but a percentage of the price (known as an *ad valorem* tax), the supply curve is still affected; but now it steepens, as shown in Figure 5.7.

Exercise 5.3

Sketch diagrams to investigate the incidence of a tax when demand is perfectly inelastic and perfectly elastic.

In some situations the government may wish to encourage production of a particular good or service, perhaps because it views the good as having strategic significance to the country. One way it can do this is by giving **subsidies**.

Such subsidies have been especially common in agriculture, which is often seen as being of strategic significance. In the early years of this century, the USA has come under pressure to reduce the subsidies that it grants to cotton producers. Analytically, a subsidy can be regarded as a sort of negative indirect tax that shifts the supply curve down, as shown in Figure 5.8. Without the subsidy, market equilibrium is at price P_0 and quantity traded Q_0. With the subsidy in place, the equilibrium price falls to P_1 and the quantity traded increases to Q_1.

Again, notice that, because the price falls by less than the amount of the subsidy, the benefits of the subsidy are shared between buyers and sellers, depending on the elasticity of demand. If the aim of the subsidy is to increase production, it is only partially successful — the degree of success also depends on the elasticity of demand.

Key terms

incidence of a tax the way in which the burden of paying a sales tax is divided between buyers and sellers

subsidy a grant given by the government to producers to encourage production of a good or service

Study tip

Remember that if you are asked to discuss an indirect tax or a subsidy in the exam, the effect is to shift the *supply curve* to the left/upwards (for a tax) or to the right/downwards (for a subsidy).

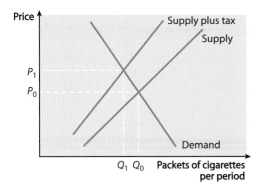

Figure 5.7 The effects of an *ad valorem* tax on cigarettes

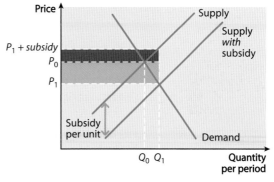

Figure 5.8 The effects of a subsidy

Do consumers always act rationally?

In discussing the way that markets work, it has been assumed that consumers act rationally, aiming to maximise their utility. Recent research in experimental and behavioural economics suggests that this may not always be the case, and that there may be situations in which consumers seem to take decisions that are economically irrational.

One example is where it is observed that consumers may not react to a price change. One reason for this may be that people develop consumption habits, which may lead to persistent behaviour, even if this is costly. This does not only apply to products that are addictive, such as tobacco, although that is an extreme example of persistence.

It has also been observed that individual consumers may exhibit herding behaviour, buying a product because others are doing so, rather than because of its intrinsic merits. People may also take decisions on impulse. For example, they may reach for a chocolate bar cunningly displayed beside the supermarket checkout queue.

People are also seen to take decisions that are altruistic in nature, such as giving to charity, or behaving in a way that is perceived to be socially responsible, but costly.

In some cases, seemingly irrational behaviour may reflect information overload. There may be more information about consumption possibilities than consumers are able to absorb and interpret. Or, indeed, it may be that information about products is difficult to gather or to analyse. People may then take decisions based on the best information that they can find, or the most information that they are capable of analysing. For example, it may be that consumers are weak at undertaking calculations, or do not have the information needed to undertake calculations. This is sometimes referred to as *bounded rationality*, where economic agents do the best that they can, given the information available.

Summary

- In agricultural markets, supply can fluctuate between seasons because of weather conditions. This causes volatility in prices.
- In commodity markets, demand may fluctuate across the business cycle, again causing volatility in prices.
- The oil market has been highly influential because of the importance of oil as a source of energy.
- The housing market can be analysed using demand and supply analysis. The level of demand may be influenced by government policy on interest rates.
- Demand and supply enable you to examine how the foreign exchange rate is determined.
- The stock market is another market to which demand and supply analysis can be applied.
- An indirect tax levied on a good or service will be seen as a shift in the supply curve. The incidence of the tax (whether the burden is borne by buyers or sellers) is determined by the elasticity of demand.
- It is important to remain aware that consumers may not always act rationally, and may take decisions that are more difficult to capture in an economic model.

Case study 5.1

Jewellery

A local craft market is populated by a variety of stalls selling a range of items — antiques, football memorabilia, second-hand books, hand-made jewellery and other items. The same sellers are present at the market every time it opens, each with their regular place, but there are some vacant stalls. The stall holders just make enough profit to make it worth their while.

One week, the craft market is featured in the local newspaper, and an item appears on local television highlighting the quality of design and value for money of the jewellery on sale at the market. The jewellery sellers suddenly find that their stock is moving very rapidly, and realise that they can increase their prices. As word gets around, some of the vacant stalls are taken up by new jewellery makers and, although the number of buyers remains high, prices drift back to their original level.

New jewellery stalls have come into the market

Follow-up question

Sketch a demand and supply diagram to track these changes in the market for jewellery.

6 Market failure and externalities

Earlier chapters have shown that prices can act as signals that help to guide the allocation of resources. However, there are situations in which markets fail to produce the ideal outcome for society. This chapter and the next discuss some key ways in which market failure can occur. The main focus of this chapter is to explore what happens if market prices are not able to reflect the full costs and benefits associated with market transactions. There are many situations in which there are costs or benefits that are external to the workings of the market mechanism.

Learning objectives

After studying this chapter, you should:
➜ recognise situations in which the free market mechanism may fail to take account of costs or benefits that are associated with market transactions
➜ be familiar with situations in which there may be a divergence between private and social costs or benefits, such that price is not set equal to marginal cost
➜ be able to use diagrams to analyse positive and negative externalities in either production or consumption
➜ be familiar with a wide range of examples of externalities

Causes of market failure

This chapter and the next explore a number of ways in which markets may fail to bring the best result for society as a whole. In each case, the failure arises because a market settles in a position in which marginal social cost diverges from marginal social benefit. This chapter introduces the most important reasons for **market failure** and examines one common form — externalities. Some other forms of market failure are discussed in Chapter 7.

Externalities

If market forces are to guide the allocation of resources, it is crucial that the costs that firms face and the prices to which they respond fully reflect the actual costs and benefits associated with the production and consumption of goods. However, there are a number of situations and markets in which this does not happen because of **externalities**. In the presence of such externalities, a price will emerge that is not equal to the 'true' marginal cost.

Information failure

If markets are to perform a role in allocating resources, it is essential that all relevant economic agents (buyers and sellers) have good information about market conditions; otherwise they may not be able to take rational decisions.

Key terms

market failure a situation in which the free market mechanism does not lead to an optimal allocation of resources, e.g. where there is a divergence between marginal social benefit and marginal social cost

externality a cost or a benefit that is external to a market transaction, and is thus not reflected in market prices

It is important that consumers can clearly perceive the benefits of consuming particular goods or services, in order to determine their own willingness to pay. Such benefits may not always be clear. For example, people may not fully perceive the benefits to be gained from education — or they may fail to appreciate the harmfulness of smoking tobacco.

In other market situations, economic agents on one side of the market may have different information from those on the other side: for example, sellers may have information about the goods that they are providing that buyers cannot discern. Chapter 7 explains that such information failure can also lead to a suboptimal allocation of resources.

Public goods

There is a category of goods known as public goods, which because of their characteristics cannot be provided by a purely free market. Street lighting is one example: there is no obvious way in which a private firm could charge all the users of street lighting for the benefits that they receive from it. Such goods are also discussed in Chapter 7.

Merit and demerit goods

There are some goods that the government believes will be underconsumed in a free market. If people do not fully perceive the benefits to be gained from consuming a good, then they will demand less than is socially desirable. In some developing countries, education may show some aspects of a merit good, if parents do not fully perceive the benefits their children could gain from education. This helps to explain low school enrolment in such countries. There are also some goods that the government believes will be overconsumed in a free market. An obvious example is addictive recreational drugs, where consumers may misperceive the benefits from consumption. Chapter 7 examines these goods in more detail.

Summary

- Free markets do not always lead to the best possible allocation of resources: there may be market failure.
- When there are costs or benefits that are external to the price mechanism, the economy will not reach allocative efficiency.
- Markets can operate effectively only when participants in the market have full information about market conditions.
- Public goods have characteristics that prevent markets from supplying the appropriate quantity.
- Merit (demerit) goods are those which government believes are under- (over-)consumed in a free market.

Study tip

Market failure is often used as a justification for government intervention in markets, so it is important to be aware of its various causes and to be able to recognise situations in which market failure may occur.

Externalities

Externality is one of those ugly words invented by economists, which says exactly what it means. It simply describes a cost or a benefit that is external to the market mechanism.

An externality will lead to a form of market failure because, if the cost or benefit is not reflected in market prices, it cannot be taken into consideration by all parties to a transaction. In other words, there may be costs (or benefits) resulting from a transaction that are borne (or enjoyed) by some third party not directly involved in that transaction. This in turn implies that decisions will not be aligned with the best interests of society. For example, if there is an element of costs that is not borne by producers, it is likely that 'too much' of the good will be produced. Conversely, where there are benefits that are not included, it is likely that too little will be produced. Later in the chapter, you will see that this is exactly what does happen.

Externalities can affect either demand or supply in a market: that is to say, they may arise either in **consumption** or in **production**.

In approaching this topic, begin by tackling Exercise 6.1, which offers an example of two types of externality.

Exercise 6.1

Each of the following situations describes a type of externality. In each case, does this affect production or consumption?

1 A factory situated in the centre of a town, and close to a residential district, emits toxic fumes through a chimney during its production process. Residents living nearby have to wash their clothes more frequently, and incur higher medical bills as a result of breathing in the fumes.

2 Residents living along a main road festoon their houses with lavish Christmas lights and decorations during the month of December, helping passers-by to capture the festive spirit.

Pollution from toxic fumes is an example of an externality

Toxic fumes

Example 1 in Exercise 6.1 is a negative production externality. The factory emits toxic fumes that impose costs on the residents (third parties) living nearby, who incur high washing and medical bills. The households face costs as a result of the production activities of the firm, so the firm does not face the full costs of its activity.

Thus, the **private costs** faced by the producer are lower than the costs faced by society as a whole. The producer will take decisions based only on its private costs, ignoring the **external costs** it imposes on society. In other words, the **social cost** of producing a good includes both private and external costs. In looking at decisions, we will often focus on **marginal social cost**, which is the cost to society of producing an extra unit of a good.

Figure 6.1 illustrates this situation under the assumption that firms operate in a competitive market (i.e. there is not a monopoly). Here, D (MSB) represents the demand curve, which was characterised in Chapter 4 as representing the marginal social benefit derived from consuming a good. In other words, the demand curve represents consumers' willingness to pay for the good, and thus reflects their marginal valuation of the product.

Producers face marginal private costs given by the line MPC, but in fact impose higher costs than this on society. Thus MSC represents the total costs imposed on society in the production of this good.

If the market is unregulated by the government, firms will choose how much to supply on the basis of the marginal (private) cost they face, shown by MPC in Figure 6.1. The market equilibrium will thus be at quantity traded Q_1, where firms just break even on the marginal unit sold. Price will be set at P_1.

This is not a good outcome for society, as it is clear that there is a divergence between the price in the market and the 'true' marginal cost — in other words, a divergence between marginal social benefit and marginal social cost. This divergence is at the heart of the market failure. The last unit of this good sold imposes higher costs on society than the marginal social benefit derived from consuming it. Too much is being produced.

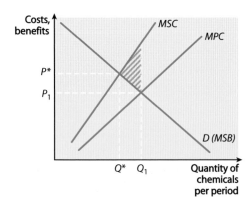

Figure 6.1 A negative productive externality

In fact, the optimum position is at $Q\star$, where marginal social benefit is equal to marginal social cost. This will be reached if the price is set equal to (social) marginal cost at $P\star$. Less of the good will be consumed, but also less pollution will be created, and society will be better off than at Q_1.

Quantitative skills 6.1

Identifying welfare loss in a diagram

The extent of the welfare loss that society suffers can be identified: it is shown by the shaded triangle in Figure 6.1. Each unit of output that is produced above $Q*$ imposes a cost equal to the vertical distance between MSC and MPC. The shaded area thus represents the difference between marginal social cost and marginal social benefit over the range of output between the optimum output and the free market level of output.

Christmas lights

Example 2 in Exercise 6.1 is an example of a positive consumption externality. Residents of this street decorate their homes in order to share the Christmas spirit with passers-by. The benefit they gain from the decorations spills over and adds to the enjoyment of others. In other words, the social benefits from the residents' decision to provide Christmas decorations go beyond the private enjoyment that they receive.

Figure 6.2 illustrates this situation. *MPB* represents the marginal private benefits gained by residents from the Christmas lights; but *MSB* represents the full marginal social benefit that the community gains, which is higher than the *MPB*. Residents will provide decorations up to the point Q_2, where their marginal private benefit is just balanced by the marginal cost of the lights. However, if the full social benefits received are taken into account, $Q\star$ would be the optimum point: the residents do not provide enough décor for the community to reach the optimum. The shaded triangle in Figure 6.2 shows the welfare loss: that is, the amount of social benefit forgone if the outcome is at Q_2 instead of $Q\star$.

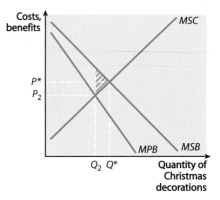

Figure 6.2 A positive consumption externality

Positive and normative revisited

Example 2 is a reminder of the distinction between positive and normative analysis, which was introduced in Chapter 1. Economists would agree that Figure 6.2 shows the effects of a beneficial consumption externality. However, probably not everyone would agree that the lavish Christmas decorations are providing such benefits. This is where a *normative judgement* comes into play. It could equally be argued that the lavish Christmas decorations are unsightly and inappropriate, or that they constitute a distraction for drivers and are therefore likely to cause accidents. After all, not everyone enjoys these lavish (and sometimes garish) displays.

Extension material

Discussion has centred on two examples of externalities: a production externality that had negative effects, and a consumption externality that was beneficial to society. In fact, there are two other possibilities.

Think about a factory that produces chemicals and is located on the banks of a river. It installs a new water purification plant that improves the quality of water discharged into the river. A trout farm located downstream finds that its productivity increases, so it has to spend less on filtering the

water. This is an example of a positive production externality, so that marginal social cost is lower than marginal private cost.

In contrast, think about Liz, a 'metal' enthusiast, who enjoys playing her music at high volume late at night, in spite of the fact that she lives in a flat with inadequate sound insulation. The neighbours prefer rock, but cannot escape the metal. This would be an example of a negative consumption externality, in which marginal social benefit is lower than marginal private benefit.

Study tip

Externalities are a common topic, so be ready to respond if questioned. Be very careful when drawing the diagram, especially in identifying the area representing welfare loss. If you understand *why* this area represents welfare loss, you should be able to check whether you have identified it correctly.

Summary

- Markets can operate effectively only if all relevant costs and benefits are taken into account in decision making.
- Some costs and benefits are external to the market mechanism, and are thus neglected, causing a distortion in resource allocation.
- Such external costs and benefits are known as 'externalities'.
- Externalities may occur in either production or consumption, thereby affecting either demand or supply.
- Externalities may be either positive or negative, but either way resources will not be optimally allocated if they are present.

Exercise 6.2

Discuss examples of some externalities that you meet in everyday situations, and classify them as affecting either production or consumption.

Examples of markets with externalities

Externalities occur in a wide variety of market situations, and constitute an important source of market failure. This means that externalities may hinder the achievement of good resource allocation from society's perspective. The rest of this chapter explores some examples of markets in which externalities may be present.

Externalities and the environment

Concern for the environment has been growing, with 'green' lobbyist groups drawing attention to the issues, sometimes through demonstrations. There are so many different facets to environmental concern that it is sometimes difficult to isolate the core issues. Externalities lie at the heart of much of the debate.

Global warming

Some of the issues are international in nature, such as global warming. At the heart of this concern is the way in which emissions of greenhouse gases are said to be warming up the planet. Sea levels are rising and major climate change seems imminent — if it is not already happening.

One reason why global warming is especially difficult to tackle is that actions taken by one country can have effects on other countries. Scientists argue that the problem is caused mainly by pollution created by transport and industry, especially in the richer countries. However, poorer nations suffer the consequences as well, especially countries such as Bangladesh. Here much of the land is low lying and prone to severe flooding almost every year. In some years up to three-quarters of the land area is under water at the height of the flooding.

In principle, this is similar to example 1 in Exercise 6.1: it is an example of a negative production externality, in which the nations causing most of the damage face only part of the costs caused by their lifestyles and production processes. The inevitable result in an unregulated market is that too much pollution is produced.

When externalities cross international borders in this way, the problem can be tackled only through international cooperation. For example, at the Kyoto World Climate

Summit held in Japan in 1997, almost every developed nation agreed to cut greenhouse gas emissions by 6% by 2010. The USA, the largest emitter of carbon dioxide, did not ratify the agreement, fearing the consequences of such a restriction for the US economy. The Kyoto Protocol was discussed at the 2012 Doha climate change talks and it was agreed to begin a new round of negotiations. However, the problems inherent in getting almost 200 countries to commit to a binding agreement seem challenging, to say the least.

Acid rain

Global warming is not the only example of international externality effects. Scandinavian countries have suffered from acid rain caused by pollution in other European countries, including the UK. Forest fires left to burn in Indonesia have caused air pollution in the neighbouring countries of Singapore and Malaysia.

River water

Another environmental issue concerns rivers. Some of the big rivers of the world, such as the Nile in Africa, pass through several countries on their way to the sea. The Nile runs through Egypt at the end of its journey, and is crucial for the economy. If countries further upstream were to increase their usage of the river, perhaps through new irrigation projects, this could have disastrous effects on Egypt. Again, the actions of one set of economic agents would be having damaging effects on others, and these effects would not be reflected in market prices, in the sense that the upstream countries would not have to face the full cost of their actions.

Part of the problem here can be traced back to the difficulty of enforcing property rights. If the countries imposing the costs could be forced to make appropriate payment for their actions, this would help to bring the costs back within the market mechanism. Such a process is known in economics as 'internalising the externality', and will be examined later in Chapter 8.

Biodiversity

Concern has also been expressed about the loss of *biodiversity*, a word that is shorthand for 'biological diversity'. The issue here is that when a section of rainforest is cleared to plant soya beans, or for timber, it is possible that species of plants, insects or even animals whose existence is not even known at present may be wiped out. Many modern medicines are based on chemicals that occur naturally in the wild. By eradicating species before they have been discovered, possible scientific advances will be forgone. Notice that when it comes to measuring the value of what is being destroyed, biodiversity offers particular challenges — namely, the problem of putting a value on something that might not even be there.

Externalities and transport

The London authorities have attempted to tackle traffic congestion in the city using the congestion charge. When traffic on the roads reaches a certain volume, congestion imposes heavy costs on road users. This is another example of an externality.

Figure 6.3 illustrates the situation. Suppose that D (MSB) represents the demand curve for car journeys along a particular stretch of road. When deciding whether or not to undertake a journey, drivers will balance the marginal benefit gained from making the journey against the marginal cost that they face. This is given by MPC — the marginal private cost of undertaking journeys. When the road is congested, a motorist who decides to undertake the journey adds to the congestion, and slows the traffic. The MPC curve

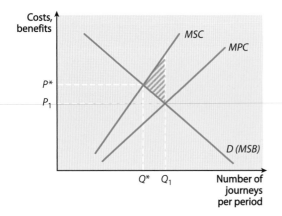

Figure 6.3 Traffic congestion

incorporates the cost to the motorist of joining a congested road, and the chosen number of journeys will be at Q_1.

However, in adding to the congestion the motorist not only suffers the costs of congestion, but also imposes some marginal increase in costs on all other users of the road. Thus, the marginal social costs (*MSC*) of undertaking journeys are higher than the cost faced by any individual motorist. *MSC* is therefore higher than *MPC*. Society would be better off with lower congestion: that is, with the number of journeys undertaken being limited to $Q^\star$, where marginal social benefit equals marginal social cost. By imposing a charge on motorists entering central London, the authorities are trying to ensure that drivers face at least part of the social costs they impose on others by using congested roads.

The congestion charge in London is an attempt to make drivers face some of the social costs of their journeys

Externalities and health

Healthcare is a sector in which there is often public provision, or at least some state intervention in support of the health services. In the UK, the National Health Service is the prime provider of healthcare, but private healthcare is also available, and the use of private health insurance schemes is on the increase. Again, externalities can help to explain why there is a need for government to intervene.

Consider the case of vaccination against a disease such as measles. Suppose an individual is considering whether or not to be vaccinated. Being vaccinated reduces the probability of that individual contracting the disease, so there are palpable potential benefits to that individual. However, these benefits must be balanced against the costs. There may be a direct charge for the vaccine, some individuals may have a phobia against needles, or they may be concerned about possible side-effects. Individuals will opt to be vaccinated only if the marginal expected benefit to them is at least as large as the marginal cost.

From society's point of view, however, there are potential benefits that individuals will not take into account. After all, if they do contract measles, there is a chance of their passing it on to others. Indeed, if lots of people decide not to be vaccinated, there is the possibility of a widespread epidemic, which would be costly and damaging to many.

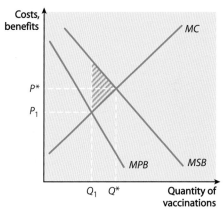

Figure 6.4 illustrates this point. The previous paragraph argues that the social benefits to society of having people vaccinated against measles exceed the private benefits that will be perceived by individuals, so that marginal social benefits exceed marginal private benefits. Private individuals will choose to balance marginal private benefit against marginal private cost at Q_1, whereas society would prefer more people to be vaccinated at $Q\star$. This parallels the discussion of a positive consumption externality. Chapter 7 considers another aspect of healthcare provision.

Figure 6.4 Vaccination

Externalities and education

As you are reading this textbook, it is reasonably safe to assume that you are following a course in economics. You have decided to demand education. This is yet another area in which externalities may be important.

When you decided to take AS/A-levels (including economics), there were probably a number of factors that influenced your decision. Perhaps you intend to demand even more education in the future, by going on to study at university. Part of your decision process probably takes into account the fact that education improves your future earnings potential. Your expected lifetime earnings depend in part upon your level of qualifications. Research has shown that, on average, graduates earn more during their lifetimes than non-graduates. This is partly because there is a productivity effect: by becoming educated, you cultivate a range of skills that in later life will make you more productive, and this helps to explain why you can expect higher lifetime earnings than someone who chooses not to demand education. There is also a signalling effect, as having a degree signals to potential employers that you have the ability to cope with university study and have gained a range of skills.

What does society get out of this? Evidence suggests that, not only does education improve productivity, but a *group* of educated workers cooperating with each other become even more productive. This is an externality effect, as it depends upon interaction between educated workers — but each individual perceives only the individual benefit, and not the benefits of cooperation.

In other words, when you decide to undertake education, you do so on the basis of the expected private benefits that you hope to gain from education. However, you do not take into account the additional benefits through cooperation that society will reap. So here is another example of a positive consumption externality. As with healthcare, some other aspects of education will be discussed in Chapter 7.

Waste disposal and recycling

A major problem faced by twenty-first-century society and governments is waste disposal. Landfill is one way of dealing with waste, but it has long-term effects on the environment, and imposes negative externalities on people living near landfill sites. Recycling is an alternative, but also suffers from externality effects. There are positive consumption externalities associated with recycling, in the sense that the benefits to society exceed the benefits to individuals (i.e. $MSB > MPB$). In such a situation, there will be 'too little' recycling relative to the best outcome for society, and the government or local authorities may need to find ways of encouraging households to recycle more.

Externalities and tourism

As international transport has become easier and cheaper, more people are wanting to travel to new and different destinations. For less developed countries, this offers an opportunity to earn much-needed foreign exchange.

There has been some criticism of this. The building of luxury hotels in the midst of the poverty that characterises many less developed countries is said to have damaging effects on the local population by emphasising differences in living standards.

However, constructing the infrastructure that tourists need may have beneficial effects on the domestic economy. Improved roads and communication systems can benefit local businesses. This effect can be interpreted as an externality, in the sense that the local firms will face lower costs as a result of the facilities provided for the tourist sector.

Summary

- Externalities arise in many aspects of economic life.
- Environmental issues are especially prone to externality effects, as market prices do not always incorporate impacts on the environment, especially where property rights are not assigned.
- Congestion on the roads can also be seen as a form of externality.
- Externalities also arise in the areas of healthcare provision and education, where individuals do not always perceive the full social benefits that arise.

Exercise 6.3

Table 6.1 shows the situation in a market where pollution is generated by the production process.

Table 6.1 A market with pollution

Quantity produced (thousands per week)	Marginal social benefit (£)	Marginal private cost (£)	Marginal social cost (£)
10	80	5	10
20	75	10	20
30	70	20	35
40	60	32	60
50	48	48	90
60	30	75	125
70	8	110	175

a At what level of output would marginal social benefit be equal to marginal private cost? (Note: this is the quantity of output that would be produced by firms in an unregulated competitive market.)

b By how much would marginal social cost exceed marginal private cost at this level of output?

c At what level of output would marginal social benefit be equal to marginal social cost?

d What amount of tax would induce firms to supply this quantity of output?

Case study 6.1

Healthcare: public or market?

In July 2013, the NHS celebrated its 65th anniversary amid continuing debate about whether healthcare should be state-provided, or whether market forces should be given a greater role. In the UK, market forces have played an increasing part in allocating resources within the public health sector through the operation of internal markets, but the debate over public vs private provision continues. So far, the proportion of health expenditure that is undertaken by the public sector has changed little.

What does economic analysis have to say about the matter? The justification for public provision of healthcare rests on the existence of market failure. There are a number of reasons why there might be some form of market failure in the provision of healthcare, whether we consider the provision of preventative or curative measures.

In the case of preventative healthcare, there may be other factors at work. Take the case of vaccination against disease. If vaccinations are provided by a private competitive market, an individual faces costs of the treatment, both financial and perhaps in the unpleasantness and possible risks of being vaccinated. The benefits of having been vaccinated may be perceived to be relatively low, if the individual sees a low probability of being infected. However, the benefits of vaccination from the point of view of society may be greater, because a widespread vaccination programme not only reduces the risk of infection for each individual, but also reduces the likelihood of an epidemic.

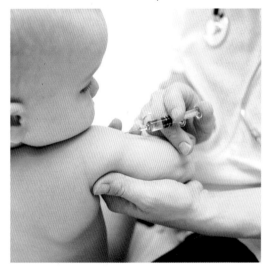

A vaccination programme has palpable benefits for society

Follow-up questions

1 Explain what is meant by **market failure**.

2 Draw a diagram to help to explain the possible market failure outlined in relation to a vaccination programme.

Market failure: public goods and information gaps

Externalities are not the only form of market failure. There are also situations where the characteristics of a good or service can affect the effective operation of a market. This chapter explores goods with unusual economic characteristics and markets that may fail as a result of problems with information.

Learning objectives

After studying this chapter, you should:
→ be aware of the distinction between private and public goods
→ understand the nature of public goods and problems that arise in their provision
→ be able to identify examples of public goods
→ appreciate how imperfect market information may be seen as a source of market failure and a misallocation of resources

Private and public goods

Private goods

Most of the goods that individuals consume are **private goods**. You buy a can of Diet Coke, you drink it, and it's gone. You may choose to share it with a friend, but you do not have to: by drinking it you can prevent anyone else from doing so. Furthermore, once it is gone, it's gone: nobody else can subsequently consume that Coke.

The two features that characterise a private good are:

● other people can be excluded from consuming it
● once consumed by one person, it cannot be consumed by another

The first feature can be described as *excludability*, whereas the second feature might be described by saying that consumption of a private good is *rivalrous*: the act of consumption uses up the good.

Public goods

Not all goods and services have the two characteristics above. There are goods that, once provided, are available to all. In other words, people cannot be excluded from consuming such goods. There are other goods that do not diminish through consumption, so they are non-rivalrous in consumption. Goods that have the characteristics of non-excludability and non-rivalry are known as **public goods**.

Examples of public goods that are often cited include street lighting, a lighthouse and a nuclear deterrent. For example, once street lighting has been provided in a

Key terms

private good a good that, once consumed by one person, cannot be consumed by somebody else; such a good has excludability and is rivalrous

public good a good that is non-exclusive and non-rivalrous in consumption — consumers cannot be excluded from consuming the good, and consumption by one person does not affect the amount of the good available for others to consume

particular street, anyone who walks along that street at night benefits from the lighting — no one can be excluded from consuming it. So street lighting is non-exclusive. In addition, the fact that one person has walked along the street does not mean that there is less street lighting left for later walkers. So street lighting is also non-rivalrous.

The key feature of such a market is that, once the good has been provided, there is no incentive for anyone to pay for it — so the market will fail, as no firm will have an incentive to supply the good in the first place. This is often referred to as the **free-rider problem**, as individual consumers can free-ride and avoid having to pay for the good if it is provided.

Key term

free-rider problem when an individual cannot be excluded from consuming a good, and thus has no incentive to pay for its provision

Extension material

A key question is how well the market for a public good is likely to operate. In particular, will a free market reach a position where there is allocative efficiency, with price equal to marginal social cost?

Think about the supply and demand curves for a public good such as street lighting. To simplify matters, suppose there are just two potential demanders of the good, a and b. Consider Figure 7.1. If it is assumed that the supply is provided in a competitive market, S represents the supply curve, reflecting the marginal cost of providing street lighting. The curves d_a and d_b represent the demand curves of the two potential demanders. For a given quantity Q_1, a would be prepared to pay P_a and b would pay P_b. If these prices are taken to be the value that each individual places on this amount of the good, then $P_a + P_b = P_T$ represents the social benefit derived from consuming Q_1 units of street lighting. Similarly, for any given quantity of street lighting, the marginal social benefit derived from consumption can be calculated as the vertical sum of the two demand curves. This is shown by the curve MSB. So the optimal provision of street lighting is given by $Q^\star$, at which point the marginal social benefit is equated with the marginal cost of supplying the good.

However, if person a were to agree to pay P_a for the good, person b could then consume Q_1 of the good free of charge, but would not be prepared to pay in order for the supply to be expanded beyond this point — as person b's willingness to pay is below

the marginal cost of provision beyond this point. So the social optimum at $Q^\star$ cannot be reached. Indeed, when there are many potential consumers, the likely outcome is that none of this good will be produced: why should any individual agree to pay if he or she can free-ride on others?

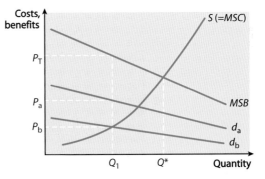

Figure 7.1 Demand and supply of a public good

The free-rider problem helps to explain why these sorts of goods have typically been provided through state intervention. This begs the question of how the state can identify the optimal quantity of the good to be provided — in other words, how the government determines $Q^\star$. The extent to which individuals value a particular good cannot be directly observed. However, by including statements about the provision of public goods in their election manifestos, politicians can collect views about public goods provision via the medium of the ballot box. This is an indirect method, but it provides some mandate for the government to take decisions.

The free-rider problem makes it difficult to charge for a public good, so the private sector will be reluctant to supply such goods. In fact, pure public goods are relatively rare, but there are many goods that have some but not all of the required characteristics. On the face of it, the lighthouse service seems to be a good example of a public good. Once the lighthouse has been constructed and is sending out its signal, all boats and ships that pass within the range of its light can benefit from the service: that is, it is non-excludable. Moreover, the fact that one ship has seen the lighthouse signal does not reduce the amount of light available to the next ship, so it is also non-rivalrous.

However, this does not mean that ships cannot be charged for their use of lighthouse services. In 2002 an article in the *Guardian* reported that ships were complaining about the high charges to which they were subjected for lighthouse services. Ships of a certain size must pay 'light dues' every time they enter or leave UK ports, and the fees collected are used to fund lighthouses, buoys and beacons around the coast. In principle, it could be argued that this renders lighthouses excludable, as ships can be prevented from sailing if they have not paid their dues, and so could not consume the lighthouse services. At the heart of the complaints from the shipping companies was the fact that leisure craft below a certain threshold did not have to pay the charges, and they made more use of the lighthouses than the larger vessels. This is one example of the way in which it becomes necessary to design a charging system to try to overcome the free-rider problem associated with the provision of public goods.

Charging ships for lighthouse services when they enter or leave ports is one way to overcome the free-rider problem

In fact, there are many goods that are either non-rivalrous or non-excludable, but not both. One example of this is a football match. If I go to watch a premiership football match, my 'consumption' of the match does not prevent the person sitting next to me from also consuming it, so it is non-rivalrous. However, if I go along without my season ticket (or do not have a ticket), I can clearly be excluded from consuming the match, so it is *not* non-exclusive.

A stretch of road may be considered non-exclusive, as road users are free to drive along it. However, it is not non-rivalrous, in the sense that as congestion builds up consumption is affected. This example is also imperfect as a public good because, by installing toll barriers, users can be excluded from consuming it.

Where goods have some features of a public good, the free market may fail to produce an ideal outcome for society. Exercise 7.1 provides some examples of goods: to what extent may each of these be considered to be non-rivalrous or non-excludable?

Exercise 7.1

For each of the following goods, think about whether they have elements of non-rivalry, non-excludability, both or neither:

a a national park

b a playground

c a theatre performance

d an apple

e a television programme

f a firework display

g police protection

h a lecture

i a DVD recording of a film

j the national defence

Tackling the public goods problem

For some public goods, the failure of the free market to ensure provision may be regarded as a serious problem — for example, in such cases as street lighting or law and order. Some government intervention may thus be needed to make sure that a sufficient quantity of the good or service is provided. Notice that this does not necessarily mean that the government has to provide the good itself. It may be that the government will raise funds through taxation in order to ensure that street lighting is provided, but could still make use of private firms to supply the good through some sort of subcontracting arrangement. In the UK, it may be that the government delegates the responsibility for provision of public goods to local authorities, which in turn may subcontract to private firms.

In some other cases, it may be that changes in technology may alter the economic characteristics of a good. For example, in the case of television programmes, originally provision was entirely through the BBC, funded by the licence fee. Subsequently, ITV set up in competition, using advertising as a way of funding its supply. More recently, the advent of satellite and digital broadcasting has reduced the degree to which television programmes are non-excludable, allowing private firms to charge for transmissions.

Summary

- A private good is one that, once consumed by one person, cannot be consumed by anyone else — it has the characteristics of excludability and rivalry.
- A public good is non-exclusive and non-rivalrous.
- Because of these characteristics, public goods tend to be underprovided by a free market.
- One reason for this is the free-rider problem, whereby an individual cannot be excluded from consuming a public good, and thus has no incentive to pay for it.
- Public goods, or goods with some of the characteristics of public goods, must be provided with the assistance of the government or its agents.

Information failures

Key term

asymmetric information
a situation in which some
participants in a market
have better information
about market conditions
than others

If markets are to be effective in guiding resource allocation, it is important that economic decision-makers receive full and accurate information about market conditions. Ideally, all traders in a market should have the same information about market conditions — a situation known as *symmetric information*. Consumers need information about the prices at which they can buy and the quality of the products for sale. Producers need to be able to observe how consumers react to prices. Information is thus of crucial significance if markets are to work. However, there are some markets in which not all traders have access to good information, or in which some traders have more or better access to it than others. This is known as a situation of **asymmetric information**, and can be a source of market failure.

Healthcare

One example of asymmetric information is in healthcare. Suppose you go to your dentist for a check-up. He tells you that you have a filling that needs to be replaced, although you have had no pain or problems with it. In this situation the seller in a market has much better information about the product than the buyer. You as the buyer have no idea whether or not the recommended treatment is needed, and without going to another dentist for a second opinion you have no way of finding out. You might think this is an unsatisfactory situation, as it seems to give a lot of power to the seller relative to the consumer. The situation is even worse where the dentist does not even publish the prices for treatment until after it has been carried out! The Office of Fair Trading criticised private dentists for exactly this sort of practice when it reported on this market in March 2003. Indeed, dentists are now required by law to publish prices for treatment.

The same argument applies in the case of other areas of healthcare, where doctors have better information than their patients about the sort of treatment that is needed.

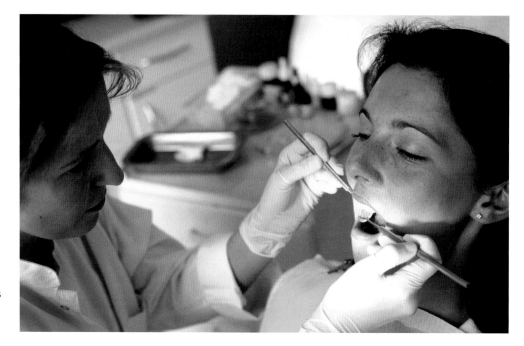

Dentists have better information than their patients about what treatments are needed

Tobacco

The market for tobacco is an interesting example of how imperfect market information can contribute to market failure. Chapter 5 discussed the effects of imposing an indirect tax on cigarettes (see Figure 5.8). If you look back at the diagram, you will see that the impact of the tax is to raise the price of cigarettes significantly, with the incidence of the tax falling mainly on consumers. The problem with using a tax in this case is that the demand for cigarettes is inelastic, so a substantial tax has only a modest effect on the consumption of cigarettes.

One reason for this is that tobacco is addictive, but there is also an information failure present. The government took the view that, although the link between tobacco and ill health was proven, smokers had not fully assimilated the dangers, or were prepared to discount the future damage to their health in the short run. As a result, the cigarette companies were required to add health warnings to cigarette packets in an attempt to correct the information failure. The controls on information became more and more stringent over time, with bans on advertising and open sales of cigarettes, not to mention the banning of smoking in public buildings — all because smokers failed to take heed of the information about the dangers of smoking and continued to rate the benefits of smoking more highly than was good for society.

Exercise 7.2

Ethel, an old-age pensioner, is sitting quietly at home when the doorbell rings. At the door is a stranger called Frank, who tells her that he has noticed that her roof is in desperate need of repair, and if she does not get something done about it very soon, there will be problems in the next rainstorm. Fortunately, he can help — for a price. Discuss whether there is a market failure in this situation, and what Ethel (or others) could do about it.

Education

The market for education is similar. Teachers or government inspectors may know more about the subjects and topics that students need to study than the students do themselves. This is partly because teachers are able to take a longer view and can see education provision in a broader perspective. Students taking economics at university may have to take a course in mathematics and statistics in their first year, and some will always complain that they have come to study economics, not maths. It is only later that they come to realise that competence in maths is crucial these days for the economics that they will study later in their course.

How could this problem be tackled? The answer would seem to be obvious — if the problem arises from an information failure, then the answer should be to improve the information flow, in this case to students. This might be achieved by providing a convincing explanation of why the curriculum has been designed in a particular way. It may also be necessary to provide incentives for students to study particular unpopular topics, perhaps by making success in them a requirement for progression to the next stage of the course. By understanding the economic cause of a problem, it is possible to devise a strategy that should go some way towards removing the market failure.

There are also externality effects present in relation to education. As explained earlier, research has shown that educated workers are better able to cooperate and work together, becoming jointly more productive than they would be if they were working individually. Furthermore, there are other external benefits. Education has health spillovers because there is a better understanding of nutrition and hygiene. It is also seen that when education levels in a society are high, crime rates tend to be lower and there is better-informed political debate and decision making. More schooling may enable more technological progress to be made. In other words, the social benefits of education may exceed the private benefits to the individuals who receive it.

Second-hand cars

One of the most famous examples of asymmetric information relates to the second-hand (or, in the latest terminology, 'pre-owned') car market. This is because the first paper that drew attention to the problem of asymmetric information, by Nobel laureate George Akerlof, focused on this market.

Akerlof argued that there are two types of car. Some cars are good runners and are totally reliable, whereas some are continually breaking down and needing parts and servicing; the latter are known as 'lemons' in the USA (allegedly from fruit machines, where lemons offer the lowest prize). The problem in the second-hand car market arises because the owners of cars (potential sellers) have better information about their cars than the potential buyers. In other words, when a car owner decides to sell a car, he or she knows whether it is a lemon or a good-quality car — but a buyer cannot tell.

In this sort of market, car dealers can adopt one of two possible strategies. One is to offer a high price and buy up all the cars in the market, knowing that the lemons will be sold on at a loss. The problem is that, if the lemons make up a large proportion of the cars in the market, this could generate overall losses for the dealers. The alternative is to offer a low price, and just buy up all the lemons to sell for scrap. In this situation, the market for good-quality used cars is effectively destroyed because owners of good-quality cars will not accept the low price — an extreme form of market failure!

Again, the solution may be to tackle the problem at its root, by finding a way to provide information. In the case of second-hand cars, AA inspection schemes or the offering of warranties may be ways of improving the flow of information about the quality of cars for sale.

Pensions

The market for pensions is another that is fraught with information problems by its very nature. A key source of information failure here arises from uncertainty and risk. Individuals face uncertainty in predicting their need for an adequate pension in the future, which depends upon their state of health in the future, their longevity and so on. There is risk involved in the sense that pension funds depend critically on movements in the stock market. There is also the fact that there is a vast array of alternative pension schemes available, many of them very complex. This makes it very difficult for individuals to know how to take a rational decision — especially when their need for a pension is many years in the future. If people make bad decisions about pensions, this creates problems for the future, and society may find that it needs to cope with care for the elderly, especially when improvements in health mean that more people are living for longer.

The insurance market

People take out insurance to cover themselves against the risk of uncertain future events. Asymmetric information can cause problems with this market in two different ways. Suppose an individual approaches an insurance company wanting health insurance. The individual knows more about his or her health and health history than the insurance company. After all, the individual knows whether they are prone to illness or if they are accident-prone. This could mean that the people most likely to take out health insurance are the ones most likely to fall ill or be involved in accidents. This is known as **adverse selection**. A second form of information failure in terms of insurance is known as **moral hazard**. An individual who has taken out insurance may be more likely to take risks, knowing that he or she is covered by insurance. For example, if someone has taken out insurance against the loss of their mobile phone, they may be less careful about leaving it around.

Merit goods

There are some goods that the government believes will be undervalued by consumers, so that too little will be consumed in a free market. In other words, individuals do not fully perceive the benefits that they will gain from consuming such goods, or do not have enough information to take decisions that are best for society. These are known as **merit goods**.

One situation in which the merit good phenomenon arises is where the government is in a better position than individuals to take a long-term view of what is good for society. In particular, governments may need to take decisions on behalf of future generations as well as the present. Resources need to be used wisely in the present in order to protect the interests of tomorrow's citizens. Notice that this may require decision-makers to make normative judgements about the appropriate weighting to be given to the present as opposed to the future.

There is a strong political element involved in identifying the goods that should be regarded as merit goods: this is because there is a subjective or normative judgement involved, since declaring a good to be a merit good requires the decision-maker to make a choice on behalf of the population, which may be seen as being paternalistic.

Examples of merit goods include museums, libraries and art galleries. These are goods that are provided or subsidised because someone somewhere thinks that communities should have more of them.

Economists are wary of playing the merit good card too often, as it entails such a high normative element. It is also sometimes difficult to disentangle merit good arguments from externality effects.

Exercise 7.3

The *Guardian* reported on 27 August 2004 that the pharmaceutical company GlaxoSmithKline had been forced to publish details of a clinical trial of one of its leading antidepressant drugs following a lawsuit that had accused the company of concealing evidence that the drug could be harmful to children. Discuss the extent to which this situation may have led to a market failure because of information problems.

Study tip

Be ready to discuss the key types of market failure that have been discussed:

- externalities
- public goods
- imperfect market information

Where possible, be ready with your own examples to show your understanding.

Exercise 7.4

Identify the form of market failure associated with each of the following:

a the use of heroin

b the provision of a police officer on the beat

c vaccination against measles

d investment in new roads

e provision of higher education

Summary

- A merit good is one that society believes should be consumed by individuals whether or not they have the means or the willingness to do so.
- There is a strong normative element in the identification of merit goods.
- Demerit goods (or 'merit bads') are goods that society believes should not be consumed by individuals even if they wish to do so.
- In the case of merit and demerit goods, 'society' (as represented by government) believes that it has better information than consumers about these goods, and about what is good (or bad) for consumers.
- Information deficiency can lead to market failure in other situations: for example, where some participants in a market have better information about some aspect(s) of the market than others.
- Examples of this include healthcare, education and second-hand cars.
- Asymmetric information can also result in problems of adverse selection and moral hazard.

Television in a digital world

In the UK, we spend an average of just under 3 hours a day, every day, watching television. That amounts to 20 hours a week; or over 43 days a year; or over 9 years in the life of an average person. Watching television comes behind only work and sleep as a pastime. It accounts for about half of our leisure time.

From an early stage, government has been intimately involved in television broadcasting. At several points, there were calls for the government to take over the BBC (notably during the General Strike of 1926 and the Suez Crisis of 1956).

The major part of the BBC's income comes through a mandatory licence, which comes to just under £3 billion per annum, or not far off one day's gross domestic product for the UK. The government grants licences (via its regulator) to broadcasters. In exchange for the right to broadcast, these companies have to fulfil a number of obligations.

Why should the government be so involved in broadcasting? The basic reason is the existence of market failure: the idea that a freely functioning market in broadcasting will not produce the socially desirable outcome. The issue is: why won't the free market, left unregulated, inform, educate and entertain? There are three main types of market failure relevant for broadcasting:

- broadcasting is a public good
- the broadcasting market is inherently concentrated, leading to market power
- consumption of broadcasting is subject to externalities

Source: adapted from Robin Mason, 'Television in the digital world', *Economic Review*, Vol. 22, No. 3 (February 2005), pp. 2–6.

The BBC is publicly funded by the television licence fee

Follow-up questions

a Discuss the three forms of market failure mentioned, and discuss why they are potentially relevant to broadcasting.

b Given that the article was written in 2005, to what extent do you think that further developments in the technology of broadcasting since then have affected these forms of market failure?

Government intervention and government failure

The previous two chapters have examined forms of market failure, and have discussed the sorts of policy intervention that might be used to try to correct these market failures. This chapter reminds us of some of these interventions and explores how some well-intentioned interventions by government can sometimes produce unintended results — a situation that may be tantamount to government failure.

> **Learning objectives**
>
> After studying this chapter, you should:
> → be familiar with ways in which governments intervene in an attempt to address market failure
> → appreciate the role of government expenditure and state provision of goods and services
> → be able to identify areas in which government actions may have unintended distortionary effects
> → be aware of some sources of government failure
> → be familiar with the effects of price controls such as minimum wage legislation and rent controls
> → be able to analyse the effects of sales taxes and subsidies

Correcting market failure

Markets fail when the price mechanism causes an inefficient allocation of resources within a society. This occurs when price is not set equal to marginal cost, or where marginal social benefit is not equal to marginal social cost. In such circumstances, it seems apparent that by improving the way in which resources are allocated, the society could become better off. In other words, market failure is often viewed as a valid reason for governments to intervene in the economy.

Externalities

Chapter 6 looked at the problems caused by externalities, and discussed how these can occur in various different contexts. An externality occurs where the price mechanism fails to reflect the true costs or benefits associated with a product. One approach to tackling this problem is to internalise the externality, by bringing its effects into the market mechanism (see page 91). For example, this might be done by making sure that firms that cause pollution face the true costs of their production activities. An alternative approach is to impose regulation that ensures that the appropriate level of output of a good is produced, perhaps through a pollution permit scheme.

Public goods

The problem with public goods arises from the free-rider problem. When goods are non-exclusive and non-rivalrous, no individual has the incentive to pay. In such circumstances, some form of intervention is needed to ensure that a sufficient quantity of such public goods is produced. This intervention need not involve direct production by the government, but could include subsidies to local authorities or other bodies.

Imperfect market information

A natural approach to tackling information problems is by providing information. This may take the form of government campaigns to spread information, or some form of regulation that forces firms to reveal information about their products. One example might be the regulations that require firms to specify ingredient lists on processed food products.

Government failure

Most governments see it as their responsibility to try to correct some of the failures of markets to allocate resources efficiently. As outlined above, this has led to a wide variety of policies being devised to address issues of market failure. Some of these have been discussed already. However, some policies have unintended effects that may not culminate in successful elimination of market failure. Indeed, in some cases government intervention may introduce new market distortions, leading to a phenomenon known as **government failure**. The remainder of this chapter examines some examples of such government failure.

Many of the measures outlined at the beginning of this chapter can cause problems if they are not carefully implemented, or if the government itself does not have sufficient information to take good decisions. For example, in the case of externalities, the government may choose to tackle pollution by a tax, or by regulation. However, if it is not possible to identify the appropriate amount of the tax that is needed to correct the market failure, or if it is not known how many pollution permits need to be issued to reach the optimum outcome for society, then it will not be possible to get the policy exactly right. Similar implementation problems may arise with other attempts to deal with market failure. However, government failure may arise in many other ways.

Sales taxes

Governments need to raise funds to finance the expenditure that they undertake. One way of doing this is through expenditure taxes such as value added tax (VAT) or excise duties on such items as alcohol or tobacco. You might think that raising money in this way to provide goods and services that would otherwise not be provided would be a benefit to society. But there is a downside to this action, even if all the funds raised by a sales tax are spent wisely.

The effects of a sales tax can be seen in a demand and supply diagram, and were discussed briefly in Chapter 5. An **indirect tax** is paid by the seller, so it affects the supply curve for a product. Figure 8.1 illustrates the case of a fixed-rate or specific tax — a tax that is set at a constant amount per litre of petrol. Without the tax, the market equilibrium is at the intersection of demand and supply with a price of P_0 and a quantity traded of Q_0. The effect of the tax is to reduce the quantity that firms are prepared to supply at any given price — or, to put it another way, for any given quantity of petrol, firms need to receive the amount of the tax over and above

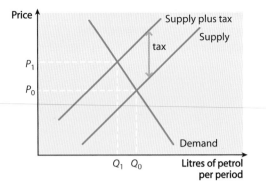

Figure 8.1 The effects of an indirect tax on petrol

the price at which they would have been prepared to supply that quantity. The effect is thus to move the supply curve upwards by the amount of the tax, as shown in the figure. We get a new equilibrium with a higher price at P_1 and a lower quantity traded at Q_1.

To what extent is this good for society? The government has raised revenue as a result of the tax, so we might argue that the funds raised can be used in a way that benefits society as a whole. However, the picture is not quite so straightforward. Recall from Chapter 4 that an efficient allocation of resources is achieved when a market reaches an equilibrium such that the price of a product is equal to the marginal cost of producing it. This suggests that the market for petrol shown in Figure 8.1 has been moved away from this ideal state of affairs. It may thus arise that by imposing a tax to raise funds for correcting market failure in one part of the economy, the government introduces a misallocation of resources elsewhere.

Of course, it may be that in this particular market, the government has some other reason for wanting to reduce the consumption of petrol — perhaps because of congestion or pollution. However, this argument cannot be applied to many other markets in which indirect taxes are levied. After all, VAT is applied to almost all goods and services sold in the UK.

Indirect taxes on petrol can be used to reduce consumption

Extension material

Is it possible to identify how a sales tax will affect total welfare in society? Consider Figure 8.2, which shows the market for DVDs. Suppose that the government imposes a specific tax on DVDs. This would have the effect of taking market equilibrium from the free market position at $P\star$ with quantity traded at $Q\star$ to a new position, with price now at P_t and quantity traded at Q_t. Remember that the price rises by less than the amount of the tax, implying that the incidence of the tax falls partly on buyers and partly on sellers. In Figure 8.2 consumers pay more of the tax (the area $P\star P_t BE$) than the producers (who pay $FP\star EG$). The effect on society's overall welfare will now be examined.

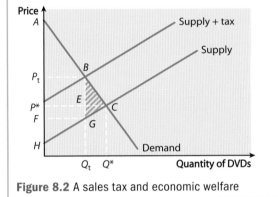

Figure 8.2 A sales tax and economic welfare

Remember that the total welfare that society receives from consuming a product is the sum of consumer and producer surplus. The situation before and after the sales tax is as follows. Before the tax, consumer surplus is given by the area $AP\star C$ and producer surplus is given by the triangle $P\star CH$. How about afterwards? Consumer surplus is now the smaller triangle $AP_t B$, and producer surplus is FGH. The area $P_t BGF$ is the revenue raised by the government from the tax, which should be included in total welfare on the assumption that the government uses this wisely. The total amount of welfare is now $ABGH$. If you compare these total welfare areas before and after the tax, you will realise that they differ by the area BCG. This triangle represents a deadweight loss that arises from the imposition of the tax. It is sometimes referred to as the excess burden of the tax.

So, even where the government intervenes to raise funding for its expenditure — and spends wisely — a distortion is introduced to resource allocation, and society must bear a loss of welfare.

Dealing with externalities

Chapter 6 showed how externalities arise in situations where there are items of cost or benefit associated with transactions, and these are not reflected in market prices. In these circumstances a free market will not lead to an optimum allocation of resources. One approach to dealing with such market situations is to bring those externalities into the market mechanism — a process known as **internalising an externality**. The London congestion charge may be seen as an attempt to internalise the externality effects of traffic congestion. In the case of pollution, this principle would entail forcing the polluting firms to face the full social cost of their production activities. This is sometimes known as the *polluter pays* principle.

> ### Key term
>
> **internalising an externality** an attempt to deal with an externality by bringing an external cost or benefit into the price system

Pollution

Figure 8.3 illustrates a negative production externality: pollution. Suppose that firms in the market for chemicals use a production process that emits toxic fumes, thereby imposing costs on society that the firms themselves do not face. In other words, the marginal private costs faced by these firms are less than the marginal social costs that are inflicted on society. As explained earlier in Chapter 6, firms in this market will choose to produce up to point Q_1 and charge a price of P_1 to consumers. At this point, marginal social benefit is below the marginal cost of producing the

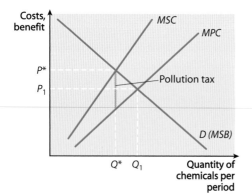

Figure 8.3 Pollution

MB, MC axis with MC and MB curves, t^* marked, e^* on Emission reduction axis

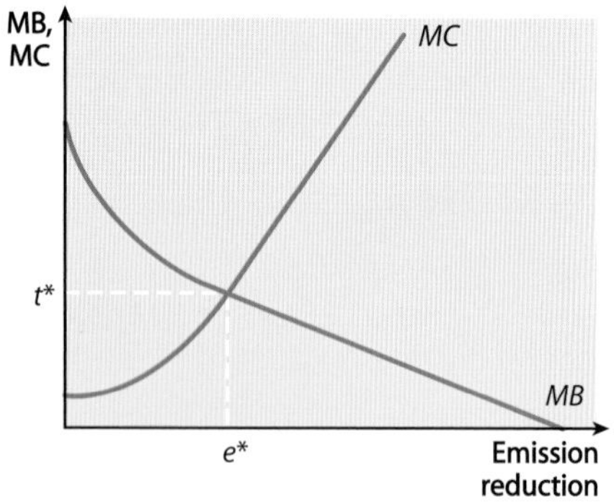

Figure 8.4 Reducing the emission of toxic fumes

chemicals, so it can be claimed that 'too much' of the product is being produced — that society would be better off if production were at $Q^\star$, with a price charged at $P^\star$.

Note that this optimum position is not characterised by zero pollution. In other words, from society's point of view it pays to abate pollution only up to the level where the marginal benefit of reducing pollution is matched by the marginal cost of doing so. Reducing pollution to zero would be too costly.

How can society reach the optimum output of chemicals at $Q^\star$? In line with the principle that the polluter should pay, one approach would be to impose a tax on firms such that polluters face the full cost of their actions. In Figure 8.3, if firms were required to pay a tax equivalent to the vertical distance between marginal private cost (MPC) and marginal social cost (MSC), they would choose to produce at $Q^\star$, paying a tax equal to the brown line on the figure.

An alternative way of looking at this question is via a diagram showing the marginal benefit and marginal cost of emissions reduction. In Figure 8.4 MB represents the marginal social benefits from reducing emissions of some pollutant and MC is the marginal costs of reducing emissions. The optimum amount of reduction is found where marginal benefit equals marginal cost, at $e^\star$. Up to this point, the marginal benefit to society of reducing emissions exceeds the marginal cost of the reduction, so it is in the interest of society to reduce pollution. However, beyond that point the marginal cost of reducing the amount of pollution exceeds the benefits that accrue, so society will be worse off. Setting a tax equal to $t^\star$ in Figure 8.4 will induce firms to undertake the appropriate amount of emission reduction.

This is not the only way of reaching the objective, however. Figure 8.4 suggests that there is another possibility — namely, to impose environmental standards, and to prohibit emissions beyond $e^\star$. This amounts to controlling quantity rather than price; and, if the government has full information about marginal costs and marginal benefits, the two policies will produce the equivalent result.

Measuring benefits and costs

Either of the approaches outlined above will be effective — *if* the authorities have full information about the marginal costs and benefits. But how likely is this? There are many problems with this proviso. The measurement of both marginal benefits and marginal costs is fraught with difficulties.

The marginal social benefits of reducing pollution cannot be measured with great precision, for many reasons. It may be argued that there are significant gains to be made in terms of improved health and lower death rates if pollution can be reduced, but quantifying this is not straightforward. Even if it were possible to evaluate the saving in resources that would need to be devoted to future medical care resulting from the pollution, there are other considerations: quantification of the direct improvements to quality of life; whether or not to take international effects into account when formulating domestic policy; and the appropriate discount rate for evaluating benefits that will be received in the future. Moreover, the environmentalist and the industrialist may well arrive at different evaluations of the benefits of pollution control, reflecting their different viewpoints.

The measurement of costs may also be problematic. For example, it is likely that there will be differences in efficiency between firms. Those using modern technology may face lower costs than those using relatively old capital equipment. Do the authorities try to set a tax that is specific to each firm to take such differences into account? If they do not, but instead set a flat-rate tax, then the incentives may be inappropriate. This would mean that a firm using modern technology would face the same tax as one using old capital. The firm using new capital would then tend to produce too little output relative to those using older, less efficient capital.

Pollution permits

Another approach is to use a *pollution permit system*, under which the government issues or sells permits to firms, allowing them to pollute up to a certain limit. These permits are then tradable, so that firms that are relatively 'clean' in their production methods and do not need to use their full allocation of permits can sell their polluting rights to other firms, whose production methods produce greater levels of pollution.

Advantages

One important advantage of such a scheme lies in the incentives for firms. Firms that pollute because of their relatively inefficient production methods will find they are at a disadvantage because they face higher costs. Rather than continuing to purchase permits, they will find that they have an incentive to produce less pollution — which, of course, is what the policy is intended to achieve. In this way, the permit system uses the market to address the externality problem — in contrast to direct regulation of environmental standards, which tries to solve pollution by overriding the market.

A second advantage is that the overall level of pollution can be controlled by this system, as the authorities control the total amount of permits that are issued. After all, the objective of the policy is to control the overall level of pollution, and a mixture of 'clean' and 'dirty' firms may produce the same amount of total emissions as uniformly 'slightly unclean' firms.

Disadvantages

However, the permit system may not be without its problems. In particular, there is the question of enforcement. For the system to be effective, sanctions must be in place for firms that pollute beyond the permitted level, and there must be an operational and cost-effective method for the authorities to check the level of emissions.

Furthermore, it may not be a straightforward exercise for the authorities to decide upon the appropriate number of permits to issue in order to produce the desired reduction in emission levels. Some alternative regulatory systems share this problem, as it is not easy to measure the extent to which marginal private and social costs diverge.

One possible criticism that is unique to a permit form of regulation is that the very different levels of pollution produced by different firms may seem inequitable — as if those firms that can afford to buy permits can pollute as much as they like. On the other hand, it might be argued that those most likely to suffer from this are the polluting firms, whose public image is likely to be tarnished if they acquire a reputation as heavy polluters. This possibility might strengthen the incentives of such firms to clean up their production. Taking the strengths and weaknesses of this approach together, it seems that on balance such a system could be effective in regulating pollution.

Global warming

Global warming is widely seen to require urgent and concerted action at a worldwide level. The Kyoto summit of 1997 laid the foundations for action, with many of the developed nations agreeing to take action to reduce emissions of carbon dioxide and other 'greenhouse' gases that are seen to be causing climate change. Although the USA withdrew from the agreement in early 2001, apparently concerned that the US economy might be harmed, in November of that year 178 other countries did reach agreement on how to enforce the Kyoto Accord. The absence of US cooperation is potentially significant, however, as the USA was the world's second largest emitter of carbon dioxide, responsible for about a quarter of the world's greenhouse gas emissions.

At the heart of the Kyoto Accord was the decision of countries to reduce their greenhouse gas emissions by an agreed percentage by 2010. The method chosen to achieve these targets was based on a tradable pollution permit system. This was seen to be especially demanding for countries such as Japan, whose industry is already relatively energy-efficient. Japan was thus concerned that there should be sufficient permits available for purchase. More explicitly, it was concerned that sloppy compliance by Russia would limit the amount of permits on offer. The issues of monitoring and compliance are thus seen as critical.

Further summit meetings were held to try to maintain the Kyoto protocol, which appeared to have been salvaged in Doha in 2012. Some progress was made, but countries such as the USA, Canada and Japan remained sceptical, and China was reluctant to negotiate beyond Kyoto. This is significant, as China has now overtaken the USA as the world's largest emitter of greenhouse gases.

Study tip

Try to keep up to date with recent developments in environmental policy, as it is good to show examiners that you can apply your economic thinking to events in the world around us.

The NIMBY syndrome

One problem that arises in trying to deal with externalities is that you cannot please all of the people all of the time. For example, it may well be that it is in society's overall interests to relocate unsightly facilities — it may even be that everyone would agree about this; but such facilities have to be located somewhere, and someone is almost bound to object because they are the ones to suffer. This is the **NIMBY (not in my back yard)** syndrome.

For example, many people would agree that it is desirable for the long-run sustainability of the economy that cleaner forms of energy are developed. One possibility is to build wind farms. People may well be happy for these to be constructed — as long as they do not happen to be living near them. This may not be the best example, however, as the effectiveness of wind farms is by no means proven, and there is a strong movement against their use on these grounds.

Key term

NIMBY (not in my back yard) a syndrome under which people are happy to support the construction of an unsightly or unsocial facility, so long as it is not in their own area

Exercise 8.1

You discover that your local authority has chosen to locate a new landfill site for waste disposal close to your home. What costs and benefits for society would result? Would these differ from your private costs and benefits? Would you object?

Property rights

The existence of a system of secure property rights is essential as an underpinning for the economy. The legal system exists in part to enforce property rights, and to provide the set of rules under which markets operate. When property rights fail, there is a failure of markets.

One of the reasons underlying the existence of some externalities is that there is a failing in the system of property rights. For example, think about the situation in which a factory is emitting toxic fumes into a residential district. One way of viewing this is that the firm is interfering with local residents' clean air. If those residents could be given property rights over clean air, they could require the firm to compensate them for the costs it was inflicting. However, the problem is that, with such a wide range of people being affected to varying degrees (according to prevailing winds and how close they live to the factory), it is impossible in practical terms to use the assignment of property rights to internalise the pollution externality. This is because the problem of coordination requires high transaction costs in order for property rights to be individually enforced. It may also be difficult to introduce property rights into a situation where none has previously existed. Therefore, the government effectively takes over the property rights on behalf of the residents, and acts as a collective enforcer.

Nobel Prize winner Ronald Coase argued that externality effects could be internalised in conditions where property rights could be enforced, and where the transaction costs of doing so were not too large.

Summary

- In seeking to counter the harmful effects of externalities, governments look for ways of internalising the externality, by bringing external costs and benefits within the market mechanism.
- For example, the 'polluter pays' principle argues that the best way of dealing with a pollution externality is to force the polluter to face the full costs of its actions.
- Attempts have been made to tackle pollution through taxation, the regulation of environmental standards and the use of pollution permits.
- In some cases the allocation of property rights can be effective in curbing the effects of externalities — so long as the transaction costs of implementing it are not too high.

Government expenditure and state provision

Expenditure taxes are not only imposed to address perceived market failure, but also in order to help finance the government's expenditure. This includes expenditure on the administration of government, but also to enable transfer payments to be made in order to affect the distribution of income in a society — protecting the vulnerable and addressing poverty that may exist.

Chapter 7 discussed public goods, and argued that the free-rider problem would prevent the provision of public goods by the private sector in a free market. This does not mean that the government itself needs to provide such goods, but expenditure may be needed to encourage the private sector to provide public goods.

Government plans to invest in the HS2 rail link has sparked large-scale protests

Maintaining an appropriate balance between the public and private sectors is one of the fundamental dilemmas of government. For private firms to operate effectively and to compete in international markets, they need access to public goods such as a good transport and communications infrastructure. If the government does not put sufficient resources into road maintenance, or the development of the rail network, then firms may face higher costs, and be disadvantaged relative to their international competitors. On the other hand, if the government over-invests, then there is an opportunity cost, because more resources used for infrastructure implies that fewer resources are available for private sector investment. The debate about the HS2 rail link between London and the north provides an example of the tension that can arise when the government seeks to invest heavily in specific projects.

Price controls

In some markets, governments have been seen to intervene to regulate price directly. This could be viewed as a response to market failure — for example, if it were apparent that price was not being set equal to marginal cost. Some governments in developing countries have at times intervened to control food prices in urban areas in response to civil unrest. This can create a form of government failure if it provides weak incentives for farmers to raise production or improve their crops.

Regulation of prices has also been introduced in other contexts, notably in the housing market, where rent controls have been used to prevent exploitation of tenants by landlords. There have also been proposals to set minimum prices for alcohol in an attempt to control drinking.

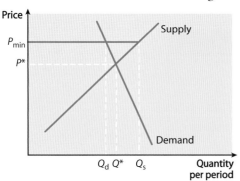

Figure 8.5 A minimum price for alcohol?

A minimum price for alcohol

Can problems caused by excessive drinking of alcohol be tackled by setting minimum prices for alcoholic drinks? Figure 8.5 represents the market.

In equilibrium, the market price would be at $P\star$, and the quantity traded would be $Q\star$. If the government want to discourage heavy drinking, they could introduce a minimum price, so that sellers were not able to charge a price below P_{min}.

Quantitative skills 8.1

Interpreting quantities on a graph

Figure 8.5 shows a market in disequilibrium, and it is helpful to be able to read off the relevant quantities. The equilibrium position is of course at the point where demand and supply intersect, at P^*, Q^*. However, if the price is set by government to be at least P_{min}, the market is held away from that equilibrium. Buyers and sellers now want different things. Buyers are only prepared to buy Q_d at this price, whereas suppliers would be prepared to sell Q_s.

One effect of the minimum price is therefore that there is excess supply, given by the distance $Q_s - Q_d$.

What is happening here is that, with the minimum price in effect, *some* consumers reduce their consumption: alcohol consumption falls by the distance $Q^* - Q_d$.

Whether this would be seen as a successful policy is a different matter. As Figure 8.5 has been drawn, the demand for alcohol is relatively inelastic with respect to the increase in price. If demand had been relatively more elastic, the impact would have been greater.

Rent controls

Another market in which governments have been tempted to intervene is the housing market. Figure 8.6 represents the market for rented accommodation. The free market equilibrium would be where demand and supply intersect, with the equilibrium rent being $R\star$ and the quantity of accommodation traded being $Q\star$.

If the government regards the level of rent as excessive, to the point where households on low incomes may be unable to afford rented accommodation, then, given that housing is one of life's necessities, it may regard this as unacceptable.

The temptation for the government is to move this market away from its equilibrium by imposing a maximum price (level of rent) that landlords are allowed to charge their tenants. Suppose that this level of rent is denoted by R_{max} in Figure 8.6. Again, there are two effects that follow. First, landlords will no longer find it profitable to supply as much rental accommodation, and so will reduce supply to Q_s. Second, at this lower rent there will be more people looking for accommodation, so that demand for rented accommodation will move to Q_d. The upshot of the rent controls, therefore, is that there is less accommodation available, and there are more homeless people.

It can be seen that the well-meaning rent control policy, intended to protect low-income households from being exploited by landlords, merely has the effect of reducing the amount of accommodation available. This is not what was supposed to happen.

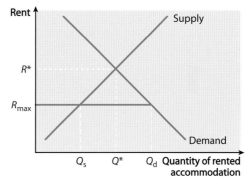

Figure 8.6 Rent controls

Legislation and regulation

In some markets, the government chooses to intervene directly through legislation and regulation, rather than by influencing prices. For example, it may limit the market power of large firms to protect consumers, or place direct controls on the emission of pollution.

Prohibition

An extreme form of this is to declare some goods illegal. This may also have unintended effects. Consider the situation in which action is taken to prohibit the consumption of a demerit good. Consider the case of a hard drug, such as cocaine. It can be argued that there are substantial social disbenefits arising from the consumption of hard drugs, and that addicts and potential addicts are in no position to make informed decisions about their consumption of them. One response to such a situation is to consider making the drug illegal — that is, to impose **prohibition**.

Figure 8.7 shows how the market for cocaine might look. You may wonder why the demand curve takes on this shape. The argument is that there are two types of cocaine user. There are the recreational users, who will take cocaine if it is available at a

> ### Key term
>
> **prohibition** an attempt to prevent the consumption of a demerit good by declaring it illegal

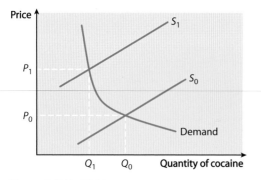

Figure 8.7 Prohibition

reasonable price, but who are not addicts. In addition, there is a hard core of habitual users who are addicts, whose demand for cocaine is highly inelastic. Thus, at low prices demand is relatively elastic because of the presence of the recreational users, who are relatively price sensitive. At higher prices the recreational users drop away, and demand from the addicts is highly price inelastic. Suppose that the supply in free market equilibrium is given by S_0; the equilibrium will be with price P_0 and quantity traded Q_0. If the drug is made illegal, this will affect supply. Some dealers will leave the market to trade in something else, and the police will succeed in confiscating a certain proportion of the drugs in the market. However, they are unlikely to be totally successful, so supply could move to, say, S_1.

In the new market situation, price rises substantially to P_1, and quantity traded falls to Q_1. However, what has happened is that the recreational users have dropped out of the market, leaving a hard core of addicts who will pay any price for the drug, and who may resort to muggings and robberies in order to finance their habit. This behaviour clearly imposes a new sort of externality on society. And the more successful the police are in confiscating supplies, the higher the price will be driven. There may thus be disadvantages in using prohibition as a way of discouraging consumption of a demerit good.

Tackling information failure

Market failure can arise from information failure, especially where there is asymmetric information or where economic agents lack information or the capacity to process the information available. In such circumstances, the solution would seem to be to find a way of providing the information to remedy the situation.

One example discussed in Chapter 7 was that of second-hand cars, where car dealers may find that they cannot find buyers for good-quality cars at a fair price if potential buyers cannot distinguish quality. The solution here may be to tackle the problem at its root, by finding a way to provide information about quality. In the case of second-hand cars, AA inspection schemes or the offering of warranties may be ways of improving the flow of information about the quality of cars for sale. Buyers may then have confidence that they are not buying a lemon.

Similarly, in the case of the insurance market, the asymmetric information problem helps to explain why insurance companies try to cover themselves by insisting on comprehensive health histories of those who take out health insurance, and include exclusion clauses that entitle them to refuse to pay out if past illnesses have not been disclosed. It also helps to explain why banks may insist on collateral to back up loans.

Information problems may also be present in respect of some demerit goods. Think back to the tobacco example discussed in Chapters 6 and 7. Tobacco is seen by government as a 'demerit' good on the grounds that smokers underestimate the damaging effects of smoking. There may also be negative externalities caused by passive smoking. At first, taxes were used to try to discourage smoking, but given the inelastic demand for tobacco, this proved ineffective. The taxes were reinforced by extensive campaigns to spread information about the damaging effects of smoking. When even this did not solve the problem, the government had to introduce regulation by prohibiting smoking in public buildings. The spread of e-cigarettes adds a new dimension to the situation.

The negative externalities caused by passive smoking led the government to introduce a no-smoking ban in public places

Costs of intervention

Some roles are critical for a government to perform if a mixed economy is to function effectively. A vital role is the provision by the government of an environment in which markets can operate effectively. There must be stability in the political system if firms and consumers are to take decisions with confidence about the future. And there must be a secure system of property rights, without which markets could not be expected to work.

In addition, there are sources of market failure that require intervention. This does not necessarily mean that governments need to substitute markets with direct action. However, it does mean that they need to be more active in markets that cannot operate effectively, while at the same time performing an enabling role to encourage markets to work well whenever this is feasible.

Such intervention entails costs. There are costs of administering and of monitoring the policy to ensure that it is working as intended. This includes the need to look out for the unintended distortionary effects that some policies can have on resource allocation in a society. It is therefore important to check that the marginal costs of implementing and monitoring policies do not exceed their marginal benefits.

Summary

- Government failure can occur when well-meaning intervention by governments has unintended effects.
- Rent controls may have the effect of reducing the amount of accommodation available.
- A sales tax imposes an excess burden on society.
- Prohibition may also have unintended effects.
- Governments have often regarded it as desirable to intervene in agricultural markets to sustain food production and stabilise prices.

Case study 8.1

Who pays taxes?

This may sound like a simple question, but many politicians do not seem to know the answer. Nor do a great many journalists. In fact, if there is one important economic concept that almost no one in the general public seems to understand, it is tax incidence — the economic study of who really pays taxes.

You might think it is easy to work out who pays tax — just look at who is handing over the money. Beer drinkers pay alcohol duties when they buy a pint, businesses pay corporation tax when they file their accounts (unless they can find a way of avoiding doing so, as highlighted by the media). It all seems so straightforward. But this is where an economist has to dig a little deeper. Consider the case of indirect taxes like VAT or the tax on alcohol. Who pays this tax?

To understand who is really paying a tax, we have to understand that both sides of the market (producers and consumers, or employers and employees) are trying to shift the burden of the tax on to the other side.

Suppose the government is worried about drunkenness in society, and introduces a new tax on vodka, intended to be paid by the consumer when they buy their bottle of Smirnoff at the off-licence. Will the vodka drinker have to bear the whole burden of the tax?

Source: adapted from Antoine Bozio, 'Who pays taxes?', *Economic Review*, Vol. 25, No. 4 (April 2008), pp. 17–19.

Follow-up question

Draw a demand and supply diagram to examine how much of the new tax will be paid by the consumer, and how much by the producer. How would your answer differ if the demand for vodka were perfectly inelastic?

The Common Agricultural Policy

The European Union (EU) attracts a lot of criticism — arguably more than its fair share — but one policy where criticism is justified is its Common Agricultural Policy (CAP). Even among farmers and their extended families, support is not universal. One suspects that for the majority of EU governments, only the threat of violent actions by some farmers prevents a rapid phasing out of what is now a highly complex system of payments and protections for the EU's farm businesses. Back in 1957, when the treaty incorporating the CAP was signed, things were very different.

The six founding members had suffered food shortages during the war and their governments were determined to become self-sufficient; moreover, they feared that a fall in agricultural incomes would drive people off the land and into urban areas, threatening a rise in urban unemployment. Thus, at its inception, the CAP had two prime objectives: to increase agricultural production of basic commodities, such as cereals, milk and beef; and to support agricultural incomes. In 1950, agricultural employment accounted for 25% of total employment in Europe; hence, the founding fathers could legitimately claim that the CAP would, by protecting rural incomes, create a balance between urban and rural living standards.

The policy instrument selected to achieve the CAP's objectives was open-ended price support. In essence, farmers would be guaranteed a price for each unit of output, such as a tonne of wheat, regardless of the amount produced. If a farm could double or treble its output of, say, cereals, it doubled or trebled its revenue. However, the

CAP could not achieve its objectives by merely announcing a target price. Two additional instruments were needed: namely, tariff barriers and intervention.

Compared to their counterparts in other parts of the world, western European farms are high cost. Setting a price to cover average unit production costs and leave sufficient for a profit necessitated protecting the prices of agricultural commodities produced within the EU from being undercut by cheaper imports from other parts of the world. The appropriate policy instrument here is a tariff or, to be strictly correct in the case of the CAP, a variable levy.

Source: adapted from Séan Rickard, 'The Common Agricultural Policy', *Economic Review*, Vol. 24, No. 3 (February 2007), pp. 17–21.

The CAP guarantees farmers a price for each unit of output

Follow-up question

Discuss the economic arguments surrounding the continuance of the CAP, and the possible presence of government failure. Do you think that the original arguments that led to the establishment of the CAP remain valid in the twenty-first century?

Theme 1 key terms

adverse selection a situation in which a person at risk is more likely to take out insurance

allocative efficiency achieved when society is producing an appropriate bundle of goods relative to consumer preferences

asymmetric information a situation in which some participants in a market have better information about market conditions than others

cartel an agreement between firms in a market on price and output with the intention of maximising their joint profits

ceteris paribus a Latin phrase meaning 'other things being equal'; it is used in economics when we focus on changes in one variable while holding other influences constant

command economy an economy in which decisions on resource allocation are guided by the state

comparative static analysis examines the effect on equilibrium of a change in the external conditions affecting a market

competitive market a market in which individual firms cannot influence the price of the good or service they are selling, because of competition from other firms

complements two goods are said to be complements if an increase in the price of one good causes the demand for the other good to fall

consumer surplus the value that consumers gain from consuming a good or service over and above the price paid

consumption externality an externality that affects the consumption side of a market, which may be either positive or negative

cross-price elasticity of demand (XED) a measure of the sensitivity of quantity demanded of a good or service to a change in the price of some other good or service

demand the quantity of a good or service that consumers choose to buy at any possible price in a given period

demand curve a graph showing how much of a good will be demanded by consumers at any given price

diminishing marginal utility describes the situation where an individual gains less additional utility from consuming a product, the more of it is consumed

division of labour a process whereby the production procedure is broken down into a sequence of stages, and workers are assigned to a particular stage

elasticity a measure of the sensitivity of one variable to changes in another variable

external cost a cost associated with an individual's (a firm or household's) production or other economic activities, which is borne by a third party and is not reflected in market prices

externality a cost or a benefit that is external to a market transaction, and is thus not reflected in market prices

factors of production resources used in the production process; inputs into production, particularly including labour, capital, land and entrepreneurship

firm an organisation that brings together factors of production in order to produce output

free-rider problem when an individual cannot be excluded from consuming a good, and thus has no incentive to pay for its provision

government failure a misallocation of resources arising from government intervention that causes a divergence between marginal social benefit and marginal social cost

gross domestic product (GDP) a measure of the economic activity carried out in an economy over a period

incidence of a tax the way in which the burden of paying a sales tax is divided between buyers and sellers

income elasticity of demand (YED) a measure of the sensitivity of quantity demanded to a change in consumer incomes

indirect tax a tax levied on expenditure on goods or services (as opposed to a direct tax, which is a tax charged directly to an individual based on a component of income)

inferior good one where the quantity demanded decreases in response to an increase in consumer incomes

internalising an externality an attempt to deal with an externality by bringing an external cost or benefit into the price system

law of demand a law that states that there is an inverse relationship between quantity demanded and the price of a good or service, ceteris paribus

luxury good one for which the income elasticity of demand is positive, and greater than 1, such that as income rises, consumers spend proportionally more on the good

macroeconomics the study of the interrelationships between economic variables at an aggregate (economy-wide) level

marginal analysis an approach to economic decision making based on considering the additional (marginal) benefits and costs of a change in behaviour

marginal cost the cost of producing an additional unit of output

marginal social benefit (MSB) the additional benefit that society gains from consuming an extra unit of a good

marginal social cost the cost to society of producing an extra unit of a good

market a set of arrangements that allows transactions to take place

market economy an economy in which market forces are allowed to guide the allocation of resources

market equilibrium a situation that occurs in a market when the price is such that the quantity that consumers wish to buy is exactly balanced by the quantity that firms wish to supply

market failure a situation in which the free market mechanism does not lead to an optimal allocation of resources, e.g. where there is a divergence between marginal social benefit and marginal social cost

merit good a good that brings unanticipated benefits to consumers, such that society believes it will be underconsumed in a free market

microeconomics the study of economic decisions taken by individual economic agents, including households and firms

mixed economy an economy in which resources are allocated partly through price signals and partly on the basis of intervention by the state

model a simplified representation of reality used to provide insight into economic decisions and events

moral hazard a situation in which a person who has taken out insurance is prone to taking more risk

necessity a good for which the income elasticity of demand is positive, and less than 1, such that as income rises, consumers spend proportionally less on the good

NIMBY (not in my back yard) a syndrome under which people are happy to support the construction of an unsightly or unsocial facility, so long as it is not in their own area

non-renewable resources natural resources that once used cannot be replenished, such as coal or oil

normal good one where the quantity demanded increases in response to an increase in consumer incomes

normative statement a statement that involves a value judgement about what *ought to be*

opportunity cost in decision making, the value of the next-best alternative forgone

positive statement a statement about what is (i.e. about facts)

potential economic growth an expansion in the productive capacity of the economy

price elasticity of demand (*PED*) a measure of the sensitivity of quantity demanded to a change in the price of a good or service. It is measured as:

$$\frac{\% \text{ change in quantity demanded}}{\% \text{ change in price}}$$

price elasticity of supply (*PES*) a measure of the sensitivity of quantity supplied of a good or service to a change in the price of that good or service

private cost a cost incurred by an individual (firm or consumer) as part of its production or other economic activities

private good a good that, once consumed by one person, cannot be consumed by somebody else; such a good has excludability and is rivalrous

producer surplus the difference between the price received by firms for a good or service and the price at which they would have been prepared to supply that good or service

production externality an externality that affects the production side of a market, which may be either positive or negative

production possibility frontier (*PPF*) a curve showing the maximum combinations of goods or services that can be produced in a given period with available resources

prohibition an attempt to prevent the consumption of a demerit good by declaring it illegal

public good a good that is non-exclusive and non-rivalrous in consumption — consumers cannot be excluded from consuming the good, and consumption by one person does not affect the amount of the good available for others to consume

relatively elastic a term used when the price elasticity of demand is greater than 1 but less than infinity

relatively inelastic a term used when the price elasticity of demand is less than 1 but greater than zero

renewable resources natural resources that can be replenished, such as forests that can be replanted, or solar energy that does not get used up

scarcity a situation that arises when people have unlimited wants in the face of limited resources

social cost private cost plus external cost

subsidy a grant given by the government to producers to encourage production of a good or service

substitutes two goods are said to be substitutes if the demand for one good is likely to rise if the price of the other good rises

supply the quantity of a good or service that firms choose to sell at any possible price in a given period

supply curve a graph showing the quantity supplied at any given price

sustainable development 'development which meets the needs of the present without compromising the ability of future generations to meet their own needs' (Brundtland Commission, 1987)

unitary elastic a term used when the price elasticity of demand is equal to 1

Theme 1 practice questions

1 The nature of economics

1 'Wants are unlimited but resources are finite.' This illustrates:

   A That all needs may be satisfied

   B The problem of scarcity

   C That a centrally planned economy is the best means of allocating resources

   D That resources are free

2 Figure 1 illustrates two production possibility frontiers.

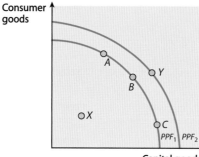

Capital goods   **Figure 1** Production possibility frontiers

   Which of the following would involve an opportunity cost? A movement from:

   A *X* to *B*

   B *B* to *Y*

   C *X* to *A*

   D *B* to *C*

3 Which of the following is a sustainable source of energy?

   A Electricity generated from coal

   B Oil from the North Sea

   C Gas from shale sands

   D Electricity generated from wind farms

4 A function of the price mechanism in a market economy is to:

   A Ensure everyone can afford food and water

   B Keep prices stable

   C Ensure that all resources are fully employed

   D Indicate changes in wants

5 *Statement 1: The UK economy has had a double-dip recession.*

   Statement 2: The government should reduce taxes to increase the rate of economic growth.

   Which of the following is correct about the above statements?

	Statement 1	Statement 2
A	Normative	Normative
B	Normative	Positive
C	Positive	Normative
D	Positive	Positive

6 Suppose that a local garage introduces division of labour for car servicing. A disadvantage of such division of labour in this process could be that:

A Workers may find it more difficult to get a job in another industry

B Labour productivity will increase

C The training required will be reduced

D Workers have to spend more time moving from one activity to another

2 The nature of demand

1 Which of the following would cause a rightward *shift* of the demand curve for cars?

A An increase in VAT on cars

B A decrease in the cost of components used in cars

C An increase in the price of petrol

D An increase in real incomes of consumers

2 Which of the following would cause a movement *along* a given demand curve for wheat?

A A subsidy given to wheat farmers

B An increase in the population

C A decrease in the demand for bread

D An increase in the popularity of rice, a substitute for wheat

3 **Table 1**

Product	Price elasticity of demand	Income elasticity of demand
Rice	−0.3	−1.2
Beef steak	−1.7	+2.8
Carrots	−0.4	+0.8

Given the information in Table 1, it can be deduced that:

A The demand for rice is more price elastic than the demand for beef steak

B Rice is an inferior good whereas carrots are a normal good

C The demand for rice is more income elastic than the demand for beef steak

D The demand for carrots is price elastic and income elastic

4 Demand for a product will become more price elastic if:

A Stocks of the product increase

B The product becomes more durable

C More consumers regard the product as being essential

D A new substitute becomes available

5 If the cross-price elasticity of demand between two products is negative then it may be deduced that they are:

A Complements

B Inferior goods

C Substitutes

D Normal goods

6 When demand is price elastic, a reduction in price will lead to:

  A A decrease in total revenue

  B An increase in total revenue

  C A more than proportionate fall in quantity demanded

  D A decrease in the profits of the firm selling the product

3 The nature of supply

1 Which of the following would cause a rightward *shift* of the supply curve for sweetcorn?

  A A severe drought in areas where sweetcorn is grown

  B An increased preference for sweetcorn by consumers

  C A fall in the price of other vegetables

  D An increase in productivity caused by increased use of fertilisers

2 Which of the following would cause a movement *along* the supply curve for beef?

  A A decrease in consumption of beef following a health scare

  B A government subsidy for beef farmers

  C A rise in the cost of animal feed

  D An increase in the number of cows

3 An increase in value added tax on petrol would cause:

  A A shift in the supply curve to the right and its gradient to get steeper

  B A shift in the demand curve to the left

  C A shift in the supply curve to the left and its gradient to get steeper

  D A movement along the supply curve

4 The supply of a product is likely to be very price inelastic if:

  A There are close substitutes for it

  B It is perishable

  C Large stocks are available

  D It forms a large percentage of consumer incomes

5 If a 10% rise in the price of copper causes a 10% increase in the quantity supplied then supply is:

  A Price inelastic

  B Perfectly inelastic

  C Perfectly elastic

  D Unitary elastic

6 A subsidy to bee-keepers would cause:

  A The demand curve for honey to shift to the left

  B A fall in the price of honey

  C A decrease in the quantity of honey supplied

  D The supply curve of honey to shift to the left

4 How markets work: price determination

1 Which of the following is **not** a function of the price mechanism in a free market economy?

  A To provide signals to producers to increase or decrease output when price changes

  B To indicate changes in consumer wants

  C To keep prices stable

  D To allocate resources

2 In a free market economy, if the current market price is above the equilibrium price then:

    A There will be an extension of supply and a contraction in demand

    B The price will rise

    C There will be an extension of demand and a contraction in supply

    D There will be a rightward shift of the demand curve

Questions 3 and 4 are based on Figure 2.

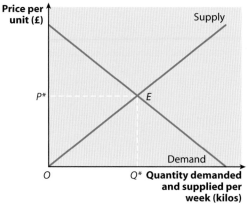

Figure 2

3 An increase in supply would cause:

    A A contraction in demand and an increase in price

    B An extension of demand and a decrease in price

    C A contraction in supply and an increase in price

    D An extension of supply and a decrease in price

4 An increase in demand would cause:

    A Consumer surplus to decrease

    B Producer surplus to decrease

    C Both consumer surplus and producer surplus to increase

    D Both consumer surplus and producer surplus to decrease

5 For an economy as a whole, efficiency in production would be achieved:

    A At any point along a productive possibility frontier

    B When there are unemployed resources

    C At a point to the right of an existing possibility frontier

    D When resources are shared equally

5 How markets work: the price mechanism in action

1 Illustrating your answer with a supply and demand diagram, explain the effect of an increase in VAT on sweets and crisps.

2 The price of coffee has fluctuated considerably over the last 5 years.

    a Analyse reasons which might explain why the price of coffee fluctuates. Illustrate your answer with a supply and demand diagram.

    b Assess the effects on consumers and producers of fluctuations in the price of coffee.

3 The UK housing market

Home ownership dropped from 68% in 2001 to 64% in 2011 partly because of the difficulties in securing mortgages from banks and building societies and the need to provide large deposits to secure the lowest interest rates. Consequently, more people are renting accommodation, causing rents to increase significantly.

Given the UK's rising and ageing population, more homes are needed. However, house builders are unwilling to build new houses when economic growth prospects are weak. Furthermore, it takes considerable time to obtain planning permission and then to build new houses.

Some economists have suggested that the government should offer subsidies to house builders to encourage them to increase the rate of house building. However, this would involve an increase in public expenditure at a time when the government is trying to reduce its expenditure in order to reduce the budget deficit.

   a Illustrating your answer with a supply and demand diagram, explain why rents have increased.

   b Analyse the factors influencing the demand for houses to buy.

   c Assess the factors influencing the elasticity of supply of houses.

   d Evaluate the effects of a decision by the government to subsidise the building of new houses.

6 Market failure and externalities

1

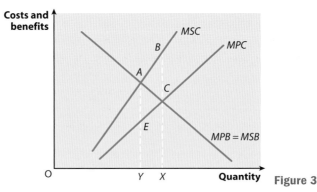

Figure 3

From Figure 3, it can be deduced that:

  A The free market level of output is *OY*

  B The welfare loss is *EAC*

  C The welfare gain from increasing output from *OY* to *OX* is *YACX*

  D A reduction in the quantity produced below *OX* would reduce the welfare loss

2 New vaccine

A new vaccine is developed to prevent the spread of coughs and colds, which are the main cause of around 130 million working days lost through absenteeism in the UK. The government decides to make this vaccine freely available to anyone who wants it, much to the delight of the pharmaceutical company that developed it.

   a What are the private benefits of the production and consumption of this new vaccine?

   b Explain the opportunity cost of providing the vaccine free to individuals.

   c Assess the external benefits of the new vaccine, illustrating your answer with an externalities diagram.

7 Market failure: public goods and information gaps

1 Market failure might occur in a free market economy when:

  A Firms enter the market in response to higher prices

  B A net welfare loss results from intervention by the government

  C Prices rise when there is excess demand

  D There is underprovision of public goods

2 The free-rider problem arises because:

  A Producers charge a price for private goods

  B There is no opportunity cost in providing a public good

  C Private goods are always free

  D Public goods are non-excludable

3 Public goods differ from private goods because:

  A Public goods are excludable

  B It is impossible to charge for private goods

  C Private goods are always underprovided in a market economy

  D Public goods are non-excludable and non-rivalrous

4 Without government intervention, it is unlikely that workers will make adequate provision for their pensions. The most likely reason is:

  A Workers have inadequate information

  B Pensions are a public good

  C Life expectancy is falling

  D There is no tax on pension contributions

8 Government intervention and government failure

1 Between 2009 and 2012, the price of maize fluctuated between $144 per tonne and $330 per tonne. The most likely explanation is that:

  A Demand and supply of maize are price elastic

  B The supply of maize is unaffected by changes in weather conditions

  C Demand and supply of maize are price inelastic

  D The demand for maize is continuously decreasing

2 Tax on tobacco

Many governments tax tobacco as a means of raising revenue. Indeed the UK government raised £12.1 billion from the tax on tobacco in 2011/12. The effect of the tax increases in the 2012 Budget was to increase the price of a packet of cigarettes by 37p. However, there is evidence that this has led to a significant increase in smuggling as people try to avoid the taxes, which account for a large proportion of the cost of a packet of cigarettes.

Similarly, heavy taxes on alcohol have led to an increase in sales on the black market. Further, it has been found that in some years, when taxes on alcohol have been increased, tax revenue has actually decreased. A different approach has been adopted by the Scottish government, which has introduced a minimum price for alcohol.

  a Giving examples, distinguish between the private costs and external costs of cigarette consumption.

  b Illustrating your answer with a supply and demand diagram, analyse the effect of an increase in tax on tobacco.

c To what extent does taxation of tobacco result in government failure?

d Assess the likely economic effects of a minimum price being set for alcoholic drinks.

e Examine two other ways in which the government might discourage the consumption of alcohol and tobacco.

THEME 2

THE UK ECONOMY — PERFORMANCE AND POLICIES

Measures of economic performance: economic growth

This part of the book switches attention to macroeconomics. Macroeconomics has much in common with microeconomics, but focuses on the whole economy, rather than on individual markets and how they operate. Although the way of thinking about issues is similar, and although similar tools are used, now it is interactions between economic variables at the level of the whole economy that are studied. This chapter will introduce economic growth; the following chapter will discuss other major concerns of the media — inflation, unemployment and the balance of payments.

Learning objectives

After studying this chapter, you should:
➡ be aware of the main economic aggregates in a modern economy
➡ understand the distinction between real and nominal variables
➡ be familiar with the use of index numbers and the calculation of growth rates
➡ understand how economic growth is measured and its limitations
➡ appreciate the inadequacy of economic growth as a measure of the standard of living
➡ be aware of problems of comparison between developed and developing countries

Economic performance

Key term

macroeconomics
the study of the interrelationships between economic variables at an aggregate (macroeconomic) level

The first part of the book emphasised the importance of individual markets in achieving allocative and productive efficiency. In a modern economy, there are so many separate markets that it is difficult to get an overall picture of how well the economy is working. When it comes to monitoring its overall performance, the focus thus tends to be on the **macroeconomic** aggregates. 'Aggregates' here means 'totals' — for example, total unemployment in an economy, or total spending on goods and services — rather than, say, unemployed workers in a particular occupation, or spending on a particular good.

There are a number of dimensions on which the economy as a whole can be monitored. One prime focus of economic policy in recent years has been the inflation rate, as it has been argued that maintaining a stable economic environment is crucial to enabling markets to operate effectively. A second focus has been unemployment, which has been seen as an indicator of whether the economy is using its resources to the full — in other words, whether there are factors of production that are not being fully utilised. In addition, of course, there may be concern that the people who are unemployed are being disadvantaged.

Perhaps more fundamentally, there is an interest in economic growth. Is the economy expanding its potential capacity as time goes by, thereby making more resources available for members of society? In fact, it might be argued that this is the most fundamental objective for the economy, and the most important indicator of the economy's performance.

Other concerns may also need to be kept in mind. In particular, there is the question of how the economy interacts with the rest of the world. The UK is an 'open' economy — one that actively engages in international trade — and this aspect of UK economic performance needs to be monitored too.

The importance of data

To monitor the performance of the economy, it is crucial to be able to observe how the economy is functioning, and for this you need data. Remember that economics, especially macroeconomics, is a non-experimental discipline. It is not possible to conduct experiments to see how the economy reacts to various stimuli in order to learn how it works. Instead, it is necessary to observe the economy, and to come to a judgement about whether or not its performance is satisfactory, and whether macroeconomic theories about how the economy works are supported by the evidence.

So, a reliable measure is needed for tracking each of the variables mentioned above, in order to observe how the economy is evolving through time. The key indicators of the economy's performance will be introduced as this chapter unfolds.

Study tip

Although data are important in economics, notice that it is *not* necessary to learn lots of detailed facts and statistics about the UK economy. However, it is of course helpful to be familiar with recent events and general trends in the performance of the economy.

Sources of data

Most of the economic statistics used by economists are collected and published by various government agencies. Such data in the UK are published mainly by the Office for National Statistics (ONS). Data on other countries are published by the International Monetary Fund (IMF), the World Bank and the United Nations, as well as national sources. There is little alternative to relying on such sources because the accurate collection of data is an expensive and time-consuming business.

Care needs to be taken in the interpretation of economic data. It is important to be aware of how the data are compiled, and the extent to which they are indicators of what economists are trying to measure. It is also important to remember that the economic environment is ever changing, and that single causes can rarely be ascribed to the economic events that are observed. This is because the ceteris paribus condition that underlies so much economic analysis is rarely fulfilled in reality. In other words, you cannot rely on 'other things remaining constant' when using data about the real world.

It is also important to realise that even the ONS cannot observe with absolute accuracy. Indeed, some data take so long to be assembled that early estimates are provisional in nature and subject to later revision as more information becomes available. Data used in international comparisons must be treated with even greater caution.

Real and nominal measurements

The measurement of economic variables poses many dilemmas for statisticians. Not least is the fundamental problem of what to use as units of measurement. Suppose economists wish to measure total output produced in an economy during successive years. In the first place, they cannot use volume measures. They may be able to count how many computers, passenger cars, tins of paint and cauliflowers the economy produces — but how do they add all these different items together to produce a total?

An obvious solution is to use the *money values*. Given prices for all the items, it is possible to calculate the money values of all these goods and thus produce a measurement of the total output produced in an economy during a year in terms of pounds sterling. However, this is just the beginning of the problem because, in order to monitor changes in total output between 2 years, it is important to be aware that not only do the volumes of goods produced change, but so too do their prices. In effect, this means that, if pounds sterling are used as the unit of measurement, the unit of measurement will change from one year to the next as prices change.

This is a problem that is not faced by most of the physical sciences. After all, the length of a metre does not alter from one year to the next, so if the length of something is being measured, the unit is fixed. Economists, however, have to make allowance for changing prices when measuring in pounds sterling or US dollars.

Measurements made using prices that are current at the time a transaction takes place are known as measurements of **nominal values**. When prices are rising, these nominal measurements will always overstate the extent to which an economic variable is growing through time. Clearly, to analyse performance, economists will be more interested in 'real' values — that is, the quantities produced after having removed the effects of price changes. One way in which these real measures can be obtained is by taking the volumes produced in each year and valuing these quantities at the prices that prevailed in some base year. This then enables allowance to be made for the changes in prices that take place, permitting a focus on the real values. These can be thought of as being measured at constant prices.

For example, suppose that last year you bought a tub of ice cream for £2, but that inflation has been 10%, so that this year you had to pay £2.20 for the same tub. Your real consumption of the item has not changed, but your spending has

How can we add together all the different items an economy produces?

increased. If you were to use the value of your spending to measure changes in consumption through time, it would be misleading, as you know that your real consumption has not changed at all (so is still £2), although its *nominal* value has increased to £2.20.

Quantitative skills 9.1

Converting nominal measurements to real

It is worth being aware that the ratio of the current (nominal) value of a variable to its constant price (real) value (multiplied by 100) is a price index. For example:

$$100 \times \frac{\text{nominal GDP}}{\text{real GDP}} \text{ is a price index}$$

So, if we know GDP at current prices and we know the relevant price index, we can calculate the real value of GDP.

For example, in 2013, GDP for the UK in current prices was estimated to be £1.613 billion, and the underlying price index was 105.2 (based on 2010 = 100). The real value of GDP can thus be calculated as:

$$100 \times \frac{1.613}{105.2} = £1.533 \text{ billion}$$

Quantitative skills 9.2

Calculating a percentage change

In macroeconomics it is often important to be able to calculate the percentage change in a variable. For example, it may be that there is interest in knowing how rapidly prices are changing, or in calculating the rate of economic growth. In the previous paragraph, the price of a tub of ice cream was supposed to have increased from £2 to £2.20. To calculate the percentage change in the price, calculate the change in price (2.20 − 2 = 0.20) and express that as a percentage of the original value. In other words, the percentage change is:

$$100 \times (2.20 - 2) \div 2 = 10\%$$

Notice that the change in the variable is always expressed as a percentage of the initial value, not the final value.

Index numbers

In some cases there is no apparent unit of measurement that is meaningful. For example, if you wished to measure the general level of prices in an economy, there is no meaningful unit of measurement that could be used. In such cases the solution is to use **index numbers**, which are a form of ratio that compares the value of a variable with some base point.

For example, suppose the price of a 250g pack of butter last year was 80p, and this year it is 84p. How can the price between the two periods be compared? One way of doing it is to calculate the percentage change using the formula introduced above:

$$100 \times (84 - 80) \div 80 = 5\%$$

Alternatively, you could create an index number as shown below.

Summary

- Macroeconomics is the study of the interrelationships between economic variables at the level of the whole economy.
- Some variables are of particular interest when monitoring the performance of an economy — for example, inflation, unemployment and economic growth.
- As economists cannot easily conduct experiments in order to test economic theory, they rely on the use of economic data: that is, observations of the world around them.
- Data measured in money terms need to be handled carefully, as prices change over time, thereby affecting the units in which many economic variables are measured.
- Index numbers are helpful in comparing the value of a variable with a base date or unit.

Economic growth

If the ultimate aim of a society is to improve the well-being of its citizens, then in economic terms this means that the resources available within the economy need to expand through time in order to widen people's choices. This requires a process of economic growth, which as we saw in Chapter 1 is an increase in the productive capacity of the economy.

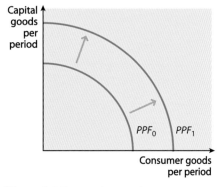

Capital goods per period

Consumer goods per period

Figure 9.1 Economic growth

From a theoretical point of view, **potential economic growth** can be thought of as an expansion of the productive capacity of an economy. If you like, it is an expansion of the potential output of the economy.

The notion of economic growth was introduced in Chapter 1 in terms of the production possibility frontier (PPF). Figure 9.1 is a reminder and reproduces Figure 1.4. Economic growth is characterised as an outward movement of the production possibility frontier from PPF_0 to PPF_1. In other words, economic growth enables a society to produce more goods and services in any given period as a result of an expansion in its resources.

Chapter 1 also briefly introduced the notion of **gross domestic product (GDP)** as representing the total output of an economy during a period of time. GDP can be seen as the total value added produced by firms in the domestic economy during a period, but it can also be measured by adding up total expenditures in the period, or by totalling the amount of income earned. In principle, these should all give the same answer, but in practice GDP is calculated as the average of the three measures.

GDP focuses on the domestic economy. However, it is also important to recognise that residents of the economy also receive some income from abroad — and some income earned in the domestic economy is sent abroad. **Gross national income (GNI)** takes into account these income flows between countries, and for some purposes is a more helpful measure — indeed, this is the standard measure used by the World Bank to compare average incomes across countries. This measure was formerly known as gross national product (GNP).

Actual economic growth is measured by the percentage rate of growth of GDP (or GNI) in a period. This may differ from potential economic growth because the economy is not always operating at full capacity. Economies tend to go through a **business cycle**, with the level of economic activity fluctuating around an underlying trend.

Figure 9.2 shows real GDP since 1948. You can see that during this period, real GDP grew in almost every year, but that there are some years where real GDP dipped. In particular, notice how real GDP fell after 2007. It is also important to note that this shows the level of real GDP, so to calculate growth it is necessary to compute the annual rate of change. This is done in Figure 9.3, which shows the annual growth rate of real GDP in the UK since 1948. You can see that it is quite difficult to determine the underlying trend because the year-to-year movements are so volatile. Figure 9.4 takes 5-yearly average growth rates over the same period, with the horizontal red line showing the underlying trend rate of growth. Again, you can see that the recession of the late 2000s was out of line with previous experience.

Key terms

potential economic growth an expansion in the productive capacity of the economy

gross domestic product (GDP) a measure of the economic activity carried out in the domestic economy over a period

gross national income (GNI) GDP plus net income from abroad

actual economic growth the rate of growth of GDP in a period

business cycle a phenomenon whereby GDP fluctuates around its underlying trend, following a regular pattern

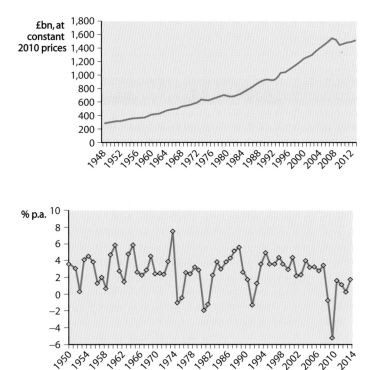

Figure 9.2 Real GDP, 1948–2013 (£ billion)
Source: ONS

Figure 9.3 Growth of real GDP, 1949–2014 (% change over previous year)
Source: ONS

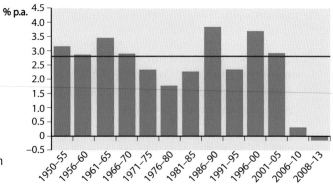

Figure 9.4 Average annual growth rates in the UK since 1950

Summary

- Economic growth is a fundamental aspect of the overall performance of an economy, as it is through growth that the citizens of a country can become better off.
- From a theoretical point of view, potential economic growth is an increase in the productive capacity of an economy — in other words, an increase in the potential output of an economy.
- GDP is a measure of the total economic activity carried out in an economy during a period by residents living on its territory.
- The rate of growth of real GDP informs us about actual economic growth, but not necessarily about the growth of potential output, which is much more difficult to measure.
- Economies tend not to grow according to a constant trend, but to fluctuate around an underlying trend, creating a business cycle.

Exercise 9.1

Table 9.1 provides data on real GDP for the period 2005–13. Convert the series to an index based on 2005 = 100. Calculate the growth rate of GDP for each year from 2005/06 to 2012/13. In which year was growth at its highest and in which year was it at its lowest?

Table 9.1 Real GDP in the UK, 2005–13 (£bn)

2005	1,549
2006	1,597
2007	1,637
2008	1,632
2009	1,562
2010	1,591
2011	1,618
2012	1,628
2013	1,656

GDP, GNI and the standard of living

GDP is a way of measuring the total output of an economy over a period of time. Although this measure can provide an indicator of the quantity of resources available to citizens of a country in a given period, as an assessment of the standard of living it has its critics.

If the intention is to monitor the standard of living in a country — in other words, the quality of life that is enjoyed by the country's residents — GNI is to be preferred to GDP, as it more closely reflects the incomes of the residents, including net flows of income between countries. This would be important for some countries such as Pakistan or the Philippines, where there are relatively large inflows of income from people working abroad and remitting income to their families. GNI also has other things going for it. First, it is relatively straightforward and thus is widely understood. Second, it is a well-established indicator and one that is available for almost every country in the world, so that it can be used to compare income levels across countries.

An important point to notice is that if we want to compare across countries, we need to recognise that different countries have differently sized populations, and we need to take this into account. This is done by calculating the average level of GNI per head of population, which is known as **GNI per capita**.

Quantitative skills 9.4

Calculating GNI per capita

Suppose you want to compare living standards in China and Malaysia. In 2012, GNI in China was US$7,748.9 billion, whereas in Malaysia it was US$286.4 billion. However, China's population was 1,351 million, compared to Malaysia's 29 million. It is more meaningful to compare average GNI per capita. For China this was US$7,748,900/1,351 = US$5,736. Notice that because GNI was measured in billions, but population was in millions, it was necessary to convert GNI into millions for this calculation to be correct. For Malaysia, GNI per capita was US$9,876.

Figure 9.5 provides data on GNI per capita for a range of countries around the world. The extreme differences that exist around the globe are immediately apparent from the data. GNI per capita in Burundi was just $240 in 2012, whereas in the USA the figure was $50,120.

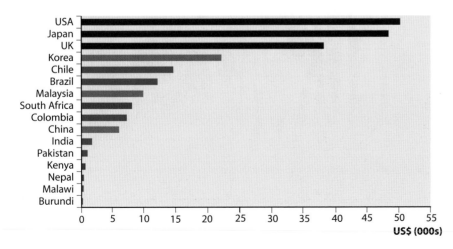

Figure 9.5 GNI per capita, 2012, in US$

Source: World Bank

In trying to interpret these data, there are a number of issues that need to be borne in mind, as the comparison is not as straightforward as it looks.

Inequality in income distribution

One important point to notice is that looking at the average level of income per person may be misleading if there are wide differences in the way in which income is distributed within countries. In other words, it cannot be assumed that every person living in Burundi receives $240, or that every US citizen receives $50,120. If income is more unequally distributed in some countries, this will affect one's perception of what the term 'average' means. For example, Chile and Hungary had broadly similar GNI per capita levels in 2012, but the income distribution in Hungary was more equitable than in Chile.

The informal sector and the accuracy of data

A further problem with undertaking international comparisons is that it is never absolutely certain that the accuracy with which data are collected is consistent across countries. Definitions of GNI and other variables are now set out in a clear, internationally agreed form, but even when countries are working to the same definitions, some data collection agencies may be more reliable than others.

In many developing countries, substantial economic activity may take place without an exchange of money

One particular area in which this is pertinent relates to the informal sector. In every economy there are some transactions that go unrecorded. In most economies, there are economic activities that take place that cannot be closely monitored because of their informal nature. This is especially prevalent in many developing countries, where substantial amounts of economic activity often take place without an exchange of money. For example, in many countries subsistence agriculture remains an important facet of economic life. If households are producing food simply for their own consumption, there is no reason for a money transaction to take place with regard to its production, and thus such activity will not be recorded as a part of GNI. Equally, much economic activity within the urban areas of less developed countries comes under the category of the 'informal sector'.

Where such activity varies in importance between countries, comparing incomes on the basis of measured GNI may be misleading, as GNI will be a closer indicator of the amount of real economic activity in some countries than in others.

Exchange rate problems

The data presented in Figure 9.5 were expressed in terms of US dollars. This allows economists to compare average incomes using a common unit of measurement. At the same time, however, it may create some problems.

Economists want to compare average income levels so that they can evaluate the standard of living, and compare standards across countries. In other words, it is important to be able to assess people's command over resources in different societies, and to be able to compare the purchasing power of income in different countries.

GNI is initially calculated in terms of local currencies, and subsequently converted into US dollars using official exchange rates. Will this provide information about the relative local purchasing power of incomes? Not necessarily.

One reason for this is that official exchange rates are sometimes affected by government intervention. Indeed, in many of the less developed countries, exchange rates are pegged to an international currency — usually the US dollar. In these circumstances, exchange rates are more likely to reflect the government's policy and actions than the relative purchasing power of incomes in the countries under scrutiny.

Where exchange rates are free to find their own equilibrium level, they are likely to be influenced strongly by the prices of *internationally traded* goods — which are likely to be very different from the prices of the goods that are typically consumed by residents in these countries. Again, it can be argued that the official exchange rates may not be a good reflection of the relative purchasing power of incomes across countries.

The United Nations International Comparison Project has been working on this problem for many years. It now produces an alternative set of international estimates of GNI based on purchasing power parity (PPP) exchange rates, which are designed to reflect the relative purchasing power of incomes in different societies more accurately. Figure 9.6 shows estimates for the same set of countries as Figure 9.5.

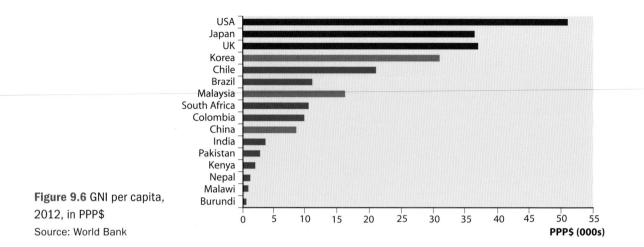

Figure 9.6 GNI per capita, 2012, in PPP$

Source: World Bank

Comparing this with Figure 9.5, you will notice that the gap between the low-income and high-income countries seems a bit less marked when PPP dollars are used as the unit of measurement. In other words, the US dollar estimates exaggerate the gap in living standards between rich and poor countries. This is a general feature of these measurements — that measurements in US dollars tend to understate real incomes for low-income countries and overstate them for high-income countries compared with PPP-dollar data. Put another way, people in the lower-income countries have a stronger command over goods and services than is suggested by US-dollar comparisons of GNI per capita. You can also see that the relative levels of GNI per capita of countries in PPP dollars are different in some cases — for example, compare Brazil with Chile, or Japan with the UK.

Social indicators

A final question that arises is whether GNI can be regarded as a reasonable indicator of a country's standard of living. You have seen that GNI provides an indicator of the total resources available within an economy in a given period, calculated from data about total output, total incomes or total expenditure. This focus on summing the transactions that take place in an economy over a period can be seen as a rather narrow view of what constitutes the 'standard of living'. After all, it may be argued that the quality of people's lives depends on more things than simply the material resources that are available.

For one thing, people need to have knowledge if they are to make good use of the resources that are available. Two societies with similar income levels may nonetheless provide very different quality of life for their inhabitants, depending on the education levels of the population. Furthermore, if people are to benefit from consuming or using the available resources, they need a reasonable lifespan coupled with good health. So, good standards of health are also crucial to a good quality of life.

It is important to remember that different societies tend to set different priorities on the pursuit of growth and the promotion of education and health. This needs to be taken into account when judging relative living standards through a comparison of GNI per capita, as some countries have higher-than-average levels of health and education as compared with other countries with similar levels of GNI per capita.

A reasonable environment in which to live may be seen as another important factor in one's quality of life, and there may be a trade-off between economic growth and environmental standards.

There are some environmental issues that can distort the GNI measure of resources. Suppose there is an environmental disaster — perhaps an oil tanker breaks up close to a beautiful beach. This reduces the overall quality of life by degrading the landscape and preventing enjoyment of the beach. However, it does not have a negative effect on GNI; on the contrary, the money spent on clearing up the damage actually adds to GNI, so that the net effect of an environmental disaster may be to *increase* the measured level of GNI!

Exercise 9.2

Table 9.2 gives some indicators for two countries, A and B. Discuss the extent to which GNI per capita (here measured in PPP$) provides a good indication of relative living standards in the two countries.

Table 9.2 Social indicators for countries A and B

Indicators	Country A	Country B
GNI per capita (PPP$)	11,578.0	11,445.0
Life expectancy (in years at birth)	56.1	75.2
Adult literacy rate (%)	93.0	98.0
Infant mortality rate (per 1,000 live births)	33.3	5.7
% of population living on less than $1 per person per day	13.77	0.21

Discuss what other indicators might be useful in this evaluation.

Economic growth: international experience

The growth performance of different regions around the world has shown contrasting patterns in recent years. As early as the 1950s, a gap had opened up between the early developing countries in North America, Western Europe and Japan and the late developers in sub-Saharan Africa and Latin America.

Between 1960 and 1980 this gap began to widen, except for a small group of countries, mainly in East Asia, that had begun to close it. Figure 9.7 gives some data for countries in different regions. These data relate to GDP rather than GNI, as GNI data are not available for all countries back to 1960. Burundi (in sub-Saharan Africa), together with Nepal and India (in South Asia) experienced relatively low growth in this period, and were among the countries with the lowest GDP per capita. Latin America showed a diverse experience: the examples shown in the figure are Colombia, which grew at 2.5% per annum, and Brazil, which achieved growth of above 4.5% per annum. However, East Asia (Korea and Malaysia) took off during this period, achieving rapid growth partly through exporting to world markets. Japan also grew rapidly at this time, while the UK and the USA grew at a more sedate pace of between 2 and 3% per annum.

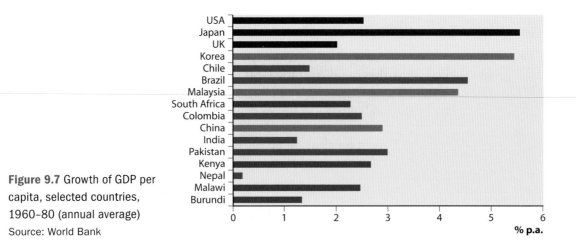

Figure 9.7 Growth of GDP per capita, selected countries, 1960–80 (annual average)

Source: World Bank

Figure 9.8 presents some more recent data for the same countries. This reveals some interesting patterns. First, the remarkable success of China in economic growth stands out very clearly in this figure, with annual growth in GDP per capita of nearly 10%. India and Korea also grew at more than 4% per annum over this period. The picture for countries in sub-Saharan Africa is far less encouraging, with Burundi even showing negative growth — meaning that real GDP per capita was lower in 2012 than it had been in 1990. The dampened performance of many countries in this period in part reflects the impact of the recession that hit many countries after the financial crisis of the late 2000s.

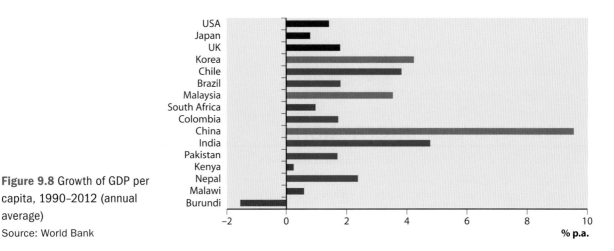

Figure 9.8 Growth of GDP per capita, 1990–2012 (annual average)

Source: World Bank

Gross national happiness?

If the intention is to measure the standard of living that is achieved by people in a society, is there a different approach that could be adopted? Many attempts have been made to do this. For example, an alternative indicator was proposed by William Nordhaus and James Tobin in 1972, known as the *Measure of Economic Welfare (MEW)*. This began with GNP (GNI) and then made various adjustments so that it only included the consumption and investment items that contribute positively to economic well-being. For example, they argued that the value of informal production should be added, but that there should be deductions for negative externalities such as environmental damage. An attempt was made to re-launch this as the *Index of Sustainable Economic Welfare (ISEW)*. It was hoped that this indicator would be able to capture key issues relating to the sustainability of economic growth, but it has yet to gain widespread support.

The fourth dragon king of Bhutan, Jigme Singye Wangchuck, went further when he came to the throne in 1972. He was intent on building an economy based on Buddhist values, so turned his back on the idea of GNI, shifting the focus of attention to GNH, gross national happiness. Can this be measured? One possibility is to ask people whether they are happy or not. The percentage of people answering positively could then be used as an indicator, and it would be possible to track how this changes through time, or across countries.

The 2007 OECD World Forum issued a declaration calling for fact-based information that could be used by a society to formulate a shared valuation of national well-being. In the UK, the ONS launched its Measuring National Well-Being Programme in 2010, to bring together a range of indicators across ten dimensions of the quality of life that would allow the monitoring of well-being through time. These indicators include measures of personal well-being, relationships, health, education and the environment, as well as some relating to the economy and personal finance. Again, these measures have not yet become fully embedded in the process of monitoring the economy, but they do allow some comparisons to be made across Europe, as similar measures are being produced for other countries.

To what extent is happiness likely to be correlated with real incomes? The relationship is not likely to be very close, as people's subjective perception of happiness will be related to a whole range of different things in addition to their material prosperity. Figure 9.9 takes data from the *World Happiness Report* of 2013 and produces a scatter plot of happiness against GNI per capita for 120 countries for which data were available. The values for happiness for each country represent the average values from interviews with individuals based on a scale of 0 to 10.

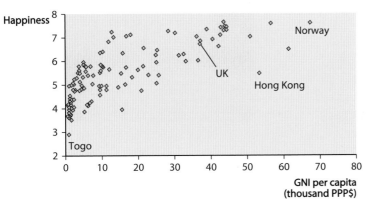

Figure 9.9 Happiness and GNI per capita

Sources: World Bank, United Nations

Summary

- GNI is a widely understood and widely available measure, but it does have some drawbacks.
- Average GNI per capita neglects the important issue of income distribution.
- There may be variation in the effectiveness of data collection agencies in different countries, and variation in the size of the informal sector.
- Converting from a local currency into US dollars may distort the use of GNI as a measure of the purchasing power of local incomes.
- GNI may neglect some important aspects of the quality of life.
- Recent research has begun to explore alternative ways of measuring well-being.

Case study 9.1

China's economic growth

Since China adopted market reforms in the late 1970s, its economy has enjoyed a period of rapid economic growth that is unprecedented by historical standards. One of the characteristics of this period of rapid growth has been the gradual move towards allowing market forces to operate after a long period of central planning. This would be expected to have benefits for the economy in terms of the efficiency of resource allocation.

Although China's success in achieving such rapid economic progress has been much admired, it has also been much criticised, for a number of reasons.

One source of criticism centres on the environmental damage that results from a rapid rate of economic growth. For example, *The Economist* ran an article in 2007 pointing to several incidents that illustrate some of the ways in which China's growth was causing externalities, some of which cross international borders. One such incident was an explosion at a chemical plant that caused pollution in the Songhua river. This affected the city of Harbin, which had to shut down its water supply, but also had effects on Russia, which is downstream from the spillage.

Such accidents may reflect local problems, but others may be related more directly to economic growth. A key ingredient of the growth process — especially in terms of industrialisation — is an expansion in energy supplies. Factories cannot operate without reliable electricity and other energy sources. Proposals to double China's production of hydroelectric power caused concerns about the effects of new dams on river levels in downstream countries in southeast Asia and in India.

Booming car ownership raises further concerns: one prediction is that the number of cars in China will reach 130 million by 2020 (from just 4 million in 2000). The effect of this on the demand for oil has already been reflected in higher world prices — China is already the world's second biggest oil importer (behind the USA). China is also the world's biggest producer of coal, which accounts for some 80% of China's energy use.

All of this means that China has now overtaken the USA as the largest emitter of carbon dioxide. It seems unlikely that environmental damage on this sort of scale is sustainable from a global perspective.

China is building hydroelectric dams at an unprecedented rate, raising enironmental concerns

Follow-up questions

a Explain why a move towards a market-based system would be expected to 'have benefits for the economy in terms of the efficiency of resource allocation'.

b Explain why the new dams would raise concerns.

c Discuss whether China should seek to restrain the growing car ownership that is a by-product of rapid economic growth, which has led to rising real incomes.

10 Measures of economic performance: inflation, unemployment and the balance of payments

The previous chapter introduced one of the most important macroeconomic indicators — economic growth. In trying to evaluate the performance of the economy at the macroeconomic level, it is also important to monitor other indicators, particularly inflation, unemployment and the balance of payments. The economy needs to perform well in these areas if economic growth is to be possible and sustainable.

Learning objectives

After studying this chapter, you should:
- → appreciate the significance of inflation for the modern economy
- → be familiar with alternative measurements of inflation in the context of the UK economy
- → be aware of the meaning and significance of unemployment, and ways in which it is measured in the UK
- → be familiar with the role and importance of the balance of payments

Inflation

Although economic growth may be seen as the most fundamental objective of macroeconomic policy, public attention in recent years has focused strongly on the control of **inflation**, principally because it is feared that instability of prices will deter firms from undertaking investment. Indeed, it would seem that the government's performance in guiding the economy at the macroeconomic level has often been judged in terms of inflation. This being so, it is important to understand how inflation is defined and measured.

> **Key term**
>
> **inflation** the rate of increase in the average price level in an economy

Inflation is defined as a change in the overall level of prices in an economy. The first step in measuring inflation is therefore to measure the average level of prices in the economy. Inflation can then be calculated as the percentage rate of change of prices over time.

Chapter 9 introduced index numbers, which are crucial when it comes to monitoring how prices change through time, or when you want to show the average level of prices at different points in time. For such a general price index, one procedure is to define a typical basket of commodities that reflects the spending pattern of a representative household. The cost of that bundle can be calculated in a base year, and then in subsequent years. The cost in the base year is set to equal 100, and in subsequent years the index is measured relative to that base date, thereby reflecting the change in prices since then. For example, if in the second year the weighted average increase in prices were 2.5%, then the index in year 2 would take on the value 102.5 (based on year 1 = 100). Such a general index of prices could be seen as an index of the cost of living for the representative household, as it would give the level of prices faced by the average household relative to the base year.

Exercise 10.1

Table 10.1 contains data on oil and petrol prices.

Table 10.1 Prices of oil and petrol

Date	Oil price ($ per barrel)	Average petrol price, London (£ per litre)	Average supermarket petrol price (£ per litre)
June 2011	112	1.361	1.346
June 2012	97	1.340	1.309
June 2013	104	1.342	1.330
June 2014	113	1.305	1.285

Source: Automobile Association

a Construct index numbers based on June 2011 = 100 and compare the movements in the price of petrol in London with the price of oil during this period.

b Construct index numbers to compare petrol prices in London with the average supermarket price for each of the periods.

The consumer price index

Key term

consumer price index (CPI) a measure of the general level of prices in the UK, the rate of change of which has been used as the government's inflation target since January 2004

The most important general price index in the UK is the **consumer price index (CPI)**, which has been used by the government in setting its inflation target since the beginning of 2004. This index is based on the prices of a bundle of goods and services measured at different points in time. A total of 180,000 individual price quotes on 680 different products are collected by the ONS each month, by visits to shops, telephone and using the internet. Data on spending from the *Household Final Monetary Consumption Expenditure* survey is used to compile the weights for the items included in the index. These weights are updated each year, as changes in the consumption patterns of households need to be accommodated if the index is to remain representative. A criticism of the index has been that it excludes housing costs of owner-occupiers, and a new index was launched in March 2013 to remedy this. The index is known as CPIH and is published alongside the CPI.

As noted above, it is important to remember that the CPI provides a measurement of the *level* of prices in the economy. This is not inflation: inflation is the *rate of change* of prices, and the percentage change in the CPI provides one estimate of the inflation rate. Notice that the CPI sets out to measure the way that inflation affects the 'average' or representative family, but individual households whose consumption pattern differs from the norm may experience inflation in different ways — for example, pensioners may have different patterns of consumption and may experience inflation in a different way.

Alternative measurements of inflation

The traditional measure of inflation in the UK for many years was the **retail price index (RPI)**, which was first calculated (under another name) in the early twentieth century to evaluate the extent to which workers were affected by price changes during the First World War. When the Blair government first set an explicit inflation target, it chose the RPIX, which is the RPI excluding mortgage interest payments. This was felt to be a better measure of the effectiveness of macroeconomic policy. It was argued that if interest rates are used to curb inflation, then including mortgage interest payments in the inflation measure will be misleading.

The CPI replaced RPIX partly because it is believed to be a more appropriate indicator for evaluating policy effectiveness. In addition, it has the advantage of being calculated using the same methodology as is used in other countries within the European Union, so that it is more useful than the RPIX for making international comparisons of inflation.

The CPI and RPI are based on a similar approach, although there are some significant differences in the detail of the calculation. Both measures set out to calculate the overall price level at different points in time. Each is based on calculating the overall cost of a representative basket of goods and services at different points in time relative to a base period. Both are produced by combining some 180,000 individual prices, which are collected each month for around 680 representative items. The result of

Key term

retail price index (RPI)
a measure of the average level of prices in the UK

The CPI and the RPI are based on a representative bundle of goods and services, reflecting consumption patterns in the UK

these calculations is an index that shows how the general level of prices has changed relative to the base year. The rate of inflation is then calculated as the percentage rate of change of the price index, whether it be the CPI or the RPI.

The indexes share a common failing, arising from the fixed weights used in calculating the overall index. Suppose the price of a particular item rises more rapidly than other prices during the year. One response by consumers is to substitute an alternative, cheaper, product. As the indexes are based on fixed weights, they do not pick up this substitution effect, and therefore tend to overstate the price level in terms of the cost of living. Some attempt is made to overcome this problem by changing the weights on an annual basis in order to limit the impact of major changes. This includes incorporating new items when appropriate — for example, 14 new items were included in the CPI in 2014, including interchangeable lens digital cameras and fresh fruit snacking pots, reflecting changes in consumer spending patterns.

Differences between the CPI and RPI

The CPI and RPI differ for a number of reasons, partly because of differences in the content of the basket of goods and services that are included, and partly in terms of the population of people who are covered by the index. For example, in calculating the weights, the RPI excludes pensioner households and the highest-income households, whereas the CPI does not. There are also some other differences in the ways that the calculations are carried out.

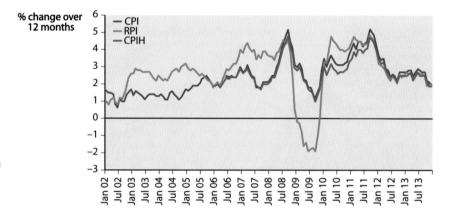

Figure 10.1 Alternative inflation measures in the UK, 2002–13
Source: ONS

Figure 10.1 shows data for the rates of change of the RPI and the CPI since 2002. These rates have been calculated on a monthly basis, computing the percentage rate of change of each index relative to the value 12 months previously.

A noticeable characteristic of Figure 10.1 (apart from in 2009) is that for much of the period the CPI has shown a lower rate of change than the RPI. In part this reflects the way in which the prices are combined, but it also reflects the fact that different items and households are covered.

Until the end of 2003, the government's target for inflation was set at 2.5% per annum in the RPIX. After that date, the target for CPI was set at 2% per annum. Since 1997, the Bank of England has had the responsibility of ensuring that inflation remains within one percentage point of this target. You can see from Figure 10.1 that inflation accelerated (on both measures) after March 2006, and in March 2007 the rate of change of CPI went above 3%, thus moving out of the permissible target range for the first time since the inflation target was introduced. Inflation then accelerated again during 2008, partly because of rising food prices in world markets, before plummeting in the global financial crisis that hit in late 2009. Notice how RPI inflation actually went negative at this time. This partly reflected the fact that interest rates were at an all-time low, which affected mortgage interest payments, causing RPI to fall for a period.

Exercise 10.2

Table 10.2 provides data on consumer prices for the UK, the USA and Italy.

a Calculate the annual inflation rate for each of the countries from 2004 to 2013.

b Plot these three inflation series on a graph against time.

c By what percentage did prices increase in each country over the whole period — that is, between 2003 and 2013?

d Which economy do you judge to have experienced most stability in the inflation rate?

Table 10.2 Consumer prices for the UK, the USA and Italy

	Consumer price index		
	UK	USA	Italy
2003	84.5	84.4	87.3
2004	85.6	86.6	89.2
2005	87.3	89.6	91.0
2006	89.4	92.4	92.9
2007	91.5	95.1	94.6
2008	94.8	98.7	97.7
2009	96.8	98.4	98.5
2010	100.0	100.0	100.0
2011	104.5	103.2	102.8
2012	107.4	105.3	105.9
2013	110.2	106.8	107.2

Source: OECD

Deflation

The recession that began to affect many advanced countries in the late 2000s raised the possibility that the overall level of prices in an economy might fall. This situation of negative inflation is known as **deflation**. Figure 10.1 showed that the UK experienced falling prices according to the RPI for a period. This is not to be confused with **disinflation**, which refers to a period in which inflation falls relative to the previous period.

Deflation is sometimes perceived to be bad for the economy on the grounds that economic agents will see this as a sign that the economy is in terminal decline. Indeed, if people expect prices to continue to fall, they may postpone purchases in the expectation of being able to buy at a lower price in the future. This would then mean a fall in demand in the economy, perpetuating the recession. However, central banks have ways of intervening to prevent deflation being long-lived, and it is not clear that consumers would actually act in the way described.

Key terms

deflation a fall in the average level of prices (negative inflation)

disinflation a fall in the rate of inflation

Inflation in the UK and throughout the world

Figure 10.2 shows a time path for the rate of change in price levels since 1949, using data for the annual change in the RPI. The figure provides the backdrop to understanding the way the UK economy evolved during this period. Apart from the period of the Korean War, which generated inflation in 1951–52, the 1950s and early 1960s were typified by a low rate of inflation, with some acceleration becoming apparent in the early 1970s. This helps to provide some context for inflation in recent years.

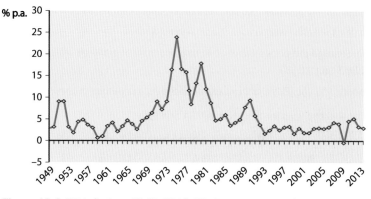

Figure 10.2 RPI inflation, 1949–2013 (% change over previous year)
Source: ONS

The instability of the 1970s was due to a combination of factors. Oil prices rose dramatically in 1973–74 and again in 1979–80, which certainly contributed to rising prices, not only in the UK but worldwide. However, inflation was further fuelled by the abandonment of the fixed exchange rate system under which sterling had been tied to the US dollar until 1972. Under a fixed exchange rate system, the government must dedicate the use of monetary policy to maintaining the value of the currency. However, the transition to a floating exchange rate system freed up monetary policy in a way that was perhaps not fully understood by the government of the day. As you can see in Figure 10.2, prices were allowed to rise rapidly — by nearly 25% in 1974–75. The diagram also shows how inflation was gradually reined in during the 1980s, and underlines the relative stability that has now been achieved, with inflation keeping well within the target range set by the government until the late 2000s, as noted above.

Figure 10.3 shows something of the extent to which the UK's experience is typical of the pattern of inflation worldwide. You can see from this how inflation in the industrial countries followed a similar general pattern, with a common acceleration in the early 1970s, and a period of gradual control after 1980. However, you can also see that the developing countries in the world experienced inflation at a much higher average level after 1974 because they proved to be less able to bring prices under control after the oil price shocks. Much of this reflects events in Latin America, which suffered especially high rates of inflation in the 1980s and 1990s. This instability in the macroeconomic environment has almost certainly hindered development in the countries affected, and makes it important to understand how inflation is generated and how to curb it.

Study tip

Although Figure 10.2 shows inflation right back to 1949, you do not need to learn about this whole period in detail. The data are provided to give you some background and context for what has happened more recently. However, it is helpful to be aware of changes and trends in the last few years.

Study tip

It is useful to be familiar with the costs of inflation, given that policy makers and commentators on the economy have regarded it as one of the most important evils that can afflict an economy, even if in recent years the onset of recession has somewhat switched the main focus of attention in other directions. These are discussed in Chapter 15.

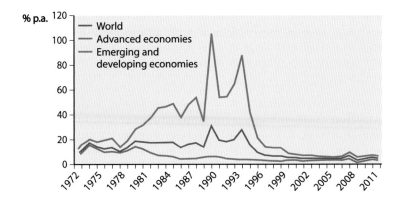

Figure 10.3 World inflation since 1972 (% change in the consumer price index)

Source: IMF

Summary

- The retail price index (RPI) is one measure of the average price level in the UK.
- In December 2003 the government adopted the consumer price index (CPI) as its preferred measure of the price level, and inflation is now monitored through the rate of change of CPI.
- The control of inflation has been the major focus of macroeconomic policy in the UK since about 1976.
- Low inflation reduces uncertainty, and may encourage investment by firms.
- Deflation is negative inflation, and may need corrective action by the central bank to avoid perpetuating a recession.

Employment and the UK workforce

In 2013, there were 40.3 million people living in the UK aged between the ages of 16 and 64. These are those considered to be of working age, although 65 is no longer seen as the normal retirement age. Figure 10.4 shows how they were distributed between three key economic categories: the employed, the unemployed and the economically inactive. Those **in employment** in this context include both those who are employed by firms or other organisations (such as government) and also the self-employed. The **economically inactive** include students, and those who have retired, are sick or are looking after family members. Also included are **discouraged workers** — people who have failed to find work and have given up looking. In other words, the economically inactive category includes all those people in the age range who are not considered to be active in the **workforce**. The **unemployed** are those who are in the workforce, but who are without jobs (a more precise definition will be provided later in the chapter).

Key terms

in employment people who are either working for firms or other organisations, or self-employed

economically inactive those people of working age who are not looking for work, for a variety of reasons

discouraged workers people who have been unable to find employment and who are no longer looking for work

workforce people who are economically active — either in employment or unemployed

unemployed people who are economically active but are not in employment

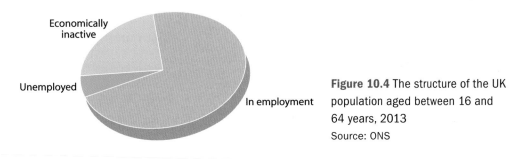

Figure 10.4 The structure of the UK population aged between 16 and 64 years, 2013

Source: ONS

Study tip

If you are confronted
with a graph such as
Figure 10.5, showing
unemployment over an
extended period, and
you need to describe the
trends over that period,
do not think that you have
to work through picking
out every observation,
but focus on the main
periods in which there
were divergences from the
norm.

The number of those employed is an important indicator, given that they contribute to the production process in their role as a factor of production: labour. Figure 10.5 shows the number of those in employment in each year since 1971. You can see that the number employed has increased substantially over this period, from just over 24 million in 1971 to nearly 29 million in 2013. It is also interesting to note that, although the number employed fell in 2009 as recession began to bite, the number employed recovered quite quickly, with employment in 2013 being slightly higher than it had been in 2008.

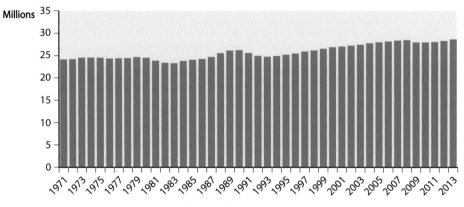

Figure 10.5 Employment in the UK, 1971–2013
Source: ONS

Key terms

full employment a
situation where people
who are economically
active in the workforce
and are willing and able
to work (at going wage
rates) are able to find
employment

**claimant count of
unemployment** the
number of people claiming
the Jobseeker's Allowance
each month

Full employment is seen as one of the core macroeconomic policy objectives. Having large numbers of people without jobs means that the economy is not making the best use of its labour resources, and is thus sacrificing potential output that could be produced. It is also undesirable from the perspective of the individuals who find themselves unemployed.

However, does this mean that everyone should have a job or be self-employed? Setting aside those who are economically inactive, there will always be some unemployment in a society, if only because there will be some people between jobs, or engaging in job search. Furthermore, if the economy were to be operating very close to full capacity, this would be likely to put upward pressure on wages and thus prices. In other words, there may be a conflict between achieving full employment and maintaining the stability of prices.

So full employment does not mean that unemployment will be zero. But it is difficult to specify a particular percentage that would constitute full employment. This may vary in different periods, and in different countries, partly reflecting the degree of flexibility in the labour market.

Measuring unemployment

The measurement of unemployment in the UK has also been contentious over the years, and the standard definition used to monitor performance has altered several times, especially during the 1980s, when a number of rationalisations were introduced.

Historically, unemployment was measured by the number of people registered as unemployed and claiming unemployment benefit (the Jobseeker's Allowance (JSA)). This measure of employment is known as the **claimant count of unemployment**.

People claiming the JSA must declare that they are out of work, and capable of, available for and actively seeking work, during the week in which their claim is made.

One of the problems with the claimant count is that, although people claiming the JSA must declare that they are available for work, it nonetheless includes some people who are claiming benefit, but are not actually available or prepared to work. It also excludes some people who would like to work, and who are looking for work, but who are not eligible for unemployment benefit, such as women returning to the labour force after childbirth.

Because of these problems, the claimant count has been superseded for official purposes by the so-called **ILO unemployment rate**, a measure based on the *Labour Force Survey*. This identifies the number of people available for work, and seeking work, but without a job. This definition corresponds to that used by the International Labour Organisation (ILO), and is closer to what economists would like unemployment to measure. It defines as being unemployed those people who are:

— *without a job, want a job, have actively sought work in the last four weeks and are available to start work in the next two weeks; or*

— *out of work, have found a job and are waiting to start it in the next two weeks*

(Labour Market Statistics, September 2004)

The ILO unemployment rate is higher than the claimant count

Quantitative skills 10.1

Calculating the percentage rate of unemployment

When calculating the percentage rate of unemployment, the key question concerns the portion of the active workforce who are unemployed at any point in time. This is calculated by expressing the number of unemployed as a percentage of the active workforce (i.e. employed plus unemployed). In March 2014 it was estimated that there were 29.437 million people in employment and 2.135 million people unemployed. The percentage rate was thus: 100 × 2.135 ÷ (29.437 + 2.135) = 6.76%.

Figure 10.6 shows the ILO unemployment rate since 1971, expressed as a percentage of the workforce. The surge in unemployment in the early 1980s stands out on the graph, when the percentage of the workforce registered as unemployed more than doubled in a relatively short period. Although this seemed to be coming under control towards the end of the 1980s, unemployment rose again in the early 1990s before a steady decline into the new millennium, rising again in the financial crisis and recession of the late 2000s.

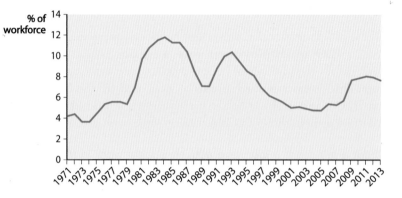

Figure 10.6 ILO unemployment rate, 1971–2013

Problems of measurement

It is important to be aware of the difficulties in measuring unemployment accurately. The claimant count is unreliable because it only captures those people who are eligible for the Jobseeker's Allowance, so it excludes some people who might be validly recognised as being unemployed. For example, it excludes people returning to the workforce after raising children or for other reasons of absence. It also excludes those who are on government training schemes and a range of other categories of people. The ILO unemployment data are based on sample evidence, and extrapolated up to give the picture for the UK as a whole. The sample cannot be guaranteed to be fully representative. From the perspective of economic analysis, it would also be helpful to know how many people are unemployed in the sense of not being able to find employment at their desired wage, but this is not covered in the definition.

Measuring unemployment in developing countries becomes even more difficult. If there is no social security system, then unemployed workers have no incentive to register as being unemployed. Furthermore, there may be people who cannot find jobs for which they are qualified, and who take jobs in second-choice occupations. This is a form of **underemployment**: for example, where qualified lawyers or doctors find themselves working as taxi drivers.

Causes of unemployment

There will always be some unemployment in a dynamic economy. At any point in time, there will be workers transferring between jobs. Indeed, this needs to happen if the pattern of production is to keep up with changing patterns of consumer demand and relative opportunity cost. In other words, in a typical period of time there will be some sectors of an economy that are expanding and others that are in decline. It is crucial that workers are able to transfer from those activities that are in decline to those that are booming. Accordingly, there will be some unemployment while this transfer takes place, and this is known as **frictional unemployment**.

Key terms

underemployment
where an individual is employed in a second-choice occupation or is only able to work part-time but would like to work full-time

frictional unemployment
unemployment associated with job search (i.e. people who are between jobs)

In some cases, this transfer of workers between sectors may be quite difficult to accomplish. For example, coal mining may be on the decline in an economy, but international banking may be booming. It is clearly unreasonable to expect coal miners to turn themselves into international bankers overnight. In this sort of situation there may be some longer-term unemployment while workers retrain for new occupations and new sectors of activity. Indeed, there may be workers who find themselves redundant at a relatively late stage in their career and for whom the retraining is not worthwhile, or who cannot find firms that are prepared to train them for a relatively short payback time. Such unemployment is known as **structural unemployment**. It arises because of the mismatch between the skills of workers leaving contracting sectors and the skills required by expanding sectors in the economy.

Unemployment could also arise in a period of recession, when the demand for workers is low. This is sometimes referred to as **cyclical unemployment**. In addition, there may be periods when the economy is in equilibrium below full employment because of a deficiency in aggregate demand, which is known as **demand–deficient unemployment**. A solution to this might be to boost aggregate demand, but not all economists believe that this is appropriate, as will be discussed later. There may also be times of the year when the demand for labour varies because of seasonal effects: for example, the tourist sector experiences quiet periods during the winter. This may give rise to **seasonal unemployment**.

A further reason for unemployment concerns the level of wages. Figure 10.7 shows a labour market in which a free market equilibrium would have wage $W^\star$ and quantity of labour $L^\star$. If for some reason wages were set at W_0, there would be disequilibrium between labour supply (at L_s) and labour demand (at L_d). Expressing this in a different way, here is a situation in which there are more workers seeking employment at the going wage (L_s) than there are firms prepared to hire at that wage (L_d). The difference is unemployment.

There are a number of reasons why this situation might arise. Trade unions may have been able to use their power and influence to raise wages above the equilibrium level, thereby ensuring higher wages for their members who remain in employment, but denying jobs to others. Alternatively, it could be argued that wages will be inflexible downwards. Thus, a supply shock that reduced firms' demand for labour could leave wages above the equilibrium, and they may adjust downwards only slowly.

Finally, if unemployment benefits are set at a relatively high level compared with wages in low-paid occupations, some people may choose not to work, thereby creating some **voluntary unemployment**. From the point of view of those individuals, they are making a rational choice on the basis of the options open to them. From society's point of view, however, there needs to be a balance between providing appropriate social protection for those unable to obtain jobs and trying to make the best use of available resources for the benefit of society as a whole.

Key terms

structural unemployment unemployment arising because of changes in the pattern of economic activity within an economy

cyclical unemployment unemployment that arises during the downturn of the economic cycle, such as a recession

demand-deficient unemployment unemployment that arises because of a deficiency of aggregate demand in the economy, so that the equilibrium level of output is below full employment

seasonal unemployment unemployment that arises in seasons of the year when demand is relatively low

voluntary unemployment situation arising when an individual chooses not to accept a job at the going wage rate

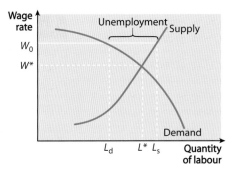

Figure 10.7 Unemployment in a labour market

Migration and unemployment

A contentious issue in recent years has been the question of migration, and the effect of an inflow of migrants on the domestic labour market. From the point of view of economic analysis, this issue turns on the characteristics of immigrant workers, especially in relation to skills. If immigrant workers have skills that are complementary to those of native workers, then a flow of in-migration can have beneficial effects on the domestic economy, by raising national income, resulting in an increase in the demand for workers. The situation is different where in-migrants are substitutes for domestic workers, such that the result may be a decrease in the equilibrium wage.

Consequences of unemployment

The costs of unemployment were mentioned earlier. From society's perspective, if the economy is operating below full capacity, then it is operating within the production possibility frontier, and therefore is not making the best possible use of society's resources. In other words, if those unemployed workers were in employment, society would be producing more aggregate output; the economy would be operating more efficiently overall.

Furthermore, there may be costs from the perspective of prospective workers, in the sense that **involuntary unemployment** carries a cost to each such individual in terms of forgone earnings and the need to rely on social security support. At the same time, the inability to find work and to contribute to the family budget may impose a cost in terms of personal worth and dignity.

Key term

involuntary unemployment situation arising when an individual who would like to accept a job at the going wage rate is unable to find employment

Exercise 10.3

Classify each of the following types of unemployment as arising from frictional, structural, demand-deficient or other causes, and decide whether they are voluntary or involuntary:

a unemployment arising from a decline of the coal mining sector and the expansion of financial services

b a worker leaving one job to search for a better one

c unemployment that arises because the real wage rate is held above the labour market equilibrium

d unemployment arising from slow adjustment to a fall in aggregate demand

e unemployment arising because workers find that low-paid jobs are paying less than can be obtained in unemployment benefit

Exercise 10.4

Visit the website of the Office for National Statistics (at **www.statistics.gov.uk**) and find out the latest data for inflation and unemployment. Has the performance of the economy in respect of these two variables improved or deteriorated in the last year?

Summary

- The population of working age is made up of the employed, the unemployed and the economically inactive.
- Full employment is an objective of macroeconomic policy, as unemployment is costly to those who are unemployed and to society as a whole.
- Unemployment is measured in two ways. The claimant count is based on the number of people claiming Jobseeker's Allowance. The ILO measure is based on a sample of the population through the *Labour Force Survey*.
- Unemployment arises for a variety of reasons, and there will always be some unemployment in the economy, even when the economy is in equilibrium.

The balance of payments

Another important dimension over which the macroeconomy needs to be monitored is in relation to a country's transactions with the rest of the world. Such transactions involve exports and imports of goods and services, but also assets, not to mention the flow of factor incomes. All of these transactions are monitored through the **balance of payments**, which is a set of accounts designed to identify international transactions between the UK economy and the rest of the world.

It is important to be able to monitor these transactions because of the increasing interconnectedness of economies through the process of international trade. This process is sometimes known as globalisation, by which economies have become more and more connected as a result of rapid changes in the technology of communications and transport, and with increasing deregulation of markets.

The transactions in the balance of payments are separated into three categories. Transactions in goods and services, together with income payments and transfers, comprise the *current account*. The *capital account* reflects transactions in fixed assets and is relatively small; it refers mainly to transactions involving migrants. The *financial account* records transactions in financial assets.

Commentators often focus on the current account. Three main items appear on this account. First, there is the balance of trade in goods and services — in other words, the balance between UK exports and imports of such goods and services. If UK residents buy German cars, this is an import and counts as a negative entry on the current account; on the other hand, if a German resident buys a British car, this is an export and constitutes a positive entry. The trade in goods is normally negative overall. However, this is partly balanced by a normally positive flow in trade in services, where the UK earns strong credits from its financial services.

BMW cars waiting to be exported at Bremerhaven habour, Germany

The second item in the current account is income. Part of this represents employment income from abroad, but the major item of income is made up of profits, dividends and interest receipts arising from UK ownership of overseas assets.

Finally, there are international transfers — either transfers through central government or transfers made or received by private individuals. This includes transactions and grants with international organisations or with the EU. The current balance combines these items together into an overall balance.

Overall, the balance of payments must always be zero, as in some way or other we have to pay for all we consume, and receive payment for all we sell. However, because data can never be entirely accurate, the accounts also incorporate a 'net errors and omissions' item, which ensures that everything balances at the end of the day.

What this really means is that any deficit in the current and capital accounts will always be balanced by a surplus on the financial account. Notice that the financial account incorporates official foreign exchange transactions undertaken by the government. In other words, if British residents buy more goods and services than they sell (i.e. if there is a current account deficit), then they must pay for them by selling financial assets or foreign exchange (i.e. there must be a financial account surplus).

There are a number of ways in which the overall balance can be achieved. 'Balance' could mean that both current and financial accounts are small, or it could mean that a deficit on one is balanced by a surplus on the other. The media tend to focus on the current balance, and a deficit on current account is sometimes seen as a matter of concern. Perhaps this harks back to the fixed exchange rate days, when a current deficit would require authorities to sell foreign exchange reserves in order to balance the accounts. This is no longer the case, as there are other ways of balancing the books. Nonetheless, a persistent deficit on the current account may pose long-term problems that need to be addressed, as it may not be desirable to continue selling UK assets indefinitely.

Table 10.3 presents the components of the UK balance of payments accounts for 2013. This was a year in which the current account was in substantial deficit. The financial account was in surplus.

Table 10.3 The UK balance of payments, 2013 (£ million at current prices)

Trade in goods and services	−32,100
Income	−13,133
Current transfers	−27,162
Current balance	−72,935
Capital account	530
Financial account	62,592
Net errors and omissions	9,273
Overall balance of payments	0

Source: ONS

Suppose the Bank of England holds interest rates high compared with other countries, in order to try to control inflation. High UK interest rates will tend to attract financial inflows from abroad, as investors find the UK attractive as a home for their funds. These flows are sometimes known as 'hot money'. This implies a surplus on the financial account — and hence a deficit on the current account. The downside of such a structure is that UK assets are being sold abroad, which might not be in the best interest of the economy in the long run.

It is this potential long-run difficulty that makes it important to monitor the current balance over time. Figure 10.8 shows the main components of the balance of payments since 1980, in current price terms, which is the form in which the data are published by the ONS. This is in the form of a stacked bar chart, and the nature of the balance of payments is that the positive and negative components exactly balance each year. The clear picture that emerges is that the current account has been negative (in deficit) for most of the period since 1980, and that this has been balanced by a positive balance (surplus) on the financial account. In other words, the UK has been importing more goods and services than it has been exporting; but this has been counterbalanced by the surplus on the financial account (i.e. of UK assets sold abroad).

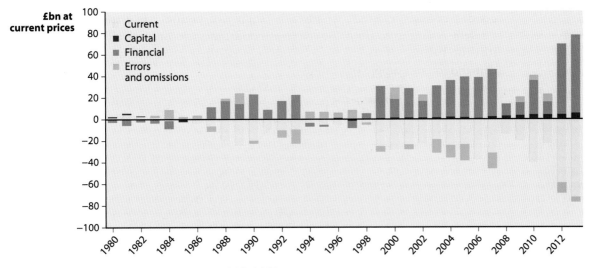

Figure 10.8 The UK balance of payments, 1980–2013

Source: ONS

The data in Figure 10.8 are measured in current prices, which means that they are nominal measurements, which make no attempt to allow for the effects of inflation. It would thus be misleading to infer too much about the magnitude of the quantities shown. A better perspective on this is provided by Figure 10.9, which shows the current account balance expressed as a percentage of nominal GDP. This helps to put the more recent data into perspective.

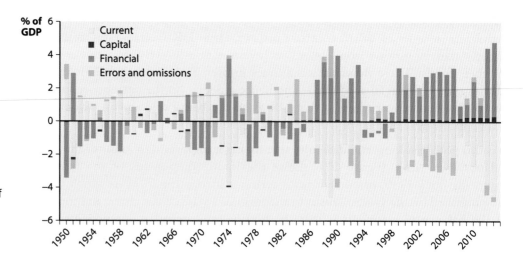

Figure 10.9 The UK balance of payments, 1950–2013

Source: ONS

Key term

exchange rate the price of one currency in terms of another

Closely associated with the balance of payments is the **exchange rate** — the price of domestic goods in terms of foreign currency. Chapter 5 introduced the notion of the demand and supply of foreign currency, shown in Figure 10.10. The demand for pounds arises from overseas residents (e.g. in the euro area) wanting to purchase UK goods, services or assets, whereas the supply of pounds emanates from domestic residents wanting to purchase overseas goods, services or assets. The connection is that the balance of payments accounts itemise these transactions, which entail the demand for and supply of pounds.

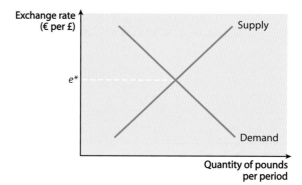

Figure 10.10 The market for pounds sterling

Summary

- The balance of payments is a set of accounts which itemises transactions that take place between an economy and the rest of the world, including goods, services, income and assets.
- The current account sets out transactions in goods, services, investment income and transfers.
- The capital account itemises transactions in fixed assets and is relatively small.
- The financial account covers transactions in financial assets and includes direct investment and official intervention in the foreign exchange market ('official financing').
- The overall balance of payments is always zero.
- However, this overall balance has often been achieved in the UK through a persistent deficit on the current account, balanced by a corresponding surplus on the financial account.
- This may be a matter for concern in the long run.

The UK economy in mid-2008

Figures 10.11 and 10.12 respectively show monthly inflation and unemployment in the UK between the beginning of 2004 and March 2008. Imagine it is mid-2008 and that you are the chancellor of the exchequer considering the state of the economy.

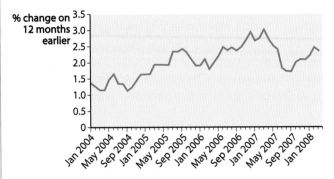

Figure 10.11 Inflation in the UK, 2004–08

Source: ONS

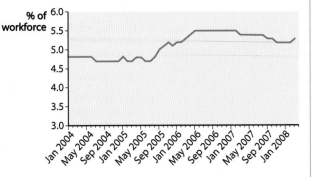

Figure 10.12 Unemployment in the UK, 2004–08

Source: ONS

Follow-up question

Discuss whether these two indicators give cause for concern about the performance of the economy. What other information would you need in order to come to a judgement?

After you have thought about this, look back at Figures 10.1 and 10.6 to see what happened next.

11 Aggregate demand

Now that you have been introduced to the main macroeconomic aggregates, it is time to start thinking about how economic analysis can be used to explore the ways in which these variables interact. The starting point is to consider the components of aggregate demand. The way in which the levels of these components are determined in practice is an important key to the operation of the economy when considered at the aggregate level.

Learning objectives

After studying this chapter, you should:
➡ understand what is meant by aggregate demand
➡ be able to identify the components of aggregate demand and their determinants
➡ be familiar with the notion of the aggregate demand curve

The components of aggregate demand

Aggregate demand is the total amount of spending on goods and services produced in an economy during a period of time. Understanding the factors that influence this is an important step in analysing the operation of the economy at the aggregate level.

It is helpful to separate aggregate demand into its key components, according to which economic agents are undertaking the spending. It is then possible to analyse how each component will be determined. The key economic agents in this context are households, firms and government. However, for an economy that engages in international trade, it is also important to take account of spending in and by the rest of the world.

From this perspective, aggregate demand comprises the combined spending of households on consumer goods and firms on investment goods, together with government expenditure (including current and capital spending). Exports (spending by the rest of the world on domestically produced goods) adds to aggregate demand, but spending by residents on goods and services from the rest of the world (imports) must be deducted. The full version of aggregate expenditure can thus be written as:

$$AD = C + I + G + X - M$$

where AD denotes aggregate demand, C is consumption, I is investment, G is government spending, X is exports and M is imports.

Figure 11.1 shows the expenditure-side breakdown of real GDP in the UK in 2013. This highlights the relative size of the components of aggregate demand. Consumption is by far the largest component, amounting to about 65% of real GDP in 2013. Government current expenditure accounted for 22.5%, but you should realise that this somewhat understates the importance of government in overall spending, as it excludes public spending on investment, which is treated together with private sector investment in the data. Combined public and private sector investment made up just under 15% of total GDP; this includes changes in the inventory holdings of firms. Notice that imports were rather higher than exports, indicating a negative balance of trade in goods and services.

Exercise 11.1

Suppose there is an economy in which the values in Table 11.1 apply.

a Calculate the level of aggregate demand.

b Calculate the trade balance.

Table 11.1 Values in an economy (all measured in £ million)

Consumption	75
Profits	60
Investment	30
Government expenditure	25
Exports	50
Private saving	50
Imports	55

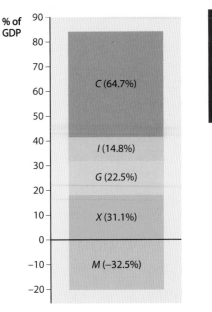

Figure 11.1 The breakdown of real GDP in 2013

Note: *C* includes spending by non-profit institutions serving households; *I* includes changes in inventory holdings; the statistical discrepancy is not shown.

Source: ONS

Consumption

Consumption is the largest single component of aggregate demand. What factors could be expected to influence the size of total spending by households? John Maynard Keynes, in his influential book *The General Theory of Employment, Interest and Money*, published in 1936, suggested that the most important determinant is **disposable income**.

In other words, as real incomes rise, households will tend to spend more. However, he also pointed out that they would not spend all of an increase in income, but would save some of it. Remember that this was important in the circular flow model. Keynes defined the **average propensity to consume** as the ratio of consumption to income, and the **marginal propensity to consume (MPC)** as the proportion of an increase in disposable income that households would devote to consumption. Similarly, the **marginal propensity to save (MPS)** is the proportion of an increase in disposable income that households would devote to saving.

J. M. Keynes's hugely influential book *The General Theory of Employment, Interest and Money* was published in 1936

Key terms

consumption total planned household spending

disposable income the income that households have to devote to consumption and saving, taking into account payments of direct taxes and transfer payments

average propensity to consume the proportion of income that households devote to consumption

marginal propensity to consume (MPC) the proportion of additional income devoted to consumption

marginal propensity to save (MPS) the proportion of an increase in disposable income that households would devote to saving

However, income will not be the only influence on consumption. Consumption may also depend partly on the *wealth* of a household. Remember that income and wealth are not the same: wealth is the accumulation of assets, which is different in concept from the flow of income received by households per period. Wealth can be thought of in terms of the asset holdings of households. If households experience an increase in the value of their asset holdings, this may influence their spending decisions. In particular, changes in house prices that affect the wealth of households may influence their expenditure: if house prices increase, households may be more prepared to consume rather than save, having the security of their property. The general state of the economy may also be a factor, as households may spend more if they have confidence in the future. Of course, in times of recession or falling house prices, the reverse may happen.

Furthermore, if part of household spending is financed by borrowing, the rate of interest may be significant in influencing the total amount of consumption spending. An increase in the rate of interest that raises the cost of borrowing may deter consumption. At the same time it may encourage saving, as the return on saving is higher when the interest rate is higher. The rate of interest may also have an indirect effect on consumption through its effect on the value of asset holdings. In addition, households may be influenced in their consumption decisions by their expectations about future inflation. Notice that some of these effects may not be instantaneous: that is, consumption may adjust to changes in its determinants only after a time lag.

This **consumption function** can be portrayed as a relationship between consumption and income. This is shown in Figure 11.2, which focuses on the relationship between consumption and household income, ceteris paribus: in other words, in drawing the relationship between consumption and income, it is assumed that the other determinants of consumption, such as wealth and the interest rate, remain constant. A change in any of these other influences will affect the *position* of the line. Notice that the marginal propensity to consume (*MPC*) is the slope of this line.

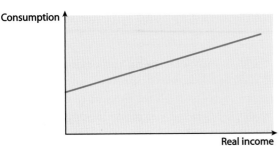

Figure 11.2 The consumption function

Quantitative skills 11.2

Interpreting the marginal propensity to consume

If the *MPC* is 0.7, this means that for every additional £100 of income received by households, £100 × 0.7 = £70 would be consumer expenditure and the remaining £30 would be saved.

In practice, it is not expected that the empirical relationship between consumption and income will reveal an exact straight line, if only because over a long time period there will be changes in the other influences on consumption, such as interest rates and expected inflation. However, Figure 11.3 shows that the hypothesis is not totally implausible, as indicated by the fact that most of the scatter points are quite close to the fitted line. However, there are some points that diverge from the pattern towards the end of the period, suggesting that the relationship was affected by the recession that followed the financial crisis of the late 2000s.

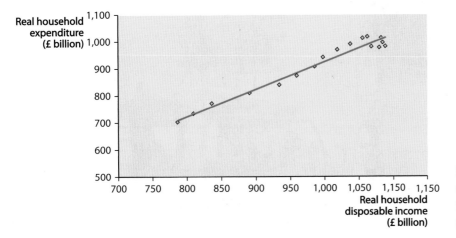

Figure 11.3 Real consumption and disposable income in the UK, 1997–2013

Source: based on data from ONS

Investment

The second major component of aggregate demand is spending by firms on **investment**. Investment leads to an increase in the productive capacity of the economy, by increasing the stock of capital available for production. This capital stock comprises plant and machinery, vehicles and other transport equipment, and buildings, including new dwellings, which provide a supply of housing services over a long period.

Part of investment by firms is to replace capital that has worn out: in other words, part of investment relates to the depreciation of old capital. However, what about investment by firms to increase productive capacity? What factors will induce firms to undertake investment?

The overall state of the economy may be an important influence. If the economy is going through a period of rapid economic growth, and this is expected to continue, then firms are likely to be optimistic about the future prospects for demand for their products, and will wish to be able to exploit the opportunities for profit. On the other hand, when the economy heads into recession, the prospects for the future will be less robust, and firms may hesitate to invest in new capacity.

This suggests that business expectations and confidence in the future path of the economy will be important in shaping their willingness to undertake investment expenditure. Keynes argued that the 'animal spirits' of firms would influence them in this situation. This could result in instability in the economy. If recession dampens the confidence with which firms view the future, such that investment expenditure falls, this will deepen the recession — or at least delay the recovery.

Expectations about future demand depend not only upon the state of the domestic economy. International competitiveness is also important where firms are involved in exporting activity. There may be firms where a buoyant demand for exports can offset the effects of low domestic demand. However, in the case of a global recession that affects many economies simultaneously, the dampening effects on confidence could be severe. The recession that followed the financial crisis of the late 2000s was a case in point, affecting many of the world's advanced countries.

Capital stock includes machinery and factory buildings, critical factors in the production process

Decisions on investment may also be influenced by government, which has an interest in encouraging investment because of its beneficial impact on expanding the economy's productive capacity and hence on economic growth. It may do this by providing incentives for firms to invest, in the form of tax concessions. It may also use regulation to influence the pattern or location of investment: for example, by targeting EU funding towards parts of the country that have found it difficult to attract private investment.

It has also been argued that inflation is damaging for an economy, as a high rate of inflation increases uncertainty about the future and may dampen firms' expectations about future demand, thereby discouraging investment.

These influences on investment focus on reasons why firms may wish to undertake investment expenditure. However, it is also important to consider how such expenditure is to be financed, given that firms must spend in the present but will reap the returns in the future. This suggests that the cost and availability of finance for investment will also affect the amount of investment that takes place.

Obtaining finance for investment

Consider the cost of obtaining finance for investment. The rate of interest represents the cost of borrowing; so, if firms need to borrow in order to undertake investment, they may be discouraged from spending on investment goods when the rate of interest is relatively high. Notice that not all investment has to be funded from borrowing — firms may be able to use past profits for this purpose. However, if firms choose to do this, they face an opportunity cost. In other words, profits can be used to buy financial assets that will provide a rate of return dependent on the rate of interest. The rate of interest is thus important, as it represents the opportunity cost of an investment project.

Figure 11.4 shows the relationship between investment and the rate of interest. The investment demand function I_{D0} is downward sloping because investment is relatively low when the rate of interest is relatively high. An improvement in business confidence for the future would result in more investment being undertaken at any given interest rate, so the investment function would move from I_{D0} to I_{D1}.

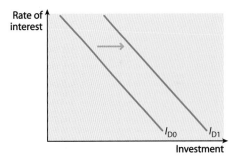

Figure 11.4 Investment and the rate of interest

Firms' willingness to borrow in order to finance their investment expenditure is only part of the story. Access to credit is also crucial. In order for firms to be able to borrow, it is necessary that financial institutions are prepared to lend and that they have funds available to lend. In the aftermath of the financial crisis, one manifestation of which was the failure of some banks, the commercial banks appeared unwilling to lend, having become more averse to taking risk. The ability of banks to provide credit also depends upon the behaviour of households, who provide bank deposits through their saving activity. With rates of interest at the low levels seen during and after the crisis, the returns on saving have been correspondingly low.

Government expenditure

By and large, you might expect government expenditure to be decided by different criteria from those influencing private sector expenditures.

From the point of view of investigating macroeconomic equilibrium, government expenditure can be regarded as mainly *autonomous*: that is, independent of the variables in the model that will be constructed in this chapter and the following ones. In some situations, the government may choose to manipulate its spending in order to influence the path of the economy.

It is also important to be aware that some parts of government expenditure are likely to vary with fluctuations in the level of overall economic activity. Think about what happens if the economy moves into a period of recession. Some workers lose their jobs, and start to claim the Jobseeker's Allowance — which affects government expenditure. Furthermore, workers who are no longer in work cease to pay income tax, so government revenue falls. The reverse effect occurs during the recovery period, so net government expenditure can be seen to vary with the business cycle.

Trade in goods and services

Finally, there are the factors that may influence the level of exports and imports. One factor that will affect both of these is the exchange rate between sterling and other currencies. This affects the relative prices of UK goods and those produced overseas. Other things being equal, an increase in the sterling exchange rate makes UK exports less competitive and imports into the UK more competitive.

The volume of international trade can also be affected by protectionist policies introduced by countries to protect their own industries. Historically, many countries imposed tariffs on imports of goods. A tariff is a tax on imports, and the period after the Second World War showed substantial reductions in tariff rates to allow countries to benefit from specialisation and trade. However, some tariffs remain, and countries have also imposed non-tariff barriers to limit their dependence on trade. This might be in the form of regulations that impose restrictive quality controls on imported goods.

However, the demand for exports and imports will also depend on the relative prices of goods produced in the UK and the rest of the world. If UK inflation is high relative to elsewhere, again this will tend to make UK exports less competitive and imports more competitive. Movements in the exchange rate can thus tend to counteract changes in relative prices between countries.

In addition, the demand for imports into the UK will depend partly upon the level of domestic aggregate income, and the demand for UK exports will depend partly upon the level of incomes in the rest of the world. Thus, a recession in the European Union will affect the demand for UK exports. The global recession that set in during the late 2000s had a noticeable effect on world trade.

The aggregate demand curve

The key relationship to carry forward from this discussion is the **aggregate demand curve**, which shows the relationship between aggregate demand and the overall price level. Formally, this curve shows the total amount of goods and services demanded in an economy at any given overall level of prices.

It is important to realise that this is a very different sort of demand curve from the microeconomic demand curves that were introduced in Chapter 2, where the focus was on an individual product and its relationship with its own price. Here the relationship is between the total demand for goods and services and the overall price level. Thus, aggregate demand is made up of all the components discussed above, and price is an average of all prices of goods and services in the economy.

Figure 11.5 shows an aggregate demand curve. The key question is why it slopes downwards. To answer this, it is necessary to determine the likely influence of the price level on the various components of aggregate demand that have been discussed in this chapter, as prices have not been mentioned explicitly (except for how expectations about inflation might influence consumer spending). First, however, the discussion needs to be cast in terms of the price *level*.

When the overall level of prices is relatively low, the purchasing power of income is relatively high. In other words, low overall prices can be thought of as indicating relatively high real income. Furthermore, when prices are low, this raises the real value of households' wealth. For example, suppose a household holds a financial asset such as a bond with a fixed money value of £100. The relative (real) value of that asset is higher when the overall price level is relatively low. From the above discussion, this suggests that, ceteris paribus, a low overall price level means relatively high consumption.

A second argument relates to interest rates. When prices are relatively low, interest rates also tend to be relatively low, which, it was argued, would encourage both investment and consumption expenditure, as interest rates can be seen as representing the cost of borrowing.

A third argument concerns exports and imports. It has been argued that, ceteris paribus, when UK prices are relatively low compared with the rest of the world, this will increase the competitiveness of UK goods, leading to an increase in foreign demand for UK exports, and a fall in the demand for imports into the UK as people switch to buying UK goods and services.

All of these arguments support the idea that the aggregate demand curve should be downward sloping. In other words, when the overall price level is relatively low, aggregate demand will be relatively high, and when prices are relatively high, aggregate demand will be relatively low.

Other factors discussed above will affect the position of the *AD* curve. It is again very important to be aware of the distinction between a movement *along* and a shift *of* the aggregate demand curve. A change in the overall price level induces a movement along the *AD* curve, but a change in any of the components of aggregate demand will result in a shift of the *AD* curve. For example, an increase in government expenditure would lead to a rightward shift of the *AD* curve. The effects of this on the macroeconomy will be analysed after we have explored the aggregate supply curve.

Summary

- Aggregate demand is the total demand in an economy, made up of consumption, investment, government spending and net exports.
- Consumption is the largest of these components and is determined by income and other influences, such as interest rates, wealth and expectations about the future.
- Investment leads to increases in the capital stock and is influenced by interest rates, past profits and expectations about future demand.
- Government expenditure may be regarded as largely autonomous.
- Trade in goods and services (exports and imports) is determined by the competitiveness of domestic goods and services compared with the rest of the world, which in turn is determined by relative inflation rates and the exchange rate. Imports are also affected by domestic income, and exports are affected by incomes in the rest of the world.
- The aggregate demand curve shows the relationship between aggregate demand and the overall price level.

Study tip

It is important to remember this difference between the aggregate demand curve and the microeconomic demand curve for a product. In the macroeconomic context, always label the vertical axis as 'Price level' as a reminder.

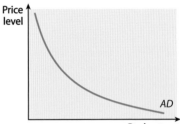

Figure 11.5 An aggregate demand curve

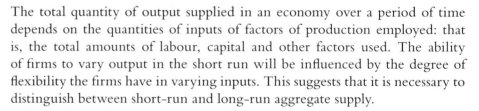

12 Aggregate supply

Having seen what is meant by aggregate demand, it is now time to investigate aggregate supply and the factors that influence it in both the short run and the long run. The different approaches adopted by the Keynesian and classical/monetarist schools of thought will be discussed.

> **Learning objectives**
>
> After studying this chapter, you should:
> → understand what is meant by aggregate supply
> → be able to identify the factors that influence aggregate supply in the short and long run
> → be familiar with the notion of the aggregate supply curve
> → be familiar with alternative Keynesian and classical views of the long-run aggregate supply curve

The aggregate supply curve

The previous chapter discussed the notion of aggregate demand and introduced the aggregate demand curve. The next stage of building a model of the macroeconomy is to derive a second relationship: that between aggregate supply and the price level.

The level of aggregate supply covers the output of all sorts of goods and services that are produced within an economy during a period of time. However, it is not simply a question of adding up all the individual supply curves from individual markets. Within an individual market, an increase in price may induce higher supply of a good because firms will switch from other markets in search of higher profits. What you now need to be looking for is a relationship between the *overall* price level and the total amount supplied, which is a different kettle of fish.

The total quantity of output supplied in an economy over a period of time depends on the quantities of inputs of factors of production employed: that is, the total amounts of labour, capital and other factors used. The ability of firms to vary output in the short run will be influenced by the degree of flexibility the firms have in varying inputs. This suggests that it is necessary to distinguish between short-run and long-run aggregate supply.

In the short run, firms may have relatively little flexibility to vary their inputs. Money wages are likely to be fixed, and if firms wish to vary output, they may need to do so by varying the intensity of utilisation of existing inputs. For example, if a firm wishes to expand output, the only way of doing so in the short run may be by paying its existing workers overtime, and it will be prepared to do this only in response to higher prices. This suggests that in the

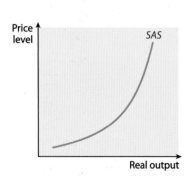

Figure 12.1 Aggregate supply in the short run

short run, aggregate supply may be upward sloping, as shown in Figure 12.1, where *SAS* represents the **short-run aggregate supply curve**.

Firms will not want to operate in this way in the long run. It is not good practice to be permanently paying workers overtime. In the long run, therefore, firms will adjust their working practices and hire additional workers to avoid this situation.

As always, it is important to be aware of the distinction between shifts *of* the aggregate supply curve, and movements *along* it. If the overall price level changes, this will induce a movement along the curve, but if something changes to affect the position of the curve, it will shift. So what factors affect the position of the short-run aggregate supply curve?

The position of the short-run aggregate supply curve

Underlying the aggregate supply curve are the decisions taken by firms about production levels at any given price. Firms are assumed to choose how much output to produce in order to maximise profits. In the short run, the strongest influence on these decisions is likely to be the costs faced by firms, as these can change quite rapidly in the short run, whereas other factors such as technological change are more significant in the long run. So, a change in the costs faced by firms may induce them to choose to supply more (or less) output.

The cost of inputs

There are several factors that could influence costs in the short run. For example, it might be that there is a change in the cost of raw materials. If a key raw material becomes more limited in supply, perhaps because reserves are exhausted, then prices will tend to

Variations in the price of oil can have an impact on aggregate supply in the short run

rise, thus raising firms' costs of production. They may then choose to supply less output at any given price — and the aggregate supply curve would shift to the left.

The price of oil has been subject to significant variations over time, as was shown in Figure 5.2. Oil is a key input for many firms, and an increase in the price of oil affects the cost of energy and transport. It also affects the economy in many other ways, as oil is a key input in the production of many fertilisers used in the agricultural sector. The price of oil may therefore have a significant impact on the position of aggregate supply in the short run.

Another key input for firms is labour, so an increase in labour costs will also cause a leftward shift of the short-run aggregate supply curve.

The exchange rate

Where firms rely on imported inputs of raw materials, energy or component parts used in production, then a change in the exchange rate could affect aggregate supply, by affecting the domestic price of imported inputs. This could be favourable, of course, depending on the direction in which the exchange rate changes. It could be that the exchange rate moves to reduce the domestic price of imports. Firms may then be prepared to supply more output at any given price, so the aggregate supply curve would shift to the right.

The exchange rate can change in the short run for a variety of different reasons, so firms may face some quite sudden changes in their costs. One way that firms can guard against this is through the nature of the contracts drawn up with their foreign suppliers, if future prices can be specified in a way that hedges against possible exchange rate fluctuations.

Government intervention

There are some forms of government intervention that can affect firms' costs in the short run. An increase in regulation that forced firms to spend more on health and safety measures would raise costs, and result in a leftward shift of the aggregate supply curve in the short run. An increase in the rate of corporation tax would have similar effects.

Exercise 12.1

For each of the following, state whether the short-run aggregate supply curve would shift to the left or to the right:

a the discovery of a new source of a raw material, reducing its price

b an increase in the exchange rate

c an increase in labour costs

d a fall in the price of oil

Summary

- The short-run aggregate supply (SAS) curve shows the relationship between aggregate supply and the overall price level.
- A change in the overall price level induces a movement along the short-run aggregate supply curve.
- Changes in the costs faced by firms result in a shift of the short-run aggregate supply curve.

Aggregate supply in the long run

The discussion so far has focused on short-run aggregate supply. However, it is also important to consider how aggregate supply can be seen in the longer term. An important debate developed during the 1970s over the shape of the aggregate supply curve, which has implications for the conduct and effectiveness of macroeconomic policy options. An influential school of macroeconomists, known as the **Monetarist School**, argued that the economy would always converge on an equilibrium level of output that they referred to as the **natural rate of output**. This was based on arguments that originated with the classical economists. Associated with this long-run equilibrium was a **natural rate of unemployment**. If this were the case, then the long-run relationship between aggregate supply and the price level would be vertical, as shown in Figure 12.2. Here $Y^\star$ is the natural rate of output: that is, the full employment level of aggregate output. In other words, a change in the overall price level does not affect aggregate output, because the economy always readjusts rapidly back to *full employment* — a position in which the aggregate economy is operating at its potential full capacity level.

An opposing school of thought (often known as the **Keynesian School**) held that the macroeconomy was not sufficiently flexible to enable continuous full employment. They argued that the economy could settle at an equilibrium position below full employment, at least in the medium term. In particular, inflexibilities in labour markets would prevent adjustment. For example, if firms had pessimistic expectations about aggregate demand, and thus reduced their supply of output, this would lead to lower incomes because of the workers being laid off. This would then mean that aggregate demand was indeed deficient, so firms' pessimism was self-fulfilling.

These sorts of argument led to a belief that there would be a range of output over which long-run aggregate supply (LRAS) would be upward sloping. Figure 12.3 illustrates such an aggregate supply curve, in which $Y^\star$ represents full employment; however, when the economy is operating below this level of output, aggregate supply is somewhat sensitive to the price level, becoming steeper as full employment is approached.

Chapter 16 discusses the operation of macroeconomic policy designed to influence the course of the macroeconomy. However, it is clear that the shape of the long-run aggregate supply curve has significant implications for policy. If the *LRAS* is indeed vertical, so that the economy always returns to its long-run equilibrium, then there would seem to be little scope for trying to use policy to affect the path of the economy. This is especially the case if the adjustment to the long-run equilibrium is rapid, which is what the Monetarist School have argued.

On the other hand, the Keynesian economists argued that the economy could find itself trapped in a position below full employment, and that intervention would be needed to get back to full employment. More discussion of this will follow in Chapter 16.

The position of the long-run aggregate supply curve

Whatever the shape of the long-run aggregate supply curve, it is important to understand the factors that may affect its *position*. Both monetarist and Keynesian versions identify a capacity level of aggregate output, so the question here centres on what affects this.

Key terms

Monetarist School a group of economists who believed that the macroeconomy always adjusts rapidly to the full employment level of output, and that monetary policy should be the prime instrument for stabilising the economy

natural rate of output the long-run equilibrium level of output to which monetarists believe the macroeconomy will always tend

natural rate of unemployment the unemployment rate that will exist when the economy is in long-run equilibrium

Keynesian School a group of economists who believed that the macroeconomy could settle at an equilibrium that was below full employment

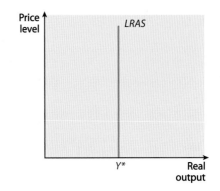

Figure 12.2 Aggregate supply in the long run (the 'monetarist' view)

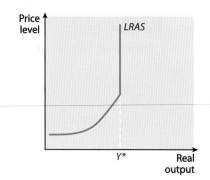

Figure 12.3 Aggregate supply in the long run (the 'Keynesian' view)

The quantity of inputs

The first obvious way in which aggregate output could be increased is if there is an increase in the availability of the factors of production. In particular, an increase in labour and/or capital inputs would lead to an increase in the amount of output that can be produced.

As far as labour input is concerned, an increase in the size of the workforce will affect the position of aggregate supply. In practice, the size of the labour force tends to change relatively slowly, which is why this affects long-run rather than short-run aggregate supply. One way in which the workforce expands is through migration. For example, the expansion of membership of the EU in May 2004 led to significant migration into the UK. This expansion of the workforce can lead to an increase in potential output.

Demographic changes can also affect the size of the workforce in the long run. The UK and many other advanced economies have been characterised by an ageing population in recent years. As more people live longer into retirement, the working population falls as a proportion of the total, and the *LRAS* may shift to the left. One response to this pattern has been the changes to the retirement age. Until 2011, the default retirement age in the UK was 65 years, but this was abolished so that those who wished to continue to work beyond 65 could do so. In many developing countries in sub-Saharan Africa, the HIV/AIDS epidemic was especially devastating to people of working age, and so reduced the size and effectiveness of the labour force.

An increase in the quantity of capital will also have the effect of increasing the capacity of the economy to produce. However, such an increase requires firms to have undertaken investment activity. In other words, the balance of spending between consumption and investment may affect the position of the aggregate supply curve in future periods.

The effective use of inputs

The effectiveness with which inputs are utilised is another important influence on the position of the aggregate supply curve. Advances in technology are one route through which inputs can be more effectively utilised. New machinery can improve the efficiency with which other inputs are used, and the development of new materials can also have an impact. Such developments can reduce firms' costs and increase the amount of aggregate output that can be produced, leading to a shift in the long-run aggregate supply curve. This is shown in Figure 12.4, where aggregate supply was originally at $LRAS_0$. Technological change that improves efficiency in the use of capital and other inputs means that firms are prepared to supply more output at any given overall price level, so the aggregate supply curve shifts to $LRAS_1$.

Labour as a factor of production can also become more effective and productive, and can be seen as a form of human capital. Improvements to education and the provision of skills training can improve the productivity of labour, again leading to a rightward shift of long-run aggregate supply. Training may be especially important for an economy that is undergoing structural change, so that workers need to be prepared to move between occupations. Government encouragement or provision of such training can improve the flexibility of the labour market and affect aggregate supply.

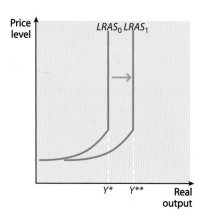

Figure 12.4 A shift in aggregate supply

An increase in congestion on the roads would raise transport costs, and lead to a less efficient use of inputs, raising the costs faced by firms. These effects would tend to result in a leftward shift of the aggregate supply curve. On the other hand, improvements to infrastructure in the domestic economy, such as improvements to the transport system, would have the opposite effect of reducing the costs faced by firms, which could then lead to a rightward shift of the aggregate supply curve.

Summary

- It is useful to distinguish between monetarist and Keynesian views about the shape of the long-run aggregate supply curve.
- Monetarist economists have argued that the economy always converges rapidly on equilibrium at the natural rate of output, implying that policies affecting aggregate demand have an impact only on prices, leaving real output unaffected. The aggregate supply curve in this world is vertical.
- The Keynesian view is that the economy may settle at an equilibrium that is below full employment, and that there is a range over which the aggregate supply curve slopes upwards.
- The position of the long-run aggregate supply curve depends upon the quantity of inputs available, and on the efficiency with which they are utilised.

Exercise 12.2

For each of the following, identify whether the change described will affect short-run or long-run aggregate supply, and whether the result is a leftward or rightward shift.

a a fall in the exchange rate that affects the price of imported inputs

b an increase in the rate of in-migration

c an increase in the price of oil

d a reduction in corporation tax

e the introduction of new super-computers

Case study 12.1

The importance of expectations

In mid-2008, the UK economy was seen to be in a state of crisis. Economic growth had slowed (although it was still positive, so technically the economy had not yet entered into recession). Inflation had been affected by a number of world events. China's economy was continuing to expand at an unprecedented rate, and was having an impact on world prices by its strong demand for oil, foodstuffs and other commodities. The growth in demand for biofuels was fuelling a rise in the prices of some key food items, including rice and wheat. This was partly because land previously used to grow food was being turned over to grow crops to be made into biofuels. These effects were beginning to take their toll on the UK economy. Surveys of business confidence showed that firms were expecting a recession, and house prices were falling.

Demand for biofuels affected the price of crops such as rice and wheat

Follow-up question

Explain how the events described above would be expected to affect aggregate demand and/or short-run and long-run aggregate supply.

National income and macroeconomic equilibrium

Gross domestic product (GDP) has been discussed as a way of measuring total income in an economy, and some of its limitations have been analysed. Income can be seen as a flow of resources in the economy. As a concept, it can be seen to be closely associated with total expenditure and total output, and this chapter begins by exploring the relationship between these three notions. There is also some discussion of the important distinction to be drawn between income and wealth. The chapter also brings together aggregate demand and aggregate supply curves to explore the nature of macroeconomic equilibrium.

Learning objectives

After studying this chapter, you should:
→ understand that national income can be represented as a circular flow of income, expenditure and output
→ be aware of the distinction between income and wealth
→ be familiar with the notion of injections and withdrawals within the circular flow
→ appreciate the potential impact and importance of investment in productive capacity
→ understand the nature of equilibrium in the macroeconomy
→ be able to undertake comparative static analysis of external shocks affecting aggregate demand and aggregate supply
→ be familiar with the multiplier and its significance

The circular flow of income, expenditure and output

Previous chapters have introduced the notion of *gross domestic product* (GDP), which was described as the total output of an economy. It is now time to examine this concept more closely, and how it can help to highlight the way that macroeconomic variables can interact.

Consider a simplified model of an economy. Assume for the moment that there are just two types of economic agent in an economy: households and firms. In other words, ignore the government and assume there is no international trade. (These agents will be brought back into the picture soon.) We also assume that all factors of production are owned and supplied to firms by households.

In this simple world, assume that firms produce goods and use factors of production (labour, capital, etc.), which are supplied by households. In return for supplying factors of production, households receive income, which they spend on consumer goods.

If you examine the monetary flows in this economy, you can see how the economy operates. In Figure 13.1 the blue arrow shows the flow of income that goes from firms to households. The orange arrow shows that output produced by firms goes to households in the form of consumer goods. The green arrow shows that the expenditure flows back to firms. This model is sometimes known as the **circular flow model**.

Key term

circular flow of income, expenditure and output a model of the economy which shows the movement of goods and services between households and firms and their corresponding payments in money terms

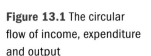

Figure 13.1 The circular flow of income, expenditure and output

As this is a closed system, these flows must balance. This means that there are three ways in which the total amount of economic activity in this economy can be measured: by the incomes that firms pay out, by the total amount of output that is produced, or by total expenditure. Whichever method is chosen, it should give the same result.

An economy such as the UK's is more complicated than this, so it is also necessary to take into account the economic activities of government and the fact that the UK engages in international trade, so that some of the output produced is sold abroad and some of the expenditure goes on foreign goods and services. Furthermore, some of the output produced by firms is made up of investment goods purchased by firms, and some household income is used for saving. These issues will be considered later in the chapter. However, the principle of measuring total economic activity is the same: GDP can be measured in three ways.

In practice, when the Office for National Statistics (ONS) carries out the measurements the three answers are never quite the same, as it is impossible to measure with complete accuracy. The published data for GDP are therefore calculated as the average of these three measures, each of which gives information about different aspects of a society's total resources.

What the three measures tell us

The expenditure-side estimate describes how those resources are being used, so that it can be seen what proportion of society's resources is being used for consumption and what for investment, etc.

The income-side estimate reports on the way in which households earn their income. In other words, it tells something about the balance between rewards to labour (e.g. wages and salaries), capital (profits), land (rents), enterprise (self-employment) and so on.

The output-side estimate focuses on the economic structure of the economy. One way in which countries differ is in the balance between primary production such as agriculture, secondary activity such as manufacturing, and tertiary activity such as services. Service activity has increased in importance in the UK in recent years, with financial services in particular emerging as a strong part of the UK's comparative advantage.

Summary

- The circular flow of income, expenditure and output describes the relationship between these three key variables.
- The model suggests that there are three ways in which the total level of economic activity in an economy during a period of time can be measured: by total income, by total expenditure and by total output produced.
- In principle, these should give the same answers, but in practice data measurements are not so accurate.

Injections and withdrawals

The circular flow diagram in Figure 13.1 was a simple model of the economy that analysed the three-way flow of resources around an economy. Households supplied factors of production in exchange for income, which was then spent on goods and services produced by firms. This model has limited applicability from a real-world perspective because it is a *closed* system, whereas in practice this is not the case, as there are **withdrawals** (or leakages) from the system and **injections** into it. These arise because of the economic activities of government and through an economy's international trade with the rest of the world.

Injections into the circular flow

The government affects the circular flow in two important ways. First, the government spends money on goods and services. For example, it may spend on the provision of public goods, and has to spend in order to carry out its other governmental obligations. In order to finance these activities, the government must raise revenue — which it can do through taxation.

International trade also affects the circular flow. Part of the expenditure on goods and services in the economy comes from abroad in the form of exports. In addition, part of the expenditure undertaken by households is on imported goods and services.

The saving activity of households also affects the circular flow, as there is a part of household income that is saved instead of being spent on goods and services. It is also important to realise that firms contribute to expenditure when they buy investment goods to add to their productive capacity.

Figure 13.2 adds all of these effects on to the circular flow diagram. The flow of expenditure is no longer just made up of household consumption expenditure on consumer goods, but is augmented by investment expenditure by firms (I), export expenditure from overseas (X) and government expenditure (G). These can be regarded as injections into the circular flow.

Key terms

withdrawals where money flows out of the circular flow in the form of savings, taxation and imports

injections where money flows into the circular flow in the form of investment, government spending and exports

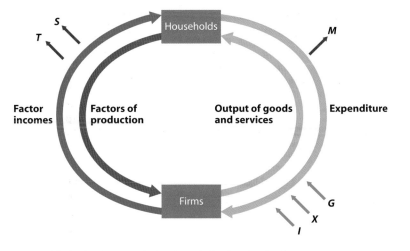

Figure 13.2 Injections and withdrawals in the circular flow

Withdrawals from the circular flow

On the other side of the coin, there are withdrawals from the circular flow, made up of spending on imports from the rest of the world (*M*), household savings (*S*) and taxes raised by the government from households (*T*). The overall economy will be in balance when planned injections are equal to planned withdrawals. Notice that there are connections between the injections and withdrawals — for example, household savings may enter financial markets, and firms borrow from financial markets in order to finance their investment expenditure.

Investment plays an important role within the macroeconomy. Investment is expenditure by firms on machinery, buildings and other productive resources. By undertaking investment expenditure, firms add to the productive capacity of the economy, and thus enable economic growth to take place. A change in the balance between investment and consumption activity therefore has an effect on the long-run path of the economy.

An increase in expenditure on investment by firms may have other effects as well. In order to meet the additional demand for machinery, other firms need to expand production. This means that they need to hire extra workers — and pay them, of course. The additional workers will then spend part of their income on consumer goods, thus unleashing a second round of expenditure. This phenomenon will be examined later in the chapter.

The circular flow model notes that total expenditure should be the same as total income and total output if all were measured fully. This might seem to suggest that the macroeconomy is always in a sort of equilibrium, in the sense that expenditure and output are always the same. However, this is misleading. When you observe the economy, you should find that expenditure and output are the same *after* the event, but this does *not* mean that equilibrium holds in the sense that all economic agents will have found that their plans were fulfilled. In other words, it is not necessarily the case that *planned* expenditure equals *planned* output.

This is the significance of the inclusion of inventory changes as part of investment. If firms find that they have produced more output than is subsequently purchased, their inventory holdings increase. Thus, although after the event expenditure always equals output, this is because any disequilibrium is reflected in unplanned inventory changes.

Summary

- In reality, the circular flow diagram needs to be expanded to accommodate injections and withdrawals.
- The government affects the circular flow through expenditure (an injection) and taxation (a withdrawal).
- International trade is important because of exports (an injection) and imports (a withdrawal).
- The circular flow is also affected by household savings (a withdrawal) and by firms' investment expenditure (an injection).
- Investment is also important because it affects the productive capacity of the economy in the long run, and is thus important for economic growth.

Income and wealth

Key terms

income a flow concept — the amount of income that is earned during a period

wealth a stock concept — the accumulation of assets, such as property or shares

In everyday parlance, it is not uncommon to use 'income' and 'wealth' as words that mean virtually the same. In economic analysis, it is important to realise that the two things are very different. **Income** has been described as a *flow*; it is the amount of income that is earned during a period. **Wealth** is a *stock* — it is the accumulated amount of assets that have been built up from past income.

Wealth is considerably less evenly distributed than income. In 2010–12, UK households in the top 10% of the income distribution owned 44% of the wealth, compared with 9.6% of the wealth owned by households in the bottom 50%. Wealth is affected by changing house prices and strongly influenced by the value of pension funds.

Notice that, although wealth and income are not the same thing, inequality in wealth can lead to inequality in income, as wealth (the ownership of assets) creates an income flow — from rents and profits — which then feeds back into a household's income stream.

A significant change in the pattern of ownership of assets in recent decades has been the increase in home ownership and the rise in house prices. For those who continue to rent their homes, and in particular for those who rent council dwellings, this is a significant source of rising inequality.

Summary

- Income is a flow, but wealth is a stock.
- Wealth is less evenly distributed than income in the UK.
- Inequality in wealth can lead to inequality in income.

The rise in home ownership has led to increasing inequality

Macroeconomic equilibrium

The circular flow diagram is useful in emphasising the importance of the interactions between households, firms and other economic factors in the macroeconomy. The next step in building a model of the macroeconomy is to bring together aggregate demand and aggregate supply in order to analyse macroeconomic equilibrium.

First consider the short-run equilibrium. In Figure 13.3, with aggregate supply given by *SAS* and aggregate demand by *AD*, equilibrium is reached at the real output level *Y*, with the price level at *P*.

This is an equilibrium, in the sense that if nothing changes then firms and households will have no reason to alter their behaviour in the next period. At the price *P*, aggregate supply is matched by aggregate demand.

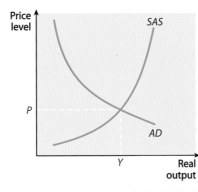

Figure 13.3 Macroeconomic equilibrium

An increase in aggregate demand

Having identified macroeconomic equilibrium, it is possible to undertake some comparative static analysis — in other words, to explore what happens if there is a change in market conditions. The position of the aggregate demand curve depends on the components of aggregate demand: consumption, investment, government spending and net exports. Factors that affect these components will affect the position of aggregate demand.

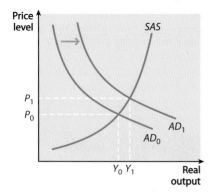

Figure 13.4 A shift in aggregate demand

Consider Figure 13.4. Suppose that the economy begins in equilibrium with aggregate demand at AD_0. The equilibrium output level is Y_0, and the price level is at P_0. An increase in government expenditure will affect the position of the aggregate demand curve, shifting it to AD_1. The economy will move to a new equilibrium position, with a higher output level Y_1 and a higher price level P_1.

An important question is whether this new equilibrium is sustainable. Suppose that the original level of real output at Y_0 had been the full employment level? Firms react in the short run by increasing their prices and raising output. However, in order to raise output in the short run, they may need to pay their workers overtime, or to hire additional office space. They will not want to continue to do this, and may also find that their suppliers are also increasing their prices. Firms then realise that their costs are rising, and will be prepared to supply less output at any given price. The short-run aggregate supply curve shifts back to the left, and the higher level of real output at Y_1 will not be sustained. This is another reason why this is an analysis of short-run equilibrium.

The effect of a supply shock

The AD/AS model can also be used to analyse the effects of an external shock that affects aggregate supply. For example, suppose there is an increase in oil prices arising from a disruption to supplies in the Middle East. This raises firms' costs, and leads to a reduction in aggregate supply. Comparative static analysis can again be employed to examine the likely effects on equilibrium.

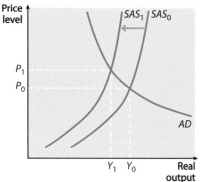

Figure 13.5 A supply shock

Figure 13.5 analyses the situation. The economy begins in equilibrium with output at Y_0 and the overall level of prices at P_0. The increase in oil prices causes a movement of the aggregate supply curve from SAS_0 to SAS_1, with aggregate demand unchanged at AD. After the economy returns to equilibrium, the new output level has fallen to Y_1 and the overall price level has increased to P_1.

At the time of the first oil price crisis back in 1973–74, the UK government of the day tried to maintain the previous level of real output by stimulating aggregate demand. This had the effect of pushing up the price level, but did not have any noticeable effect on real output. Such a result is not unexpected, given the steepness of the aggregate supply curve.

Long-run equilibrium

Long-run equilibrium is analysed in the same way, as shown in Figure 13.6 with a Keynesian long-run aggregate supply curve.

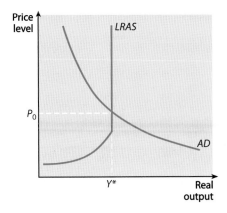

Figure 13.6 Macroeconomic equilibrium at full employment

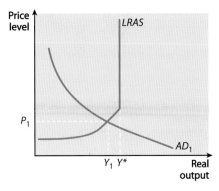

Figure 13.7 Macroeconomic equilibrium below full employment

Equilibrium occurs at the intersection of AD and $LRAS$, with price at P_0 and real output at Y^*. The figure has been drawn with equilibrium real output occurring at the full employment level, where the $LRAS$ is vertical. But can it be guaranteed that the macroeconomic equilibrium will always occur at the full employment level of output? For example, suppose that the intersection of AD and $LRAS$ had occurred at a level of real output below Y^*? Keynesians would argue that this is possible, as shown in Figure 13.7, but monetarists would hold that the $LRAS$ is vertical at Y^*, so that equilibrium is always at full employment.

Summary

- The aggregate supply (SAS) curve shows the relationship between aggregate supply and the overall price level.
- Macroeconomic equilibrium in the short run is reached at the intersection of *AD* and *SAS*.
- An increase in the equilibrium level of real output and the price level may not be sustainable if real output moves beyond the full employment level in the short run.
- Shifts in aggregate demand and aggregate supply curves lead to a new equilibrium price level and real output.
- Long-run equilibrium is found at the intersection of *AD* and *LRAS*.

The multiplier

In his *General Theory*, Keynes pointed out that there may be **multiplier** effects in response to certain types of expenditure. Suppose that the government increases its expenditure by £1 billion, perhaps by increasing its road-building programme. The effect of this is to generate incomes for households — for example, those of the contractors hired to build the road. Those contractors then spend part of the additional income (and save part of it). By spending part of the extra money earned, an additional income stream is generated for shopkeepers and café owners, who in turn spend part of *their* additional income, and so on. Thus, the original increase in government spending sparks off further income generation and spending, causing the multiplier effect. In effect, equilibrium output may change by more than the original increase in expenditure.

> **Key term**
>
> **multiplier** the ratio of a change in equilibrium real income to the autonomous change that brought it about; it is defined as 1 divided by the marginal propensity to withdraw

Government spending on road building may increase spending in other areas of the economy due to the multiplier effect

Key terms

marginal propensity to import the proportion of additional income that is spent on imports of goods and services

marginal propensity to tax the proportion of additional income that is taxed

marginal propensity to withdraw the proportion of additional income that is withdrawn from the circular flow — the sum of the marginal propensities to save, import and tax

The size of this multiplier effect depends on a number of factors. Most importantly, it depends on the size of *withdrawals* or *leakages* from the system. In particular, it depends on how much of the additional income is saved by households, how much is spent on imported goods, and how much is returned to the government in the form of direct taxes. These items constitute withdrawals from the system, in the sense that they detract from the multiplier effect. For example, if households save a high proportion of their additional income, then this clearly reduces the multiplier effect, as the next round of spending will be that much lower. This seems to go against the traditional view that saving is good for the economy.

In the same way that the marginal propensity to consume was defined as the proportion of additional income devoted to consumer expenditure, the **marginal propensity to import** is the proportion of additional income that is spent on imported goods and services, and the **marginal propensity to tax** is the proportion of additional income that is taxed. The sum of the marginal propensities to save, import and tax is the **marginal propensity to withdraw**.

However, there are also *injections* into the system in the form of autonomous government expenditure, investment and exports. One condition of macroeconomic equilibrium is that total withdrawals equal total injections. The fact that injections can have this multiplied effect on equilibrium output and income seems to make the government potentially very powerful, as by increasing its expenditure it can have a multiplied effect on the economy.

Calculating the multiplier

A numerical value for the multiplier can be calculated with reference to the withdrawals from the circular flow. Suppose that the marginal propensity to save is 0.25, the marginal propensity to import is 0.1 and the marginal propensity to tax is 0.15. The marginal propensity to withdraw is then 0.25 + 0.1 + 0.15 = 0.5. The multiplier formula is 1 divided by the marginal propensity to withdraw ($1/MPW$). If the MPW is 0.5, then the value of the multiplier is 2, so for every £100 million injection into the circular flow, there will be a £200 million increase in equilibrium output.

It is worth noting that the size of the withdrawals may depend in part upon the domestic elasticity of supply. If domestic supply is inflexible, and therefore unable to meet an increase in demand, more of the increase in income will spill over into purchasing imports, and this will dilute the multiplier effect.

Exercise 13.1

Identify each of the following as an injection or a leakage, and state whether it increases or decreases the impact of the multiplier:

a saving by households

b expenditure by central government

c spending by UK residents on imported goods and services

d expenditure by firms on investment

e spending by overseas residents on UK goods and services

f income tax payments

The multiplier and aggregate demand (*AD*)

What does the existence of the multiplier imply for aggregate demand? As we have seen, the multiplier is the idea that an increase in autonomous expenditure, such as government expenditure or investment expenditure by firms, will have *multiplier* effects through successive rounds of additional expenditure. In the context of the *AD/AS* model, this will affect the extent to which the *AD* curve shifts to the right following an increase in autonomous expenditure. In other words, the initial shift of *AD* will be augmented in following periods by further shifts as the successive rounds of additional expenditure work themselves through the system.

All of this seems to suggest that the government can always reach full employment, simply by increasing its expenditure. However, you should be a little cautious in reaching such a conclusion, as the effect on equilibrium output and the price level will depend on how close the economy is to the full employment level. Notice that the aggregate supply curve becomes steeper as output and the price level increase. In other words, the closer the economy is to the full employment level, the smaller is the elasticity of supply, so an increase in aggregate demand close to full employment will have more of an effect on the price level (and hence potentially on inflation) than on the level of real output. Indeed, if the economy is in equilibrium at the full employment level of real output before the increase in aggregate demand, the multiplier simply means more upward pressure on the equilibrium price level.

Exercise 13.2

State whether each of the following statements about aggregate demand and/or the aggregate demand curve is true or false.

a The aggregate demand curve shows the relationship between the level of aggregate demand and the overall price level in an economy.

b The aggregate demand curve shows planned expenditure in an economy at any given possible overall price level.

c As the aggregate price level falls, the demand for goods and services in the economy rises and more of each good or service will be demanded.

d Government expenditure is regarded as autonomous, and affects the shape of the aggregate demand curve.

e The value of the multiplier depends upon the level of government spending.

f An increase in government spending may induce a multiplier effect.

g The way in which consumption and investment respond to changes in the interest rate affects the shape of the aggregate demand curve.

h Investment expenditure by firms is the largest component of aggregate demand in an economy.

Exercise 13.3

For each of the following, decide whether the change affects aggregate demand or aggregate supply, and sketch a diagram to illustrate the effects on equilibrium real output and overall price level. Undertake this exercise first for a starting position in the steep part of the *AS* curve, and then for an initial position further to the left, where *LRAS* is more elastic:

a an advancement in technology that improves the efficiency of capital

b a financial crisis in Asia that reduces the demand for UK exports

c an improvement in firms' expectations about future demand, such that investment expenditure increases

d the introduction of new health and safety legislation that raises firms' costs

For each of these changes, indicate whether the result is a shift of or a movement along the *AD* and *AS* curves.

Summary

- Autonomous spending, such as government expenditure, may give rise to a magnified impact on equilibrium output through the multiplier effect.
- The magnitude of the multiplier effect depends upon the marginal propensity to withdraw.
- The presence of the multiplier affects the impact of an increase in autonomous expenditure on the resulting shift of the aggregate demand curve.

14 Economic growth

One of society's prime responsibilities is to provide a reasonable standard of living for its citizens and to promote their well-being. Hence one of the major objectives for economic policy in the long run is to enable improvements in well-being. In order to do this, it is first necessary to expand the resources available within society. A key element in this process is to achieve economic growth, which is the subject of this chapter. However, there may be more to well-being than just growth, and the chapter also explores some of the limitations of a strategy that aims to maximise GDP growth.

Learning objectives

After studying this chapter, you should:

→ be able to understand the meaning of economic growth and productivity
→ be familiar with factors that can affect the rate of economic growth, particularly the role of investment
→ be able to evaluate the importance to a society of economic growth and the costs that such growth may impose
→ understand the meaning and significance of sustainable growth

Defining economic growth

From a theoretical point of view, potential economic growth can be thought of as an expansion of the productive capacity of an economy. Earlier, this was discussed in terms of a shift in the production possibility frontier (*PPF*): economic growth enables a society to produce more goods and services in any given period as a result of an expansion in its resources. Actual economic growth (measured by the rate of growth of GDP) may also reflect a movement towards the frontier: for example, when an economy is recovering from a period of recession.

A second way of thinking about economic growth is to use the *AD/AS* model. For example, in Figure 14.1, an increase in the skills of the workforce will enable firms to produce more output at any given price, so that the aggregate supply curve will shift outwards from $LRAS_0$ to $LRAS_1$. This entails an increase in full employment output (or capacity output) from $Y^\star$ to $Y^{\star\star}$. This again can be characterised as economic growth. Chapter 16 investigates policies that might be introduced to affect aggregate supply. In this chapter the focus is on a broader perspective within which long-run growth can be achieved.

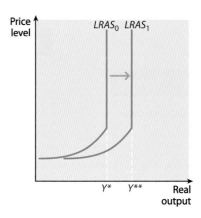

Figure 14.1 A shift in aggregate supply

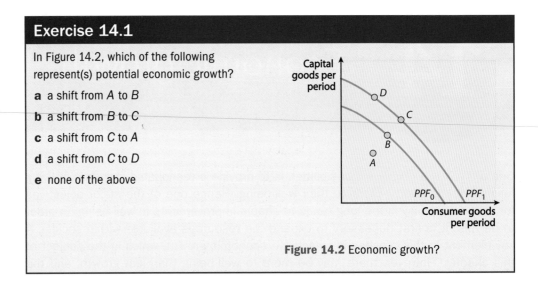

Figure 14.2 Economic growth?

Figure 14.3 shows the actual time path of real GDP in the UK since 1948, together with its underlying trend. The trend shown is based on the average growth rate between 1948 and 2012. Although the two series do not diverge by very much for most of the period, you can see the way in which the actual path of real GDP fluctuates around the trend, especially in the middle part of the period. Also very apparent in the figure is the recession that started in 2008, when GDP dipped significantly below its trend value.

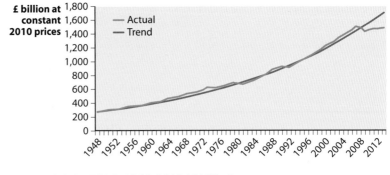

Figure 14.3 Real GDP, 1948–2013 (£ billion)   Source: ONS

The business cycle

The fluctuation of real GDP around an underlying trend is known as the **business cycle**. At any point in time, GDP may be below or above its trend value, the difference being known as the **output gap**. This is defined as the actual level of output minus the potential level. If actual GDP is below potential GDP, then the gap is negative; if actual GDP is above the trend level, the gap is positive.

Notice that actual GDP is something that we observe, whereas potential GDP represents the level of GDP that could be achieved if the economy were using all its resources effectively. You might think that the output gap could be calculated as the difference between the actual series and the underlying trend, but that is not really the case. After all, it could be that the economy never reaches full capacity, in which case it is never possible to observe potential output directly.

The output gap can be illustrated using an *AD/AS* diagram. If you look back at Figure 13.7, you will see an economy that is in equilibrium below full employment, under Keynesian assumptions. In this case, Y_1 is actual GDP and $Y^\star$ is the potential level that could be achieved at full employment. The output gap in this case is the difference between them.

Consider an economy at point *A* on Figure 14.4. At this stage in the cycle, the economy is entering a period of recession, in which GDP is falling. This continues until point *B*, the trough of the cycle, at which point GDP stops falling and begins to grow again. At point *C*, the economy is showing growth in actual GDP, but GDP is still below its trend value; only at point *D* does the economy hit the trend. In other words, between points *A* and *D*, the output gap is negative. Beyond point *D* the economy moves into a boom period (as at point *E*), where GDP grows more rapidly than its trend value, and the level of GDP is above its trend value; the output gap is positive. At point *F*, the cycle reaches its peak and stops increasing; beyond this point actual GDP again begins to fall, and then the story repeats.

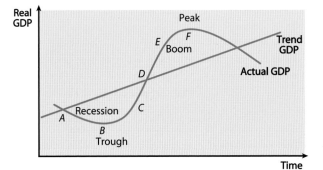

Figure 14.4 The business cycle

From a policy perspective, it is important to know at what stage the economy is located. When the output gap is negative, and the level of output is below trend, then it may be tempting for policy-makers to try to 'fill the gap' by stimulating aggregate demand. However, this would be dangerous when the output gap is positive, as the main effect would be on the price level. One classic example of a cycle occurred from 1984 to 1993, as shown in Figure 14.5; here the output gap was positive from 1985 to 1988, then becoming negative as the economy went into recession. Notice that a **recession** is said to occur when GDP falls for two or more consecutive quarters. The horizontal line on this graph and Figure 14.6 shows the average growth rate over the period.

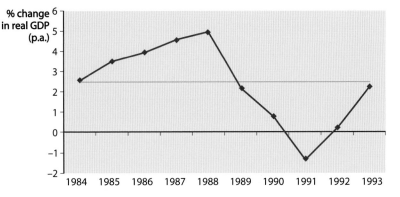

Figure 14.5 A classic business cycle

Source: ONS

In mid-2008, the chancellor of the exchequer took the unprecedented step of stating publicly that the UK was heading for its biggest recession since the Second World War. This was unprecedented because most chancellors shy away from saying anything that will damage expectations about the economy. Figure 14.6 shows quarterly data for the period 2003 to 2008, showing the information that was available to the chancellor when he made this claim. He proved to be correct.

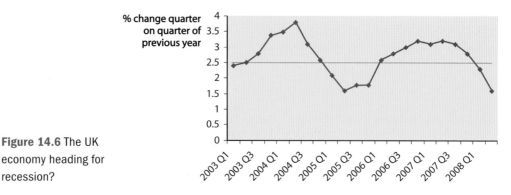

Figure 14.6 The UK economy heading for recession?

Figure 14.7 shows the growth rates of GDP per capita in selected countries from 1971 to 2009. Although the graph looks a little congested, it is useful because it shows that there are some periods when fluctuations occur simultaneously across countries. For example, look at what happened in 1974/75, when all countries shown were negatively affected by the oil price shock of 1973/74. Notice that all countries enjoyed a more stable period of growth between about 1984 and 1990. So there may be periods in which there are common cycles across countries. On the other hand, there are also exceptions to this — for example, Japan's negative growth in 1998 and 1999, which was not shared by the other countries in the graph.

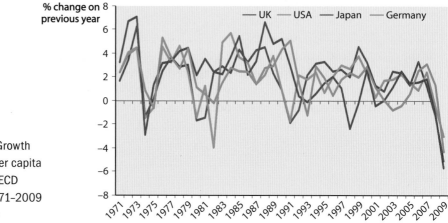

Figure 14.7 Growth of real GDP per capita in selected OECD countries, 1971–2009
Source: OECD

It is important to be aware that if countries do follow common patterns — at least in some periods — then this implies that domestic economic policy may not be the only influence on an economy's performance.

Figure 14.8 shows the actual growth rate of the UK economy since 1950. The recession that began in the late 2000s is clearly seen here. You can see that it is quite difficult to determine the underlying trend because the year-to-year movements are so volatile.

Figure 14.9 takes 5-yearly average growth rates over the same period, with the horizontal red line showing the underlying trend rate of growth. This puts the recession of the late 2000s into sharp focus, as it seems out of line with the rest of the period.

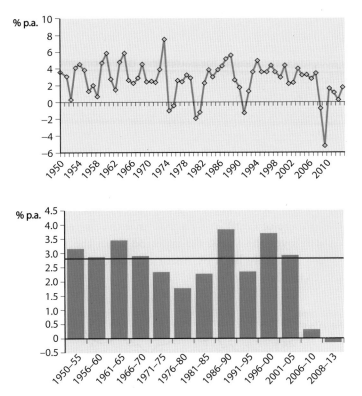

Figure 14.8 The UK's actual growth rate, 1950–2014

Source: ONS

Figure 14.9 Average annual growth rates in the UK since 1950

Sources of economic growth

At a basic level, production arises from the use of factors of production — capital, labour, entrepreneurship and so on. Capacity output is reached when all factors of production are fully and efficiently utilised. From this perspective, an increase in capacity output can come either from an increase in the quantity of the factors of production, or from an improvement in their efficiency or productivity. **Productivity** is a measure of the efficiency of a factor of production. For example, **labour productivity** measures output per worker, or output per hour worked. The latter is the more helpful measure, as clearly total output is affected by the number of hours worked, which does vary somewhat across countries. **Capital productivity** measures output per unit of capital. **Total factor productivity** refers to the average productivity of all factors, measured as the total output divided by the total amount of inputs used.

An increase in productivity raises aggregate supply and the potential capacity output of an economy, and thus contributes to economic growth.

Capital

Capital is a critical factor in the production process. An increase in capital input is thus one source of economic growth. In order for capital to accumulate and increase the capacity of the economy to produce, **investment** needs to take place.

Key terms

productivity a measure of the efficiency of a factor of production

labour productivity a measure of output per worker, or output per hour worked

capital productivity a measure of output per unit of capital

total factor productivity the average productivity of all factors, measured as the total output divided by the total amount of inputs used

investment expenditure undertaken by firms to add to the capital stock

Notice that in economics 'investment' is used in this specific way. In common parlance the term is sometimes used to refer to investing in shares or putting money into a deposit account at the bank. Do not confuse these different concepts. In economics 'investment' relates to a firm buying new capital, such as machinery or factory buildings. If you put money into a bank account, that is an act of saving, not investment.

In the national accounts, the closest measurement that economists have to investment is 'gross fixed capital formation'. This covers net additions to the capital stock, but it also includes **depreciation**. Some of the machinery and other capital purchased by firms is to replace old, worn-out capital: that is, to offset depreciation. It does not therefore represent an addition to capital stock. As depreciation cannot be observed easily, the convention in the accounts is to measure gross investment (i.e. including depreciation) and then make an adjustment for depreciation to arrive at **net investment**.

Figure 14.10 shows the time path for gross investment in the UK since 1950, expressed as a percentage of GDP. You can see that the share of investment in GDP has fluctuated a little over the years; for a period from the mid-1990s it settled at about 17%, which is relatively high by historical standards, before falling with the onset of recession in the late 2000s.

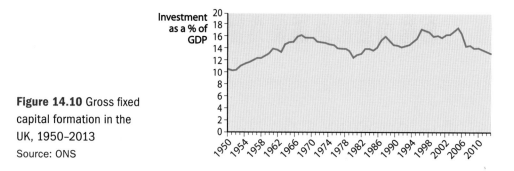

Figure 14.10 Gross fixed capital formation in the UK, 1950–2013
Source: ONS

The choice that any society makes here is between using resources for current consumption and using resources for investment. Investment thus entails sacrificing present consumption in order to have more resources available in the future.

Different countries give investment very different priorities. Something of this can be seen in Figure 14.11, which shows gross fixed capital formation in a selection of countries around the world in 2012. The diversity is substantial, ranging from just 15% in Pakistan to 49% in China. Given its high rate of investment, it is perhaps not surprising to discover that China is among the fastest-growing economies in the world in the early twenty-first century — but it must also be remembered that there is a cost to this, as it means sacrificing present consumption in China.

The contribution of capital to growth is reinforced by technological progress, as the productivity of new capital is greater than that of old capital that is being phased out. For example, the speed and power of computers has increased enormously over recent years, which has had a great impact on productivity. Effectively, this means

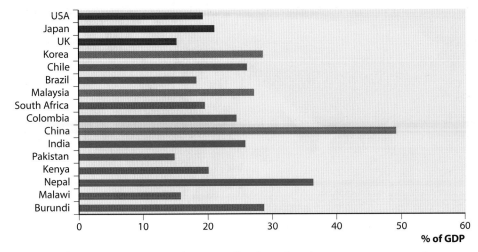

Figure 14.11 Gross fixed capital formation in 2012

Note: countries are in descending order of GNI per capita.

Source: World Bank

that technology is increasing the contribution that investment can make towards enlarging capacity output in an economy.

Innovation can also contribute, through the invention of new forms of capital and new ways of using existing capital, both of which can aid economic growth.

Labour

Capital has sometimes been seen as the main driver of growth, but labour too has a key contribution to make. There is little point in installing a lot of high-tech equipment unless there is the skilled labour to operate it.

There is relatively little scope for increasing the size of the labour force in a country, except through international migration. (Encouraging population growth is a rather long-term policy!) Nonetheless, the size of the workforce does contribute to the size of capacity output. A number of sub-Saharan African countries have seen this effect in reverse in recent years, with the impact of HIV/AIDS. The spread of this epidemic has had a devastating impact in a number of countries in the region. It has had a serious effect on capacity output because the disease affects people of working age disproportionately, diminishing the size of the workforce and the productivity of workers.

The quality of labour input is more amenable to policy action. Education and training can improve the productivity of workers, and can be regarded as a form of investment in **human capital**.

Chapter 6 discussed how education and healthcare may have associated externalities. In particular, individuals may not perceive the full social benefits associated with education, training and certain kinds of healthcare, and thus may choose to invest less in these forms of human capital than is desirable from the perspective of society as a whole. Another such externality is the impact of human capital formation on economic growth; this is a justification for viewing education and healthcare as merit goods, as discussed in Chapters 6 and 7.

For many developing countries, the provision of healthcare and improved nutrition can be seen as additional forms of investment in human capital, since such investment can lead to future improvements in productivity.

> **Key term**
>
> **human capital** the stock of skills and expertise that contribute to a worker's productivity; it can be increased through education and training

A mobile clinic in rural Uganda — investing in healthcare can lead to improvements in productivity

Growth and international trade

International trade can contribute to economic growth. Indeed, for many relatively small countries, international trade is a key part of achieving economic growth. If the domestic market is not sufficiently large, effective demand may not allow economies of scale to be reaped. By engaging in international trade, a country is able to specialise, and thus produce goods more efficiently, reaping the gains from large-scale production.

For many less developed countries, this is especially important, as not only is it crucial to be able to reach a large market, but also it is important to be able to earn the foreign exchange needed to import physical capital that cannot be produced domestically.

The countries that have been most successful in achieving economic growth in the last few decades are all countries that have relied on being able to expand rapidly through promoting exports — a process known as **export-led growth**. Examples include the east Asian 'Tiger' economies that enjoyed rapid growth from the 1960s onwards — countries like Korea, Singapore, Hong Kong and Taiwan. More recently, China has enjoyed unprecedented success in economic growth, founded upon the rapid expansion of exports.

> **Key term**
>
> **export-led growth** a strategy for achieving rapid economic growth through the promotion of export activity

Growth and the *AD/AS* model

Notice that this discussion of the sources of economic growth has focused on potential economic growth and the factors that affect aggregate supply, as in Figure 14.1. This is because the productive capacity of the economy can increase only when the *AS* curve shifts to the right. An increase in aggregate demand can lead to higher real output in the economy if the initial equilibrium is below full capacity output, but this is equivalent to a move *towards* the *PPF*, so it does not affect overall productive capacity in the economy. The only exception to this is where the increase in aggregate demand is due to an increase in investment expenditure that will later enable an increase in productive capacity. This will be important in Chapter 16, which analyses policy instruments available to the government.

If the economy is in equilibrium below full employment, then an increase in aggregate demand can also result in actual economic growth as the economy moves closer to full capacity. Indeed, in some situations it may be vital that there is an increase in aggregate demand in order to accommodate the increase in aggregate supply. One recent example of this is the rapid expansion of the Chinese economy, based upon a rapid growth in exports. This export-led growth has created one of the most dramatic examples of sustained economic growth in history. The growth could not have been based on the domestic market alone. The high level of investment suggests that growth in China came from a combination of rightward shifts in both aggregate demand and aggregate supply.

Summary

- Economic growth is the expansion of an economy's productive capacity.
- This can be envisaged as a movement outwards of the production possibility frontier, or as a rightward shift of the aggregate supply curve.
- Economic growth can be seen as the underlying trend rate of growth in real GDP.
- Over time, real GDP tends to fluctuate around its trend, a phenomenon known as the business cycle.
- Economic growth can stem from an increase in the inputs of factors of production, or from an improvement in their productivity: that is, the efficiency with which factors of production are utilised.
- Investment contributes to growth by increasing the capital stock of an economy, although some investment is to compensate for depreciation.
- The contribution of capital is reinforced by the effects of technological progress.
- Labour is another critical factor of production that can contribute to economic growth: for instance, education and training can improve labour productivity. This is a form of human capital formation.

The importance of economic growth

Expanding the availability of resources in an economy enables the standard of living of the country to increase. For developing countries this may facilitate the easing of poverty, and may allow investment in human capital that will improve standards of living further in the future. In the industrial economies, populations have come to expect steady improvements in incomes and resources. For households, economic growth may bring higher incomes, for firms it may bring higher profits, for governments it may bring higher tax revenue and an improved capacity to provide public goods.

Thus for any society economic growth is likely to be seen as a fundamental objective — perhaps even the most important one. It may be argued that other policy objectives should be regarded as subsidiary to the growth target. In other words, the control of inflation, the maintenance of full employment and the achievement of stability in the current account of the balance of payments are seen as important short-run objectives, because their achievement facilitates long-run economic growth.

Growth vs basic needs

In some less developed countries the perspective may be different, and there has been a long-running debate about whether a society in its early stages of development should devote its resources to achieving the growth objective or to catering for basic needs. By making economic growth the prime target of policy, it may be necessary in the short run to allow inequality of incomes to continue, in order to provide the incentives for entrepreneurs to pursue growth. With such a 'growth-first' approach, it is argued that eventually, as growth takes place, the benefits will trickle down: in other words, growth is necessary in order to tackle poverty and provide for basic needs. However, others have argued that the first priority should be to deal with basic needs, so that people gain in human capital and become better able to contribute to the growth process. It is also important to realise that economic growth does not necessarily translate into improvements in living standards: for example, where the benefits from growth are concentrated in certain groups within a society, rather than being spread widely.

Recession in the late 2000s

For the industrial countries, the importance of economic growth has been brought into sharp focus through the crisis of the late 2000s, which is still affecting many economies. After a period of relative stability during the 2000s, the onset of financial crisis initiated not only a slowdown in the growth of GDP, but a period of recession.

Figure 14.12 shows how recession affected the UK in late 2008, with GDP growth being negative for six consecutive quarters. The UK was not the only economy affected by recession, and many advanced countries followed a similar pattern — indeed, countries like Greece were more severely hit in this period. The consequences of such a recession are significant. If output is falling, and firms are reducing their production, it is likely that they are laying off workers, so that unemployment rises. This then leads to falling incomes, which reduces aggregate demand and may lead to further drops in output, prolonging the recession. You can see from Figure 14.12 that the recovery from recession has been sluggish.

Study tip

Notice that it is *negative* growth that defines a recession: in Figure 14.12 the *growth rate* of GDP fell in 2011, but it did not go negative, so this would not count as a recession.

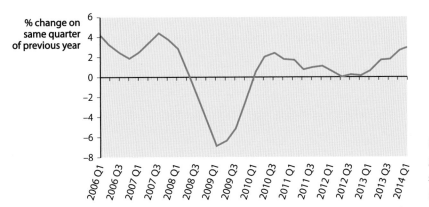

Figure 14.12 Economic growth in the UK since 2006
Source: ONS

The costs of economic growth

Economic growth also brings costs, perhaps most obviously in terms of pollution and degradation of the environment. In designing long-term policy for economic growth, governments need to be aware of the need to maintain a good balance between enabling resources to increase and safeguarding the environment. Pollution reduces the quality of life, so pursuing economic growth without regard to this may be damaging. This means that it is important to consider the long-term effects of economic growth — it may even be important to consider the effects not only for today's generation of citizens, but also for future generations.

These costs have been highlighted in recent years by the growing concerns that have been expressed about global climate change and the pressures on non-renewable resources such as oil and natural gas. For example, the rapid growth rates being achieved by large emerging economies such as China and India have raised questions about the sustainability of economic growth in the long run. China in particular has experienced a period of unprecedented growth since about 1978, which is shown in Figure 14.13. This shows the average growth in China over 5-year periods since 1978. No other economy in recent history has been able to achieve an average growth rate of 8.72% per annum over such a long period.

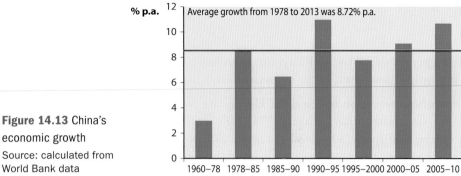

Figure 14.13 China's economic growth

Source: calculated from World Bank data

% p.a.

Average growth from 1978 to 2013 was 8.72% p.a.

Key term

sustainable development
'development that meets the needs of the present without compromising the ability of future generations to meet their own needs' (Brundtland Commission, 1987)

Economic growth may thus have important effects on the environment, and in pursuing growth, countries must bear in mind the need for **sustainable development**, safeguarding the needs of future generations as well as the needs of the present.

Another aspect of environmental degradation concerns *biodiversity*. This refers to the way in which misuse of the environment is contributing to the loss of plant species — not to mention those of birds, insects and mammals — which are becoming extinct as their natural habitat is destroyed. Some of the lost species may not even have been discovered yet. Given the natural healing properties of many plants, this could mean the destruction of plants that might provide significant new drugs for use in medicine. But how can something be valued when its very existence is as yet unknown?

Environmental capital

One way of viewing the environment is as a factor of production that needs to be used effectively, just like any other factor of production. In other words, each country has a stock of *environmental* capital that needs to be utilised in the best possible way.

However, if environmental capital is to be used appropriately, it must be given an appropriate value and this can be problematic. If property rights are not firmly established — as they are not in many less developed countries — it is difficult to enforce legislation to protect the environment. Furthermore, if the environment (as a factor of production) is underpriced, then 'too much' of it will be used by firms.

There are externality effects at work here too, in the sense that the loss of biodiversity is a global loss, and not just something affecting the local economy. In some cases there have been international externality effects of a more direct kind, such as when forest fires in Indonesia caused the airport in Singapore to close down because of the resulting smoke haze.

In August 2004, *The Economist* reported that 16 of the world's most polluted cities are now located in China, and that around half of China's population (i.e. some 600 million people) have water supplies that are contaminated by animal and human waste. River systems are heavily polluted, and air pollution is becoming a serious issue, partly as a result of the country's heavy reliance on coal-fired electricity generation. Shanghai's environmental protection bureau estimated that 70% of the 1 million cars in Shanghai do not reach even the oldest European emissions standard.

Air pollution is a serious issue in many Chinese cities

The trade-off between economic growth and environmental protection

This illustrates the trade-off between rapid economic growth and protection of the environment. The other factor in the equation is the desire to alleviate poverty. The World Bank estimated that in 2003, some 216 million people in China were living in poverty — defined then as living on less than $1 per day. The need to bring so many people out of extreme poverty lends urgency to the drive for economic growth. However, this needs to be balanced against the need to ensure sustainable development. In other words, economic growth must be achieved in such a way that it does not destroy the environment for future generations.

There are many aspects to this issue, of which protecting the environment is just one. Sustainable development also entails taking account of the depletion rates of non-renewable resources, and ensuring that renewable resources are renewed in the process of economic growth.

So, although economic growth is important to a society, the drive for growth must be tempered by an awareness of the possible trade-offs with other important objectives.

Other concers

There may be other kinds of concern about the desirability of economic growth. It is possible that economic growth could increase inequality in society, if the benefits from growth are restricted to some groups. If economic growth entails structural change in the economy, there may be workers who are displaced from declining sectors who find that they do not have the right skills for redeployment in expanding sectors. In other words, there may be structural unemployment, although hopefully this could be a transitional problem. There may also be times when economic growth has an effect on the balance of payments, if the marginal propensity to import is high — in other words, if rising incomes lead to a rapid increase in imports.

Exercise 14.3

Discuss with your fellow students the various benefits and costs associated with economic growth, and evaluate their relative importance.

Summary

- The experience of economic growth has varied substantially in different regions of the world.
- There is a gap in living standards between countries that industrialised early and countries that are now classified as being less developed.
- A few countries, mainly in east Asia, went through a period of rapid growth from the 1960s that has allowed them to close the gap. This was achieved partly through export-led growth, although other factors were also important.
- However, countries in sub-Saharan Africa have stagnated, and remain on very low incomes.
- Economic growth remains important for all countries, at whatever stage of development.
- There may be costs attached to economic growth, particularly in respect of the environment.

15 Macroeconomic policy objectives

Inevitably, there is a policy dimension to the study of the performance of the macroeconomy. Indeed, in evaluating such performance, it is the success of macroeconomic policy that is under scrutiny. However, the success of macroeconomic policy can be judged only if you are aware of what it is that the policy is trying to achieve. This chapter introduces and analyses the main objectives of policy at the macroeconomic level and explores the possibility that there may be conflict between some of the targets.

Learning objectives

After studying this chapter, you should:
→ be familiar with the principal objectives of macroeconomic policy
→ understand the reasons for setting these policy objectives
→ be aware of some potential obstacles that may inhibit the achievement of the targets
→ appreciate that the targets may sometimes conflict with each other

Targets of policy

Chapters 9 and 10 discussed some key measures of an economy's performance, particularly economic growth, inflation, unemployment and the balance of payments. If the performance of an economy at the macroeconomic level is found to be wanting in some way, then it is reasonable to ask whether some policy intervention might improve the situation.

The areas mentioned all raise policy questions that need to be addressed. In addition, it is pertinent to ask whether governments should be concerned about inequality of income distribution within a society. There is also a growing concern about the need to preserve the environment in which we live; Chapter 6 pointed out that an externality element in connection with the environment may be a cause of market failure, and commented that there may be international externalities that need to be considered. As this issue has a macroeconomic dimension to it, it will also need to be analysed in conjunction with a discussion of macroeconomic policy objectives.

These aspects of the macroeconomy that might be regarded as legitimate targets for policy action will now each be considered in turn. Chapter 16 then analyses the policy actions that might be introduced, and evaluates their possible effectiveness.

Economic growth

If the ultimate aim of a society is to improve the well-being of its citizens, then in economic terms this means that the resources available within the economy need to

> ### Study tip
>
> When considering (or revising) macroeconomic policy, structure your thinking around these six key objectives:
> - increased economic growth
> - control of inflation
> - a reduction in unemployment
> - restoration of equilibrium in the balance of payments
> - making the distribution of income more equal
> - protection of the environment
>
> Each of these is discussed in this chapter, although not in this order.

expand through time in order to widen people's choices. This requires a process of economic growth, which as we saw in Chapter 14 is an increase in the productive capacity of the economy. If you like, it is an expansion of the potential output of the economy.

This is such an important policy objective for an economy that the whole of Chapter 14 was devoted to it. Recall that the nearest measure that economists have of the resources available to members of a society is GDP; so in looking for economic growth, they are looking for sustained growth in real GDP over time.

As has been argued, economic growth may be regarded as the most fundamental of all macroeconomic policy objectives, with other policy objectives being subsidiary to it. For example, one of the key reasons for maintaining low inflation is to encourage firms to undertake investment — because this enables economic growth. Maintaining full employment ensures the best possible use of a society's resources, enabling it to reach the production possibility frontier — and failure to do this may have indirect consequences for economic growth. Running a sustained current account deficit on the balance of payments that requires the sale of UK assets may limit the future growth prospects of the economy. This chapter explores these and other issues more carefully.

A wide choice of goods for shoppers is a sign of economic growth

Full employment (low unemployment)

For an economy to be operating on the production possibility frontier, the factors of production need to be fully employed. From society's point of view, surplus capacity in the economy represents waste. In the macroeconomic policy arena, attention in this context focuses on achieving low unemployment. For example, Figure 15.1 shows that it is possible for the economy to be in macroeconomic equilibrium at a level of output Y_1 that is below the potential full employment level at Y^*. This may be seen as an unnecessary waste of potential output. In addition, there may be a cost suffered by the people who are unemployed in this situation and who could have been productively employed. The causes and consequences of unemployment were discussed in Chapter 10.

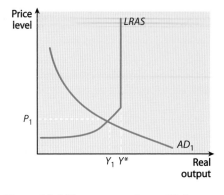

Figure 15.1 Macroeconomic equilibrium below full employment

Summary

- Full employment occurs when an economy is operating on the production possibility frontier, with full utilisation of factors of production.
- An economy operating below full capacity is characterised by unemployment.

Price stability

One of the most prominent objectives of macroeconomic policy in recent years has been the need to control inflation. Indeed, this has been at the heart of governments' stated policy objectives since 1976.

Causes of inflation

Chapter 10 defined inflation as a rise in the general price level. However, it is important to distinguish between a one-off increase in the price level and a sustained rise over a long period of time. For example, a one-off rise in the price of oil may have an effect on the price level by shifting aggregate supply, thus affecting the equilibrium price level — as shown in Figure 15.2. However, this takes the economy to a new equilibrium price level, and if nothing else were to change, there would be no reason for prices to continue to rise beyond P_1.

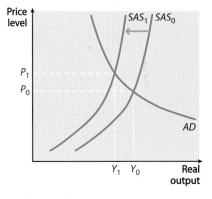

Figure 15.2 A supply shock

Nonetheless, this is one reason why prices may begin to increase. Inflation thus may be initiated on the supply side of the macroeconomy, arising from an increase in the costs faced by firms, perhaps through an increase in the price of oil, or increases in wage costs. This is sometimes referred to as **cost-push inflation**, as the increase in the overall level of prices is cost driven.

In terms of the *AD/AS* model, it is clear that an alternative explanation of a rise in the general price level could come from the demand side, where an increase in aggregate demand leads to a rise in prices, especially if the *AS* curve becomes so steep in the long run as to become vertical, as some macroeconomists believe. An increase in aggregate demand could come, for example, from an expansion of money supply that causes interest rates to be lower than would have been the case, thus encouraging higher consumption and investment expenditure. This is shown in

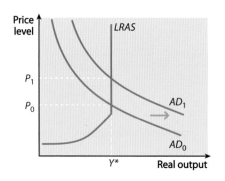

Figure 15.3 An increase in aggregate
demand

Figure 15.3, where the increase in aggregate demand from AD_0 to AD_1 leads to a rise in the overall price level from P_0 to P_1 with no change at all in real output. An increase in the price level emanating from the demand side of the macroeconomy is sometimes referred to as **demand–pull inflation**.

But why should there be *persistent* increases in prices over time? One-off movements in either aggregate demand or aggregate supply may lead to one-off changes in the overall price level, but unless the movements continue in subsequent periods there is no reason to suppose that inflation will continue. One explanation for continuing inflation is provided by changes in the supply of money circulating in an economy.

Persistent inflation can take place only when the **money supply** grows more rapidly than real output. This can be shown in terms of aggregate demand and aggregate supply. If the money supply increases, firms and households in the economy find they have excess cash balances: that is, for a given price level they have more purchasing power than they expected to have, and are holding more money than they intended. Their impulse will thus be to increase their spending, which will cause the aggregate demand curve to move to the right. They will probably also save some of the excess, which will tend to result in lower interest rates — which will then reinforce the increase in aggregate demand. However, as the AD curve moves to the right, the equilibrium price level will rise, returning the economy to equilibrium.

If the money supply continues to increase, the process repeats itself, with prices then rising persistently. One danger of this is that people will get so accustomed to the process that they speed up their spending decisions, which simply accelerates the whole process.

To summarise, the analysis suggests that, although a price rise can be triggered on either the supply side or the demand side of the macroeconomy, persistent inflation can arise only through persistent excessive growth in the money supply, which can be seen in terms of persistent movements of the aggregate demand curve.

Costs of inflation

A crucial question is why it matters if an economy experiences inflation. The answer is that very high inflation gives rise to a number of costs.

The fact that firms have to keep amending their price lists raises the costs of undertaking transactions. These costs are often known as the *menu costs* of inflation; however, these should not be expected to be significant unless inflation really is very high. A second cost of very high inflation is that it discourages people from holding money because, at the very high nominal interest rates that occur when inflation is high, the opportunity cost of holding money becomes great. People therefore try to keep their money in interest-bearing accounts for as long as possible, even if it means making frequent trips to the bank — for which reason these are known as the *shoe-leather costs* of inflation.

This reluctance to use money for transactions may inhibit the effectiveness of markets. For example, there was a period in the early 1980s when inflation in Argentina was so high that some city parking fines had to be paid in litres of petrol rather than in cash. Markets will not work effectively when people do not use money and the economy begins to slip back towards a barter economy. The situation may be worsened if taxes or pensions are not properly indexed, so that they do not keep up with inflation. If pensions do not keep up with inflation, this means that pensioners lose out, and income inequality worsens. If tax revenue fails to keep up with government expenditure, then the authorities may be drawn into printing even more money in order to finance their spending plans.

These costs are felt mainly when inflation reaches the *hyperinflation* stage. This has been rare in developed countries in recent years, although many Latin American economies were prone to hyperinflation for a period in the 1980s, and some of the transition economies also went through very high inflation periods as they began to introduce market reforms; one example of this was the Ukraine, where inflation reached 10,000% per year in the early 1990s. Another example of hyperinflation is the African country of Zimbabwe, where inflation became almost impossible to measure because it was so rapid. The BBC claimed that inflation had reached 231,000,000% in 2008.

However, there may be costs associated with inflation even when it does not reach these heights, especially if inflation is volatile. If the rate of change of prices cannot be confidently predicted by firms, the increase in uncertainty may be damaging, and firms may become reluctant to undertake the investment that would expand the economy's productive capacity. This is important for economic growth.

Furthermore, as Chapter 5 emphasised, prices are very important in allocating resources in a market economy. Inflation may consequently inhibit the ability of prices to act as reliable signals in this process, leading to a wastage of resources and lost business opportunities.

It is these last reasons that elevated the control of inflation to being one of the central planks of UK government macroeconomic policy. However, it should be noticed

A Zimbabwean looks at a new 50 billion dollar bank note issued in 2009

that the target for inflation has not been set at zero. During the period when the inflation target was set in terms of RPIX (as explained in Chapter 10), the target was 2.5%; from 2004 the target for CPI inflation was 2%. The reasoning here is twofold. One argument is that it has to be accepted that measured inflation will overstate actual inflation, partly because it is so difficult to take account of quality changes in products such as PCs, where it is impossible to distinguish accurately between a price change and a quality change. Second, wages and prices tend to be sticky in a downward direction: in other words, firms may be reluctant to reduce prices and wages. A modest rate of inflation (e.g. 2%) thus allows relative prices to change more readily, with prices rising by more in some sectors than in others. This may help price signals to be more effective in guiding resource allocation.

Summary

- The control of inflation has been the major focus of macroeconomic policy in the UK since about 1976.
- Inflation can be initiated on either the supply side of an economy or the demand side.
- However, sustained inflation can take place only if there is also a sustained increase in money supply.
- High inflation imposes costs on society and reduces the effectiveness with which markets can work.
- Low inflation reduces uncertainty, and may encourage investment by firms.

Exercise 15.1

Suppose that next year inflation in the UK economy suddenly takes off, reaching 60% per annum — in other words, prices rise by 60% — but so do incomes. Discuss how this would affect your daily life. Why would it be damaging for the economy in the future?

The balance of payments

Lists of macroeconomic policy objectives invariably include equilibrium on the balance of payments as a key item. Unlike inflation and unemployment, it is not so obvious why disequilibrium in the balance of payments is a problem that warrants policy action.

Figure 15.4 shows the market for pounds relative to euros. Here, as we saw in Chapter 10, the demand for pounds arises from residents in the euro area wanting to buy UK goods, services and assets, whereas the supply arises from UK residents wanting to buy goods, services and assets from the euro area. If the exchange rate is at its equilibrium level, this implies that the demand for pounds (i.e. the foreign demand for UK goods, services and assets) is equal to the supply of pounds (i.e. the domestic demand for goods, services and assets from the euro area).

In a free foreign exchange market, the exchange rate can be expected to adjust in order to bring about this equilibrium position. Even under a fixed exchange rate system in which the government pledges to hold the exchange rate at a particular level, any discrepancy between the demand for and supply of pounds would have to be met by the monetary authorities buying or selling foreign exchange reserves. Thus, the overall balance of payments is always in equilibrium. So why might there be a problem?

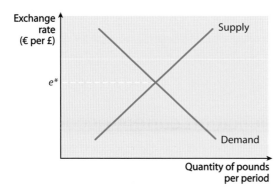

Figure 15.4 The market for pounds sterling

The problem arises not with the *overall* balance of payments, but with an imbalance between components of the balance of payments. In particular, attention focuses on the balance of the current account, which shows the balance of the trade in goods and services together with investment income flows and current transfers.

A deficit on current account

If the current account is in deficit, UK residents are purchasing more in imports of goods and services than the economy is exporting. Another way of expressing this is that UK earnings from exports are not sufficient to pay for UK imports. This is a bit like a household spending beyond its income, which can be sustained only by selling assets or by borrowing.

The concern for the economy is that a large and sustained deficit on the current account implies that the financial account must be experiencing a large and sustained surplus. This in turn means that the UK is effectively exporting assets. And this means that overseas residents are buying up UK assets, which in turn may mean a leakage of investment income in the future. Alternatively, overall balance could be achieved through the sale of foreign exchange reserves. This soaks up the excess supply of pounds that arises because UK residents are supplying more pounds in order to buy imports than overseas residents are demanding in order to buy UK exports.

However the current account deficit is financed, a large deficit cannot be sustained indefinitely. This begs the question of what is meant by a 'large' deficit. Figure 10.9 showed the current account balance as a percentage of GDP, which gives some idea of the relative magnitude of the deficit. This shows that, although the current account has been in deficit every year since 1984, the deficit has been less than 4.5% of GDP since 1990. This might be regarded as tolerable.

A critical issue is whether UK assets remain attractive to foreign buyers. Running a sustained deficit on current account requires running a surplus on financial account. If foreign buyers of UK assets become reluctant to buy, UK interest rates might have to rise in order to make UK assets more attractive. A by-product of this would be a curb in spending by UK firms and consumers. Given that part of this reduction in spending would have an impact on imports, this would begin to reduce the current account deficit.

One way in which the balance of payments is important from a policy perspective occurs when a government wishes to stimulate the economy, perhaps because it regards the level of unemployment as being excessive. An expansionary policy may be intended to increase domestic aggregate demand. However, in designing such a policy it is vital to remember that some of the increased demand will go not on domestic goods, but on imports, which is likely to dilute the effect of the expansion.

The initial effect of the financial crisis that began in the late 2000s was a reduction in the current account deficit for the UK, but this was short-lived, with the deficit increasing again in 2010.

Causes of a deficit on current account

The quantity of exports of goods and services from the UK depends partly on income levels in the rest of the world and partly on the competitiveness of UK goods and services, which in turn depends partly on the sterling exchange rate and partly on relative price levels in the UK and elsewhere. Similarly, the level of imports depends partly on domestic income and partly on the international competitiveness of UK and foreign goods and services.

This suggests that a fundamental cause of a deficit on the current account is a lack of competitiveness of UK goods and services, arising from an overvalued exchange rate or from high relative prices of UK goods and services. Alternatively, UK incomes may be rising more rapidly than those in the rest of the world.

Summary

- If the exchange rate is free to reach its equilibrium value, the overall balance of payments will always be zero.
- However, a deficit on the current account of the balance of payments must always be balanced by a corresponding surplus on the financial account.
- A persistent deficit on the current account means that in the long run domestic assets are being sold to overseas buyers, or that foreign exchange reserves are being run down. Neither situation can be sustained in the long run.
- A key cause of a deficit on the current account is the lack of competitiveness of domestic goods and services.

A balanced government budget

The financial crisis of the late 2000s focused attention on the government budget position. If the government spends more than it raises in revenue, the resulting deficit has to be financed in some way. The government deficit is the difference between public sector spending and revenues, and is known as the *public sector net cash requirement* (PSNCR). Part of the PSNCR is covered by borrowing, and the government closely monitors its *net borrowing*. Over time, such borrowing leads to *net debt*, which is the accumulation of past borrowing. The Labour government that was in power from 1997 to 2010 aimed to keep this below 40% — and was successful in achieving this until the financial crisis hit.

A major argument in favour of controlling the level of public sector net debt arose from a concern for the long-run effects of policy on spending and borrowing. It was argued that sustainable economic growth has to take into account the needs of future generations. The Labour government thus took the view that its current spending should be met out of current revenues, and that only investment for the future should be met through borrowing. In other words, future generations should not have to meet the cost of the consumption of the present population.

Figure 15.5 shows the impact of the financial crisis on this policy target. The crisis was first manifest in the banking system. In the UK, this began with the failure of Northern Rock in 2008, followed by problems in other commercial banks. The bail-out for these banks needed to safeguard the financial system led to the enormous increase in public sector net debt evident in Figure 15.5.

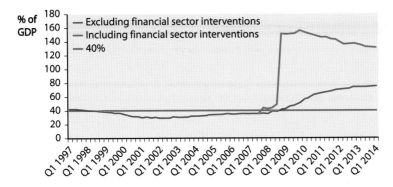

Figure 15.5 Public sector net debt in the UK, 1997–2014
Source: ONS

Concern for the environment

International externalities pose problems for policy design because they require coordination across countries. If pollution caused by the UK manufacturing sector causes acid rain elsewhere in Europe, the UK is imposing costs on other countries that are not fully reflected in market prices. Furthermore, there may be effects that are felt across generations. If the environment today is damaged, it may not be enjoyed by future generations — in other words, there may be intergenerational externality effects.

The growing concerns about global warming have drawn attention to the possible harm caused by rapid economic growth. It is this relationship between the environment and the rate of economic growth that has highlighted the macroeconomic dimension to concern for the environment, and led to growing calls for growth to be sustainable — as was pointed out in the previous chapter.

Income redistribution

The final macroeconomic policy objective to be considered concerns attempts to influence the distribution of income within a society. These may entail transfers of income between groups in society — that is, from richer to poorer — in order to protect the latter. Income redistribution may work through progressive taxation (whereby those on high incomes pay a higher proportion of their income in tax) or through a system of social security benefits such as the Jobseeker's Allowance and Income Support.

Causes of inequality

Some degree of inequality in the income distribution within a society is inevitable. People have different innate talents and abilities, and choose to undergo different types and levels of education and training, such that they acquire different sets of skills. Market forces imply that different payments will be made to people in different sectors of economic activity and different occupations. Income inequality also arises because of inequality in the ownership of assets. However, people in identical circumstances and with identical skills and abilities *may* receive identical income. This notion is sometimes known as *horizontal equity*, which most people would agree is desirable.

One category of policy measures is designed to encourage horizontal equity. Equal opportunities legislation tries to ensure that members of society do not suffer discrimination that might deny them equal pay for equal work, or equal access to employment. Nonetheless, there remain significant differences in earnings and employment between ethnic groups and between men and women.

Setting this aside, the key question remaining is the extent to which the government needs to intervene at the macroeconomic level in order to influence the distribution of income and protect vulnerable groups by redistributing from richer to poorer. Indeed, are there economic effects of inequality which suggest that redistribution of income is needed for reasons other than the purely humanitarian objective of alleviating poverty and protecting the vulnerable?

The costs of inequality

In a society where there is substantial inequality in the distribution of income, there are likely to be groups of people who are disadvantaged in various ways: for example, they may find it more difficult to obtain education for themselves or for their children. In the UK it remains the case that a lower proportion of students from low-income families go to university. It may also be that some potential entrepreneurs find it more difficult to obtain the credit needed to launch their business ideas.

Women demonstrating for equal pay in London in 2014 — there still remain significant differences in earnings between men and women

If this is so, it suggests that there are people in society who are inhibited from developing their productive potential — which in turn implies that economic growth in the future will be lower than it might be. This could provide a justification for redistributing income — or at least for trying to ensure that there is equality of opportunity for all members of society. However, it might be argued that redistribution can be taken too far. If the higher-income groups in society face too high a marginal tax rate on their income — in other words, if additions to income are very heavily taxed for the rich — this could remove their incentive to exploit income-earning opportunities, which could have a damaging impact on economic growth. Getting the right balance between protecting the vulnerable and providing appropriate incentives for enterprise is a tricky task for policy-makers.

Too much inequality may also lead to high crime rates and social discontent, which in turn may lead to political instability in a society. This could affect the security of property rights and inhibit economic growth.

There is some evidence that inequality has been widening in many countries in recent years. In particular, the way that technology has been progressing places a higher premium on skills, so that the gap between the earnings of skilled and unskilled workers has been widening.

Summary

- A balanced government budget is needed to avoid increases in the stock of public sector debt.
- There may be a need to moderate the pursuit of economic growth in order to protect the environment.
- Macroeconomic policy may also encompass the redistribution of income within society, on grounds of equity and also because extreme inequality may inhibit economic growth.

Exercise 15.2

Discuss which of the objectives of macroeconomic policy *you* think to be of most importance.

Conflicts between policy objectives

Having reviewed the main macroeconomic policy objectives, it should be clear that the designing of economic policy is likely to be something of a juggling act. This is especially so because there may be conflict and trade-offs between some of the targets of policy.

For example, it has already been noted that there may be a conflict between economic growth and the environment, so that the pursuit of economic growth may need to be tempered by concern for the environment. Policy must therefore be designed bearing in mind that there may be a trade-off between these two objectives — at some point, it could be that more economic growth is possible only by sacrificing environmental objectives, or that protecting the environment can only be achieved at the cost of a slower rate of economic growth.

Unemployment and inflation

This notion of trade-off between conflicting objectives applies in other areas too. One important trade-off was discovered by the New Zealand-born economist Bill Phillips. In 1958 Phillips claimed that he had found an 'empirical regularity' that had existed for almost a century and that traced out a relationship between the rate of unemployment and the rate of change of money wages. This was rapidly generalised into a relationship between unemployment and inflation (by arguing that firms pass on increased wages in the form of higher prices).

Figure 15.6 shows what became known as the **Phillips curve**. Although Phillips began with data, he also came up with an explanation of why such a relationship should exist. At the heart of his argument was the idea that, when the demand for labour is high (and unemployment is low), firms will be prepared to bid up wages in order to attract labour. To the extent that higher wages are then passed on in the form of higher prices, this would imply a relationship between unemployment and inflation: when unemployment is low, inflation will tend to be higher, and vice versa.

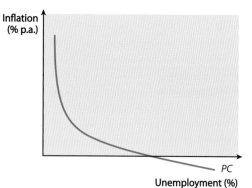

Figure 15.6 The Phillips curve

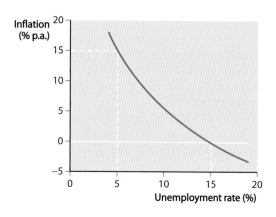

Figure 15.7 The Phillips curve inflation–unemployment trade-off

From a policy perspective, this suggests a trade-off between unemployment and inflation objectives. If the Phillips curve relationship holds, attempts to reduce the rate of unemployment are likely to raise inflation. On the other hand, a reduction in inflation is likely to result in higher unemployment. This suggests that it might be difficult to maintain full employment and low inflation at the same time. For example, Figure 15.7 shows a Phillips curve that is drawn such that to achieve an unemployment rate of 5%, inflation would need to rise to 15% per annum; this would not be acceptable these days, when people have become accustomed to much lower inflation rates. Having said that, as recently as 1990 the UK economy was experiencing inflation of nearly 10% and unemployment of 7%, which is not far from this example. To bring inflation down to zero would require an unemployment rate of 15%.

Nonetheless, the Phillips curve trade-off offers a tempting prospect to policy-makers. For example, if an election is imminent, it should be possible to reduce unemployment by allowing a bit more inflation, thereby creating a feel-good factor. After the election the process can be reversed. This suggests that there could be a political business cycle induced by governments seeking re-election. In other words, the conflict between policy objectives could be exploited by politicians who see that in the short run an electorate is concerned more about unemployment than inflation.

The 1970s provided something of a setback to this theory, when suddenly the UK economy started to experience both high unemployment and high inflation simultaneously, suggesting that the Phillips curve had disappeared. This combination of stagnation and inflation became known as **stagflation**. One possibility that was put forward was that the Phillips curve had not in fact disappeared, but had moved. Suppose that wage bargaining takes place on the basis of *expectations* about future rises in retail prices. As inflation becomes embedded in an economy, and people come to expect it to continue, those expectations will be built into wage negotiations. Another way of viewing this is that expectations about price inflation will influence the *position* of the Phillips curve.

Figure 15.8 shows some empirical data for the UK since 1986. From 1986 until 1993 (or even until 1995), the pattern seems consistent with a Phillips curve relationship. However, after that time inflation began to stabilise, and unemployment to fall — as if, with stable inflation, people's expectations have kept adjusting and allowed unemployment to fall. It could be that the Phillips curve shifted, showing a more typical pattern between 1999 and 2009, with points after 2010 again departing from the pattern.

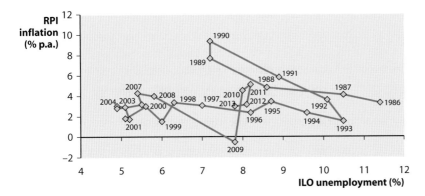

Figure 15.8 Unemployment and inflation in the UK, 1986–2013
Source: ONS

Economic growth and sustainability

It is clear that there may be conflict between achieving economic growth and protecting the environment. Nowhere is this better seen than in the case of China in the early part of the twenty-first century. China's persistently rapid growth has had consequences for the quality of the environment. Figure 15.9 shows one aspect of this — the emissions of carbon dioxide, which is one of the key so-called greenhouse gases that contribute to the process of global warming. The acceleration of emissions in China in the early 2000s is very apparent in the figure, and China became the largest emitter of carbon dioxide in 2005.

The link between economic growth and environmental degradation is a clear one. In the case of China, there are several aspects to notice. During the process of industrialisation, it is crucial to ensure that energy supplies keep pace with demand, as factories cannot operate effectively without reliable electricity and other energy sources. China has become the world's biggest oil importer (having overtaken the USA), and is the world's largest producer of coal, which accounts for some 80% of its total energy use — and is not the cleanest of energy technologies. It is also possible that inadequate regulation can add to environmental degradation, as in the case of the explosion at a chemical plant that caused pollution in the Songhua river; this not only affected the city of Harbin, but also affected part of Russia, which was downstream from the incident.

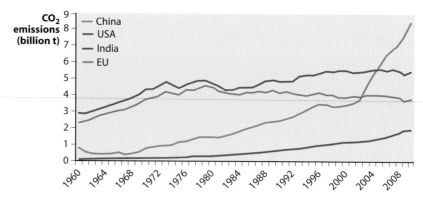

Figure 15.9 Carbon dioxide emissions
Source: World Bank

For economic growth to be sustainable, these environmental effects must be taken into account, or there is a real danger that the improved standard of living that flows from the growth process will be obtained only at the expense of the quality of life of future generations. This may require growth to be slowed in the short run in order to devote resources to the development of renewable and cleaner energy sources. However, it is politically and morally difficult to impose this on newly emerging societies in which there is widespread poverty, especially when the richer nations of the world continue to enjoy high standards of living while causing pollution of their own.

Economic growth and the current account of the balance of payments

In some circumstances, conflict can also arise between achieving economic growth and attaining equilibrium on the current account of the balance of payments. An increase in economic growth resulting in higher real incomes could lead to an increase in imports of goods and services, if UK residents spend a high proportion of their additional income abroad. This was seen as a major problem during the fixed exchange rate era of the 1950s and 1960s, when any deficit on the current account had to be met by running down foreign exchange reserves. This led to a 'stop–go' cycle of macroeconomic policy, where every time growth began to accelerate, the current account went into deficit, and policy then had to be adjusted to slow down the growth rate to deal with the deficit.

Exercise 15.3

Given the following list of policy objectives, discuss the possible conflicts that may arise between them, and how these might be resolved:

a low inflation

b low unemployment

c high economic growth

d a low deficit on the current account of the balance of payments

e maintenance of a high environmental quality

f equity in the distribution of income

Summary

- There may be conflict and trade-offs between policy objectives.
- The Phillips curve describes a trade-off between unemployment and the inflation rate, which suggests that in the short run, lower unemployment can be achieved only at the expense of a higher rate of inflation.
- There may also be a conflict between attaining a high rate of economic growth and sustainability, although some forms of growth may be less problematic in this respect.
- Economic growth may also lead to problems with the current account of the balance of payments in some circumstances.

Case study 15.1

Policy dilemmas

Imagine you are the economic leader of a country called Nowhere. The economy has been experiencing a period of prosperity, with low inflation and unemployment and steady economic growth. However, you are aware that you soon face re-election, and there are some problems on the horizon. Imports of consumer goods from China are growing rapidly, and unemployment has begun to creep up as some firms go out of business. Global commodity prices are rising, putting additional pressures on the prices of some key strategic imports. There is a growing environmental lobby putting pressure on you to reduce the environmental impact of economic growth and tackle carbon dioxide emissions. Inflation is towards the top end of the acceptable range. A house price bubble is threatening to burst.

Follow-up question

Discuss to which objective you should give top priority.

16 Macroeconomic policies

Previous chapters have shown that there may be a range of macroeconomic policy objectives, from economic growth, full employment, the control of inflation and equilibrium on the current account of the balance of payments, to concerns for the environment and for the distribution of income. Attention now turns to the sorts of policy that might be implemented to try to meet these targets. Policies at the macroeconomic level are designed to affect either aggregate demand or aggregate supply, and each will be examined in turn.

> **Learning objectives**
>
> After studying this chapter, you should:
> → understand and be able to evaluate policies that affect aggregate demand, including fiscal, monetary and exchange rate policies
> → understand and be able to evaluate policies that affect aggregate supply
> → be able to appraise the relative merits of policies applied to the demand and supply sides of the macroeconomy
> → be familiar with how macroeconomic policy has been conducted in the UK in recent years

Macroeconomic policy instruments

The government has three main types of policy instrument with which to attempt to meet its macroeconomic objectives:

1 *Fiscal policy*: the term 'fiscal policy' covers a range of policy measures that affect government expenditures and revenues through the decisions made by the government on its expenditure, taxation and borrowing. Fiscal policy is used to influence the level and structure of aggregate demand in an economy. As this chapter unfolds, you will see that the effectiveness of fiscal policy depends crucially on the whole policy environment in which it is utilised, and on the interrelationship between the three types of policy.

2 *Monetary policy*: this entails the use of monetary variables such as money supply and interest rates to influence aggregate demand. Remember that under a fixed exchange rate system, monetary policy becomes wholly impotent, as it has to be devoted to maintaining the exchange rate. So here again, the effectiveness of monetary policy will depend on the policy environment in which it is used.

3 *Supply-side policies*: such policies comprise a range of measures intended to have a direct impact on aggregate supply — specifically, on the potential capacity output of the economy. These measures are often microeconomic in character and are designed to increase output and hence economic growth.

Fiscal policy

The term **fiscal policy** covers a range of policy measures that affect government expenditures and revenues. For example, an expansionary fiscal policy would be seen as an increase in government spending (or reduction in taxes) that shifts the aggregate demand curve to the right.

In Figure 16.1 macroeconomic equilibrium is initially at the intersection of aggregate supply ($LRAS$) and the initial aggregate demand curve (AD_0), so that real output is at Y_0, which is below the full employment level of output at $Y^\star$. As government expenditure is one of the components of aggregate demand, an increase in such expenditure moves the aggregate demand curve from AD_0 to AD_1. In response, the economy moves to a new equilibrium, in which the overall price level has risen to P_1 but real output has moved to Y_1, which is closer to the full employment level $Y^\star$.

In this scenario, government expenditure is treated as an injection into the circular flow, and it will be reinforced by the multiplier effect. In the present context, an increase in government expenditure is effective in raising the level of real output in the economy, although some of the increase is dissipated in the form of an increase in the overall level of prices. Notice that, if the multiplier is relatively low, the reinforcement of fiscal policy through this route will also be relatively weak. Remember that the strength of the multiplier effect depends on the size of withdrawals from the circular flow. For example, if consumers have a high propensity to import, this will weaken the impact of the multiplier.

This kind of policy is effective only if the aggregate demand curve intersects the aggregate supply curve in the upward-sloping segment of AS. If the economy is already at the full employment level of output, an increase in aggregate demand merely results in a higher overall level of prices. This would also be the case with a vertical (monetarist) AS curve. The effective use of such policy thus requires policy-makers to have good information about the current state of the economy; in particular, they need to know whether the economy is at or below full employment. Otherwise, the results could be damaging for the price stability target. In other words, there is a danger that an expansionary fiscal policy will lead to inflation, but not affect output very much if the AS curve is relatively steep.

Looking more closely at what is happening, there are some forces at work that are acting to weaken the multiplier effect of an increase in government expenditure. One way in which this happens is through interest rates. If the government finances its deficit through borrowing, a side-effect is to put upward pressure on interest rates, which then may cause private sector spending — by households on consumption and by firms on investment — to decline, as the cost of borrowing has been increased. This process is known as the **crowding out** of private sector activity by the public sector. It limits the extent to which a government budget deficit can shift the aggregate demand curve, especially if the public sector activity is less productive than the private sector activity that it replaces.

The effect on the balance of payments must also be borne in mind. Part of an increase in aggregate demand is likely to be spent on imports, but there is no immediate reason for exports to change, so in the short run there is likely to be an increase in the current account deficit on the balance of payments.

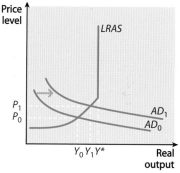

Figure 16.1 The use of fiscal policy

Although the focus of the discussion so far has been on government expenditure, fiscal policy also refers to taxation. In fact, the key issue in considering fiscal policy is the balance between government expenditure and government revenue, as it is this balance that affects the position of aggregate demand directly.

An increase in the **government budget deficit** (or a decrease in the **government budget surplus)** moves the aggregate demand curve to the right. The budget deficit may arise either from an increase in expenditure or from a decrease in taxation, although the two have some differential effects.

Chancellor of the Exchequer George Osborne announcing the 2014 budget — fiscal policy is used to influence aggregate demand in an economy

To a certain extent, the government budget deficit changes automatically, without active intervention from the government. If the economy goes into a period of recession, unemployment benefit payments will rise, thereby increasing government expenditure. At the same time, tax revenues will decrease, partly because people who lose their jobs no longer pay income tax. In addition, people whose income is reduced — perhaps because they no longer work overtime — also pay less tax. This is reinforced by the progressive nature of the income tax system, which means that people pay lower rates of tax at lower levels of income. Furthermore, VAT receipts will fall if people are spending less on goods and services.

The opposite effects will be evident in a boom period, preventing the economy from overheating. For example, tax revenues will tend to increase during the boom, and the government will need to make fewer payments of social security benefits. By such **automatic stabilisers**, government expenditure automatically rises during a recession and falls during a boom.

In the past there was a tendency for governments to use fiscal policy in a discretionary way in order to influence the path of the economy. A government might use its discretion to increase government expenditure to prevent a recession, for example. Indeed, there have been accusations that governments have sometimes, in some countries, used fiscal policy to create a 'feel-good' factor in the run-up to a general election, by allowing the economy to boom as the election approaches, only to impose a clampdown afterwards.

Such intervention has been shown to be damaging to the long-run path of the economy because of its effect on inflation. Furthermore, there are other problems with using fiscal policy in this way. Apart from anything else, it takes time to collect data about the performance of the economy, so its current state is never known for certain. Because the economy responds quite sluggishly to policy change, it is often the case that the policy comes into effect just when the economy is already turning around of its own accord. This is potentially destabilising, and can do more harm than good.

Exercise 16.1

Use *AD/AS* analysis to consider the effect of an expansionary fiscal policy on the equilibrium level of real output and the overall price level. Undertake this exercise with different initial positions along the aggregate supply curve, first analysing an economy that begins at full employment and then one in which aggregate demand creates an equilibrium that is below full employment. Discuss the differences in your results.

Fiscal policy in the UK

If the government spends more than it raises in revenue, the resulting deficit has to be financed in some way. As explained in the previous chapter, the government deficit is the difference between public sector spending and revenues, and when the deficit is covered by net borrowing, the result is an accumulation of debt. The financial crisis led to a substantial increase in public sector net debt (see Figure 15.5). The turmoil of the late 2000s required rethinking of fiscal policy. The Coalition government responded to the high level of public sector net debt by imposing cuts in public expenditure, in an attempt to reduce the debt.

Balance between the public and private sectors

Even if the size of the budget deficit limits the government's actions in terms of fiscal policy, there are still decisions to be made about the overall balance of activity in the economy. A neutral government budget can be attained either with high expenditure and high revenues, or with relatively small expenditure and revenues. Such decisions affect the overall size of the public sector relative to the private sector. Over the years, different governments in the UK have taken different decisions on this issue — and different countries throughout the world have certainly adopted different approaches.

In part, such issues are determined through the ballot box. In the run-up to an election, each political party presents its overall plans for taxation and spending, and typically they adopt different positions as to the overall balance. It is then up to those voting to give a mandate to whichever party offers a package that most closely resembles their preferences.

Direct and indirect taxes

Fiscal policy, and taxation in particular, has not only been used to establish a balance between the public and private sectors of an economy. Taxation remains an important weapon against some forms of market failure, and it also influences the distribution of income. In this context, the choice between using direct and indirect taxes is important.

Remember that direct taxes are taxes levied on income of various kinds, such as personal income tax. Such taxes are designed to be progressive and so can be effective in redistributing income: for example, a higher income tax rate can be charged to those earning high incomes. In contrast, indirect taxes — taxes on expenditure, such as VAT and excise duties — tend to be regressive. As poorer households tend to spend a higher proportion of their income on items that are subject to excise duties, a greater share of their income is taken up by indirect taxes. Even VAT can be regressive if higher-income households save a greater proportion of their incomes.

Indirect taxes can be targeted at specific instances of market failure; hence the high excise duties on such goods as tobacco (seen as a demerit good) and petrol (seen as damaging to the environment because of the externality of greenhouse gas emissions).

Exercise 16.2

Discuss the extent to which the major British political parties adopt differing stances towards establishing a balance between the private and public sectors: in other words, the extent to which each is 'high tax/high public spending' or 'low tax/low public spending'. Analyse the economic arguments favouring each of the approaches.

Summary

- Fiscal policy is concerned with the decisions made by government about its expenditure, taxation and borrowing.
- As government expenditure is an autonomous component of aggregate demand, an increase in expenditure will shift the *AD* curve to the right.
- If *AD* intersects *AS* in the vertical segment of *AS*, the effect of the increase in aggregate demand is felt only in prices.
- However, if the initial equilibrium is below the full employment level, the shift in *AD* will lead to an increase in both equilibrium real output and the overall price level.
- In fact, it is net spending that is important, so government decisions on taxation are also significant.
- The government budget deficit (surplus) is the difference between government expenditure and revenue.
- The budget deficit varies automatically through the business cycle because of the action of the automatic stabilisers.
- If the government runs a budget deficit, it may need to undertake net borrowing, which over time affects the net debt position.
- Direct taxes help to redistribute income between groups in society, but if too progressive they may dampen incentives to provide effort.

Key term

monetary policy the decisions made by government regarding monetary variables such as the money supply or the interest rate

Monetary policy

Monetary policy is the approach currently favoured by the UK government to stabilise the macroeconomy. It entails the use of monetary variables such as the money supply and interest rates to influence aggregate demand.

It is important at the outset to realise that it is not possible to control money supply and interest rates simultaneously and independently. Firms and households choose to hold some money. They may do this in order to undertake transactions, or as a precaution against the possible need to undertake transactions at short notice. In other words, there is a *demand for money*. However, in choosing to hold money they incur an opportunity cost, in the sense that they forgo the possibility of earning interest by purchasing some form of financial asset.

This means that the interest rate can be regarded as the opportunity cost of holding money; put another way, it is the price of holding money. At high rates of interest, people can be expected to choose to hold less money, as the opportunity cost of holding money is high. *MD* in Figure 16.2 represents such a money demand curve. It is downward sloping.

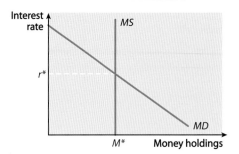

Figure 16.2 The demand for money

Suppose the government wants to set the money supply (*MS*) at *M**★** in Figure 16.2. This can be achieved in two ways. If the government controls the supply of money at *M**★*, then equilibrium will be achieved only if the interest rate is allowed to adjust to *r**★*. An alternative way of reaching the same point is to set the interest rate at *r**★* and then allow the money supply to adjust to *M**★*. The government can do one or the other — but it cannot set money supply at *M**★* and hold the interest rate at any value *other than r**★* without causing disequilibrium.

A problem with attempting to control the money supply directly is that the complexity of the modern financial system makes it quite difficult to pin down a precise definition or measurement of money. For this and other reasons, the chosen instrument of monetary policy is the interest rate.

Through the interest rate, monetary policy affects aggregate demand. At higher interest rates, firms undertake less investment expenditure and households undertake less consumption expenditure. This is partly because when the interest rate is relatively high, the cost of borrowing becomes high and people are discouraged from borrowing for investment or consumption purposes. There are reinforcing effects that operate through the exchange rate if UK interest rates are high relative to elsewhere in the world. If the exchange rate rises because of high interest rates, this will reduce the competitiveness of UK goods, and attract inflows of financial capital ('hot money'). This interaction of the money supply, interest rates and the exchange rate makes policy design a complicated business.

Suppose the government believes that the economy is close to full employment and is in danger of overheating. Overheating could push prices up without any resulting benefit in terms of higher real output. An increase in the interest rate will lead to a fall in aggregate demand, thereby relieving the pressure on prices. This is illustrated in Figure 16.3, where the initial position has aggregate demand relatively high at AD_0, real output at the full employment level Y_0 and the overall price level at P_0. The increase in interest rates shifts aggregate demand to the left, to AD_1. Real output falls slightly to Y_1 and the equilibrium price level falls to P_1.

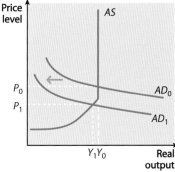

Monetary policy in the UK

One of the first steps taken by Tony Blair's government after it was first elected in 1997 was to devolve the responsibility for monetary policy to the

Figure 16.3 The use of monetary policy

Bank of England, which was given the task of achieving the government's stated inflation target, initially set at 2.5% for RPIX inflation. As noted in Chapter 10, the target was amended in 2004, when it became 2% per annum as measured by the CPI.

According to this arrangement, the **Monetary Policy Committee** (MPC) of the Bank of England sets interest rates in such a way as to keep inflation within 1 percentage point (either way) of the 2% target for CPI inflation. If it fails to achieve this, the Bank has to write an open letter to the chancellor of the exchequer to explain why the target has not been met. Such a letter became necessary for the first time in March 2007, when CPI inflation touched 3.1%. This was to become the norm in the early 2010s, although inflation came back into the target range in mid-2012.

Operationally, the MPC sets the interest rate which it pays on commercial bank reserves. This is known as the **bank rate**. The commercial banks tend to use this rate as their own base rate, from which they calculate the rates of interest that they charge to their borrowers. Thus, if the MPC changes the bank rate, the commercial banks soon adjust the rates they charge to borrowers. These will vary according to the riskiness of the loans — thus credit cards are charged at a higher rate than mortgages — but all the rates are geared to the base rate set by the commercial banks, and hence indirectly to the bank rate set by the Bank of England.

Figure 16.4 summarises the **transmission mechanism of monetary policy**. The Bank of England sets the bank rate, which affects both market rates of interest and the exchange rate. These in turn influence other asset prices and expectations about the future, and the degree of confidence among economic agents. These factors then affect both domestic and net external demand, and hence aggregate demand. An increase (decrease) in aggregate demand puts upward (downward) pressure on prices, thus affecting the amount of domestic inflationary pressure, while at the same time changes in the exchange rate have an effect on import prices, which also affect inflation. As you can see, there is a long and complicated chain of linkages that enables a change in monetary policy to affect inflation.

Figure 16.4 The transmission mechanism of monetary policy

Note: For simplicity, this figure does not show all interactions between variables, but these can be important.

Source: Bank of England

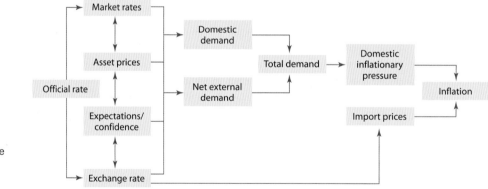

Although inflation remained within the 1% band from 1997 right through until March 2007, the following period showed a much more unstable pattern. Figure 16.5 shows bank rate and the inflation rate since 2004.

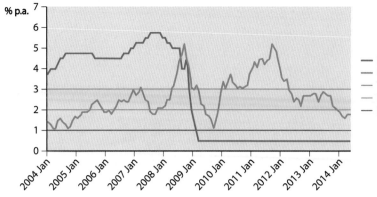

Figure 16.5 UK bank rate and the inflation target, 2004–14

Sources: ONS, Bank of England

Monetary policy until 2007

In the first part of this period, inflation seemed under control. The association between the bank rate and movements in the inflation rate is not very close. This is partly because the relationship between them is obscured by other influences. It also reflects the fact that the MPC took into account a wide range of factors when deciding whether to move the bank rate or to leave it as it was in the previous month. At a typical meeting, the MPC would discuss financial market developments, the international economy, money, credit, demand and output, and costs and prices. In other words, the inflation target was considered within the broad context of developments in various aspects of the economy. All of these factors would be discussed in some detail before a decision on the bank rate was taken. In the interests of transparency, the minutes of the regular MPC meetings are published on the internet — you can see them at **www.bankofengland.co.uk**. This means that you can readily check recent developments in the economy.

The underlying idea is that by influencing the level of aggregate demand, the MPC could affect the rate of inflation so as to keep it within the target range, although the effects of a change in the bank rate are not likely to happen immediately. One reason for giving the Bank of England such independence was that it increases the credibility of the policy. If firms and households realise that the government is serious about controlling inflation, they will have more confidence in its actions, and will be better able to form expectations about the future path the economy will take. In particular, firms will be encouraged to undertake more investment, and this will have a supply-side effect, shifting the aggregate supply curve to the right in the long run.

When inflation began drifting towards 3% in early 2007, you can see that bank rate was increased in an attempt to bring inflation down — and you can also see that this did indeed happen during 2007, with inflation coming back down to around 2%.

A Monetary Policy Committee briefing led by Mark Carney, Governor of the Bank of England

Monetary policy from 2008

Inflation accelerated during 2008, but the MPC considered that this was likely to be a temporary surge. The financial crisis began to bite, and with many commercial banks finding themselves in trouble and being bailed out, the MPC was all too aware that credit in the economy was tight. Instead of raising bank rate in order to curb inflation, the MPC reduced bank rate, and by early 2009 bank rate had reached 0.5%, which was effectively as low as it could go.

Key term

quantitative easing a process by which liquidity in the economy is increased when the Bank of England purchases assets from banks

With the economy heading into recession, reducing bank rate in order to boost aggregate demand was no longer an option, and the Bank of England instead turned to a policy that became known as **quantitative easing**. This was a process by which the Bank of England purchased assets (mainly government securities) from the banks, thus affecting the banks' liquidity positions. The aim of this was to encourage lending by the banks, which had dried up during the credit crunch, thus making it difficult for firms to borrow. Quantitative easing was effectively a way in which the Bank of England could increase money supply in order to boost aggregate demand and help to counter the recession. Bank rate remained at 0.5%, even though inflation accelerated beyond its target during parts of 2011. You can see this very clearly in Figure 16.5.

Meanwhile, in the USA, the Federal Reserve (the USA's central bank) has also taken measures to safeguard the financial system, by expanding the amount of credit provided to the banking system and by increasing the money supply by purchasing long-term securities. The crisis had begun in the housing market, and mortgage lenders Fannie Mae and Freddie Mac were nationalised in 2008.

The Great Depression of the interwar years

Some parallels can be drawn with the Great Depression of the period between the two world wars. A stock market crash in New York in 1929 spread rapidly to the UK. World trade contracted and unemployment in the UK rose to 3 million. Figure 16.6 shows the unemployment rate in the UK in this period. Unemployment rose after the First World War, and the process of recovery and adjustment to peace was slow. Unemployment through much of the 1920s was around 10%. However, this rocketed as the depression took hold, and only fell below the level of the early 1920s as the Second World War approached.

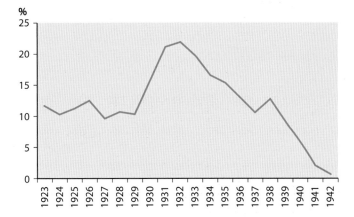

Figure 16.6 Unemployment in the UK during the Great Depression
Source: ONS

The government of the day was committed to classical economic ideas, and was determined to maintain balance in the government budget. In order to achieve this, it cut government spending. In addition, the theory suggested that unemployment would only fall if labour costs were reduced so that employers would be prepared to hire labour. They thus encouraged people to take wage cuts. This had the effect of reducing aggregate demand. As these measures took effect, the economy fell further into depression. It was in this context that Keynes published his *General Theory*, which pointed to the multiplier effects of autonomous spending, and suggested that a boost to aggregate demand could assist the recovery. This debate was renewed in the late 2000s, when some commentators argued for cuts in public expenditure in order to reduce the burden of public sector debt, whilst others advocated a stimulus to aggregate demand to speed the recovery.

Exercise 16.3

Visit the Bank of England website and check whether the MPC chose to change the interest rate at its most recent meeting. Take a look at the minutes of the meeting to see the factors that were considered in taking this decision.

Study tip

Make sure that you practise drawing the *AD/AS* diagram and manipulating the curves to illustrate the alternative policy approaches, using both monetarist and Keynesian shapes for the *AS* curve.

Summary

- Monetary policy is concerned with the decisions made by government on monetary variables such as money supply and the interest rate.
- A change in the interest rate influences the level of aggregate demand through the investment expenditure of firms, the consumption behaviour of households and (indirectly) net exports.
- In 1997, the Bank of England was given independent responsibility to set interest rates in order to meet the government's inflation target.
- The Monetary Policy Committee (MPC) of the Bank sets the bank rate, which is then used as a base rate by the commercial banks and other financial institutions.
- Giving independence to the Bank of England in this way increases the credibility of monetary policy.
- If this encourages investment, there may be a long-run impact on aggregate supply.
- With the financial crisis of the late 2000s a new approach was needed.
- Quantitative easing was introduced to help manage an economy in recession.

Policies affecting aggregate supply

Key terms

supply-side policies
a range of measures intended to have a direct impact on aggregate supply — and specifically the potential capacity output of the economy

market-based policies
policies that rely on allowing markets to work more freely and providing incentives for enterprise and initiative

interventionist policies
policies by which the government intervenes to stimulate aggregate supply

Demand-side policies have been aimed primarily at stabilising the macroeconomy in the relatively short run, but with the intention of affecting aggregate supply in the long run, by influencing firms' and households' confidence in the future path of the economy. However, there are also a number of policies that can be used to influence the aggregate supply curve directly. These **supply-side policies** can take two forms. The classical economists recommend **market-based policies**, based on freeing up markets, and providing improved incentives for enterprise and initiative. Others advocate **interventionist policies** by which the authorities should intervene directly in ways that stimulate aggregate supply.

Chapter 12 indicated that the position of the long-run aggregate supply curve depends primarily on the quantity of factor inputs available in the economy, and on the efficiency of those factors. Supply-side policies thus focus on affecting these determinants of aggregate supply in order to shift the AS curve to the right.

Investment is one key to this in the long run, and this chapter has already shown how demand-side policies that stabilise the macroeconomy in the short run may also have long-run effects on aggregate supply by encouraging investment.

Education and training

Investment is also needed in human capital, and one form that this can take is education and training. An important supply-side policy therefore takes the form of encouraging workers (and potential workers) to undertake education and training to improve their productivity.

This takes place partly through education in schools and colleges in preparation for work. It is important, therefore, that the curriculum is designed to provide key skills that will be useful in the workplace. However, this does not mean that all education has to be geared directly to providing skills; problem-solving and analytical skills, for example, can be developed through the study of a wide range of disciplines.

Adult education is also important. When the structure of the economy is changing, retraining must be made available to enable workers to move easily between sectors and occupations. This is crucial if structural unemployment is not to become a major problem. For example, workers displaced from manufacturing industry are likely to need retraining to develop new skills if they are to find jobs in the service sector. Workers released from agriculture in a less developed country will need training before they can become productive members of the industrial workforce.

The market may not deliver the training that is necessary, as firms will not invest in training workers unless they can be sure that they will not be poached by competitors once they have completed their training. The government may thus need to provide incentives. One particular concern in the UK has been the number of young people aged between 16 and 18 who are not in education, employment or training (known as NEETs). At the end of 2011 it was estimated that 9.9% of 16–18-year-olds were in this category. The Department for Education has piloted a number of initiatives to tackle this problem.

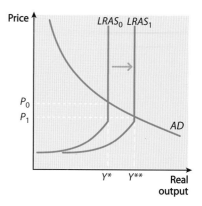

Figure 16.7 shows how such a policy can affect the aggregate supply curve, moving it from $LRAS_0$ to $LRAS_1$. This move enables an increase in the potential output capacity of the economy, and it need not be inflationary. Indeed, in the figure the overall price level falls from P_0 to P_1 following the shift in aggregate supply, with real output increasing from $Y^\star$ to $Y^{\star\star}$.

Figure 16.7 A shift in aggregate supply

An apprentice working on the wing of an Airbus A320 — education and training is an investment in human capital

Flexibility of markets

The rationale for including retraining as a supply-side policy rests partly on the argument that this provides for greater flexibility in labour markets, enabling workers to switch between economic activities to improve the overall workings of the economy.

There are other ways of improving market flexibility. One is to limit the power of the trade unions, whose actions can sometimes lead to inflexibility in the labour market, either through resistance to new working practices that could improve productivity or by pushing up wages so that the level of employment is reduced.

Indeed, maintaining the flexibility of markets is one way in which the macroeconomic stability promoted by disciplined fiscal and monetary policy can improve aggregate supply. Macroeconomic stability enables price signals to work more effectively, as producers are better able to observe changes in relative prices. This can promote allocative efficiency.

Unemployment benefits

An important influence on labour supply, particularly for low-income workers, is the level of unemployment benefit. If unemployment benefit is provided at too high a level, it may inhibit labour force participation, in that some workers may opt to live on unemployment benefit rather than take up low-skilled (and low-paid) employment. In such a situation, a reduction in unemployment benefit may induce an increase in labour supply, which again will move the aggregate supply curve to the right.

However, such a policy needs to be balanced against the need to provide protection for those who are unable to find employment. It is also important that unemployment benefit is not reduced to such a level that workers are unwilling to leave their jobs to search for better ones, as this may inhibit the flexibility of the labour market.

Promotion of competition

A recurrent theme in many policy statements from governments and international organisations like the World Bank and IMF has been the importance of promoting competition. There are several reasons why this might be important in influencing aggregate supply. One possibility is that a monopoly firm in a market may be able to use its market power to maximise profits by restricting output and raising price. If such a firm is forced to confront competition from other firms, it may have to temper its use of that market power, and reduce price in order to sell more output and protect its market share. The intensity of competition may also affect firms' willingness to improve productivity. It is possible that in some markets the lack of competition will produce complacency, depriving firms of the incentive to operate at maximum efficiency. This was especially true in the UK for the formerly nationalised industries such as electricity and gas supply, which were widely believed to have operated with widespread productive inefficiency.

Policies that promote competition may thus lead to improvements in both allocative and productive efficiency. This was one of the motivations behind the privatisation drive that began in the 1980s under Margaret Thatcher. However, it should be noted that there is not wholesale agreement on whether privatisation has invariably led to improvements in efficiency in industries such as the railways and water supply.

Incentive effects

Similarly, there are dangers in making the taxation system too progressive. Most people accept that income tax should be progressive — that is, that those on relatively high incomes should pay a higher rate of tax than those on low incomes — as a way of redistributing income within society and preventing inequality from becoming extreme. However, there may come a point at which marginal tax rates are so high that a large proportion of additional income is taxed away, reducing incentives for individuals to supply additional effort or labour. This could also have an effect on aggregate supply. Again, however, it is important to balance these incentive effects against the distortion caused by having too much inequality in society.

Supply-side policies can be important in shifting aggregate supply and enabling an increase in the productive capacity of the economy. However, it is important to remember that these are policies for the long term, and many of them take time to become effective. For each of the policies discussed, there may be problems in evaluating the magnitude of the effects that can be anticipated.

Study tip

Be prepared to evaluate each of these alternative supply-side policies. In other words, be aware of their strengths and weaknesses.

Exercise 16.4

For each of the supply-side policies outlined above, discuss whether they are market-based or interventionist.

Exercise 16.5

For each of the following policies, identify whether it is an example of fiscal, monetary or supply-side policy. Discuss how each policy affects either aggregate demand or aggregate supply (or both), and examine its effects on equilibrium real output and the overall price level:

a an increase in government expenditure

b a decrease in the rate of unemployment benefit

c a fall in the rate of interest

d legislation limiting the power of trade unions

e encouragement for more students to attend university

f provision of retraining in the form of adult education

g a reduction in the highest rate of income tax

h measures to break up a concentrated market

i an increase in the bank rate

Summary

- Policies to shift the aggregate supply curve may be used to encourage economic growth.
- Education and training can be viewed as a form of investment in human capital, which is designed to improve the productivity of workers.
- Measures to improve the flexibility of labour and product markets may lead to an overall improvement in productivity and thus may affect aggregate supply.
- Promoting competition can also improve the effectiveness of markets in the economy.
- Incentive effects are an important influence on aggregate supply. For example, if unemployment benefits are set too high, this may discourage labour force participation. An over-progressive income taxation structure can also have damaging incentive effects.

Conflicts in the implementation of policy

With the range of policy instruments available to the authorities, it is important to investigate whether they will be mutually compatible, or whether conflict could arise between them.

It was seen earlier that fiscal policy may have implications for the interest rate. If the government increases its expenditure, perhaps with the intention of improving infrastructure or subsidising education and training, one side-effect could be to require higher borrowing and push up interest rates. This could in turn lead to an inflow of hot money, affecting the exchange rate and the competitiveness of domestic goods in international markets. This suggests that there may be circumstances in which fiscal and monetary policy may come into conflict, given that interest rates are a key part of the transmission of monetary policy. Consequently, a way must be found of coordinating fiscal and monetary policy. This is naturally difficult to do, given the way that the Bank of England is intended to act independently of the government in conducting monetary policy in order to meet the inflation target.

An important aspect of monetary policy since 1997 has been the delegation of responsibility for it to the Bank of England's Monetary Policy Committee. The rationale for this is that the effectiveness of monetary policy depends quite heavily on people's expectations. It operates much more effectively if people believe it is going to work, because then they will amend their behaviour more quickly, speeding up the process of adjustment to equilibrium. By delegating responsibility for monetary policy to the Bank of England, the credibility of policy is enhanced and it thereby becomes more effective, and the government cannot be tempted to buy election success by increasing spending financed through the inflationary printing of money.

In creating a stable macroeconomic environment, the ultimate aim of monetary policy is not simply to keep inflation low, but to improve the confidence of decision-makers. This will encourage firms to invest in order to generate an increase in productive capacity — which will stimulate economic growth and create an opportunity to improve living standards. In other words, the hope is to stimulate investment and thus enable an increase in the productive capacity of the economy by shifting the AS curve. The problem is that high interest rates may be needed at times in order to achieve the inflation target — and high interest rates will tend to discourage investment. The financial crisis seemed to herald a new era of monetary policy, with interest rates so low that they became ineffective as a policy instrument. This reflected the problems that emerged in the financial sector, which necessitated a change in the focus of policy and a new regulatory framework. This will be explored in Book 2.

Designing the policy mix

In the context of the aggregate demand/aggregate supply model, it is clear that demand- and supply-side policies are aimed at achieving rather different objectives.

The primary rationale for monetary and fiscal policies is to stabilise the macroeconomy. In this, fiscal policy has come to take on a subsidiary role, supporting monetary policy. This was not always the case, and there have been periods in which fiscal policy has been used much more actively to try to stimulate the economy. There are still some countries in which such policies are very much the vogue: for example, it has been suggested that much of Latin America's problem with high inflation has stemmed from fiscal indiscipline, although not all Latin American economists accept this argument. The fact that fiscal policy has not always been well implemented does not mean that such policies cannot be valuable tools — but it does warn against their misuse.

In the UK, the use of monetary policy with the support of fiscal policy seemed to be working reasonably effectively in the early years of the twenty-first century, at least until the financial crisis pushed the economy into recession.

Supply-side policies aim to influence aggregate supply directly, either raising the supply of factor inputs or improving productivity and efficiency.

The design and conduct of economic policy may therefore be seen as an elaborate balancing act. Differing policy objectives need to be prioritised, as in many cases there may be conflict between them. Choices have to be made about the balance to be achieved between fiscal, monetary and supply-side policies.

The consensus view in the early part of the twenty-first century was that fiscal policy should be used to achieve the desired balance between the public and private sectors. Monetary policy should be devoted to meeting the government's inflation target in order to create a stable macroeconomic environment; this would then encourage growth and enable improvements in the standard of living. Problems arose when fiscal policy was forced into action in order to protect the financial system, resulting in an escalation of public debt.

In the long run, supply-side policies are perhaps the most important, as these contribute to raising efficiency and increasing the productive capacity of the economy. The keynote in policy design lies in enabling markets to operate as effectively as possible.

Summary

- Demand-side and supply-side policies have different objectives.
- Demand-side policies such as fiscal and monetary policy are aimed primarily at stabilising the economy.
- Supply-side policies are geared more towards promoting economic growth.
- There are situations in which different policies have conflicting impacts on the economy.
- The financial crisis and the recession that it triggered have led to some rethinking of the relationship between monetary and fiscal policy, with fiscal policy being invoked to protect the financial system.

Case study 16.1

Macroeconomic policy instruments

Governments in a modern economy have three main types of policy instrument for affecting the macroeconomy — monetary policy, fiscal policy and supply-side policy. Monetary policy is dedicated to ensuring the stability of the economy by influencing aggregate demand. Fiscal policy is used to maintain balance in the economy between public and private sectors and between present and future generations of citizens. Supply-side policies are dedicated to affecting the productive capacity of the economy, operating primarily through microeconomic incentives.

Follow-up question

Explain these distinctions between the types of policy instrument. Which type do you consider to be of most importance?

Theme 2 key terms

actual economic growth the rate of growth of GDP in a period

aggregate demand the total amount of spending on goods and services produced in an economy during a period of time

aggregate demand (*AD*) curve the relationship between the level of aggregate demand and the overall price level; it shows planned expenditure at any given possible overall price level

automatic stabilisers effects by which government expenditure adjusts to offset the effects of recession and boom without the need for active intervention

average propensity to consume the proportion of income that households devote to consumption

balance of payments a set of accounts showing the transactions conducted between residents of a country and the rest of the world

bank rate the interest rate that is set by the Monetary Policy Committee of the Bank of England in order to influence inflation

business cycle a phenomenon whereby GDP fluctuates around its underlying trend, following a regular pattern

capital productivity a measure of output per unit of capital

circular flow of income, expenditure and output a model of the economy which shows the movement of goods and services between households and firms and their corresponding payments in money terms

claimant count of unemployment the number of people claiming the Jobseeker's Allowance each month

consumer price index (CPI) a measure of the general level of prices in the UK, the rate of change of which has been used as the government's inflation target since January 2004

consumption total planned household spending

consumption function the relationship between consumption and disposable income; its position depends on the other factors that affect how much households spend on consumption

cost-push inflation inflation initiated by an increase in the costs faced by firms, arising on the supply side

crowding out a process by which an increase in government expenditure crowds out private sector activity by raising the cost of borrowing

cyclical unemployment unemployment that arises during the downturn of the economic cycle, such as a recession

deflation a fall in the average level of prices (negative inflation)

demand-deficient unemployment unemployment that arises because of a deficiency of aggregate demand in the economy, so that the equilibrium level of output is below full employment

demand-pull inflation inflation initiated by an increase in aggregate demand

depreciation the fall in value of physical capital equipment over time as it is subject to wear and tear

discouraged workers people who have been unable to find employment and who are no longer looking for work

disinflation a fall in the rate of inflation

disposable income the income that households have to devote to consumption and saving, taking into account payments of direct taxes and transfer payments

economically inactive those people of working age who are not looking for work, for a variety of reasons

exchange rate the price of one currency in terms of another

export-led growth a strategy for achieving rapid economic growth through the promotion of export activity

fiscal policy decisions made by the government on its expenditure, taxation and borrowing

frictional unemployment unemployment associated with job search (i.e. people who are between jobs)

full employment a situation where people who are economically active in the workforce and are willing and able to work (at going wage rates) are able to find employment

GNI per capita the average level of GNI per head of population

government budget deficit (surplus) the balance between government expenditure and revenue

gross domestic product (GDP) a measure of the economic activity carried out in the domestic economy over a period

gross national income (GNI) GDP plus net income from abroad

human capital the stock of skills and expertise that contribute to a worker's productivity; it can be increased through education and training

ILO unemployment rate a measure of the percentage of the workforce who are without jobs, but are available for work, willing to work and looking for work

in employment people who are either working for firms or other organisations, or self-employed

income a flow concept — the amount of income that is earned during a period

index number a device for comparing the value of a variable in one period or location with a base observation (e.g. the consumer price index measures the average level of prices relative to a base period)

inflation the rate of increase in the average price level in an economy

injections where money flows into the circular flow in the form of investment, government spending and exports

interventionist policies policies by which the government intervenes to stimulate aggregate supply

investment expenditure undertaken by firms to add to the capital stock

involuntary unemployment situation arising when an individual who would like to accept a job at the going wage rate is unable to find employment

Keynesian School a group of economists who believed that the macroeconomy could settle at an equilibrium that was below full employment

labour productivity a measure of output per worker, or output per hour worked

macroeconomics the study of the interrelationships between economic variables at an aggregate (macroeconomic) level

marginal propensity to consume (MPC) the proportion of additional income devoted to consumption

marginal propensity to import the proportion of additional income that is spent on imports of goods and services

marginal propensity to save (MPS) the proportion of an increase in disposable income that households would devote to saving

marginal propensity to tax the proportion of additional income that is taxed

marginal propensity to withdraw the proportion of additional income that is withdrawn from the circular flow – the sum of the marginal propensities to save, import and tax

market-based policies policies that rely on allowing markets to work more freely and providing incentives for enterprise and initiative

Monetarist School a group of economists who believed that the macroeconomy always adjusts rapidly to the full employment level of output, and that monetary policy should be the prime instrument for stabilising the economy

monetary policy the decisions made by government regarding monetary variables such as the money supply or the interest rate

Monetary Policy Committee the body within the Bank of England responsible for the conduct of monetary policy

money supply the quantity of money in the economy

multiplier the ratio of a change in equilibrium real income to the autonomous change that brought it about; it is defined as 1 divided by the marginal propensity to withdraw

natural rate of output the long-run equilibrium level of output to which monetarists believe the macroeconomy will always tend

natural rate of unemployment the unemployment rate that will exist when the economy is in long-run equilibrium

net investment gross investment *minus* depreciation

nominal value the value of an economic variable based on current prices, taking no account of changing prices through time

output gap the difference between actual real GDP and potential real GDP

Phillips curve an empirical relationship suggesting that there is a trade-off between unemployment and inflation

potential economic growth an expansion in the productive capacity of the economy

productivity a measure of the efficiency of a factor of production

quantitative easing a process by which liquidity in the economy is increased when the Bank of England purchases assets from banks

real value the value of an economic variable, taking account of changing prices through time

recession occurs when GDP falls for two or more consecutive quarters

retail price index (RPI) a measure of the average level of prices in the UK

seasonal unemployment unemployment that arises in seasons of the year when demand is relatively low

short-run aggregate supply curve a curve showing how much output firms would be prepared to supply in the short run at any given overall price level

stagflation a situation describing an economy in which both unemployment and inflation are high at the same time

structural unemployment unemployment arising because of changes in the pattern of economic activity within an economy

supply-side policies a range of measures intended to have a direct impact on aggregate supply – and specifically the potential capacity output of the economy

sustainable development 'development that meets the needs of the present without compromising the ability of future generations to meet their own needs' (Brundtland Commission, 1987)

total factor productivity the average productivity of all factors, measured as the total output divided by the total amount of inputs used

transmission mechanism of monetary policy the process by which a change in the bank rate affects inflation

underemployment where an individual is employed in a second-choice occupation or is only able to work part-time but would like to work full-time

unemployed people who are economically active but are not in employment

voluntary unemployment situation arising when an individual chooses not to accept a job at the going wage rate

withdrawals where money flows out of the circular flow in the form of savings, taxation and imports

wealth a stock concept – the accumulation of assets, such as property or shares

workforce people who are economically active – either in employment or unemployed

9 Measures of economic performance: economic growth

1 Which of the following is **not** an indicator of macroeconomic performance?

A Economic growth

B The balance of payments

C Food prices

D The rate of inflation

2 Which of the following statements is true?

A Volume measures provide an invaluable way of observing how much output is produced in an economy in a year

B Measuring macroeconomic variables in nominal terms tends to understate the extent to which they are growing through time

C Measuring macroeconomic variables at constant prices provides an indicator of their real values

D The value of an index number for the current period is calculated as the base year value divided by the current year value, multiplied by 100

3 Suppose that a good that last year was priced at £20 is now priced at £22. What is the percentage change in the price since last year?

A 1.1%

B 10%

C 2%

D 22%

4 Suppose that a good that last year was priced at £20 is now priced at £22. Calculate an index number to represent the price in the current year using last year as the base year.

A 101.1

B 102

C 110

D 122

5 Explain the difference between nominal and real GDP.

6 *'China's rate of economic growth fell from 9.2% in 2011 to 7.8% in 2012.'*
With reference to the above statement, explain what happened to China's output between 2011 and 2012.

7 Using a production possibility diagram, show the impact of economic growth.

8 Table 1

Country	GDP per capita at PPP ($)	HDI
Mali	1,300	0.463
Chile	16,100	0.805
Norway	53,300	0.943

a With reference to the information in Table 1, explain the term 'GDP per capita based on purchasing power parity'.

b Discuss two reasons why GDP is inadequate as a measure of changes in living standards over time.

10 Measures of economic performance: inflation, unemployment and the balance of payments

1 In an economy, the consumer price index changed from 150 in one year to 180 in the following year. What was the rate of inflation?

  A 20%

  B 15%

  C 10%

  D 30%

2 An economy has a working population of 500,000, of whom 400,000 are economically active. There are 50,000 unemployed people. What is the percentage unemployment rate?

  A 5.6%

  B 10%

  C 12.5%

  D 20%

3 Explain how the consumer price index measure of inflation is constructed.

4 Outline three differences between the claimant count and ILO measures of unemployment.

5 How will each of the following affect the exchange rate of the pound sterling?

  a A fall in demand for UK goods and services

  b A decrease in the demand for foreign imports

6 a *'Brazil's rate of inflation fell from 6.5% in 2011 to 5.5% in 2012.'*

  With reference to the above statement, explain what happened to the level of prices in Brazil between 2011 and 2012.

  b 'In November 2012, the UK had a balance of trade deficit in goods and services of £3.5bn whereas it was £3.7bn in October 2012.'

  With reference to the above statement, explain what happened to the UK's balance of trade in goods and services between 2011 and 2012.

11 Aggregate demand

1 Which one of the following does **not** help to explain why the aggregate demand curve slopes downwards?

  A When the overall level of prices is relatively low, the purchasing power of income is relatively high

  B When prices are relatively low, this raises the real value of households' wealth

  C When prices are relatively low, government expenditure will tend to be relatively high

  D When prices are relatively low compared with the rest of the world, the international competitiveness of domestic goods will be strong

2 Aggregate demand

At the time of the economic crisis in 2008 and 2009, the savings ratio increased significantly from just over 2% to nearly 9%. Consumer expenditure fell, following falling real incomes, even though interest rates were reduced to just 0.5%. Investment has remained low since 2009 because confidence has been low — partly because of the crisis in the euro zone, which has resulted in slow growth in those countries. Despite a 25% fall in the value of sterling, the UK's trade balance remained in deficit and between 2011 and 2012 the deficit increased from £23bn to £37bn.

Although house prices fell sharply in 2009 and again slightly in 2011, there is an expectation that they will increase from 2013.

a With reference to the information provided, outline the components of aggregate demand.

b Discuss **two** factors which influence consumer expenditure.

c Explain the impact on aggregate demand of the change in the UK's trade deficit between 2011 and 2012.

d Examine the likely effect of a fall in the rate of interest on investment.

e Apart from the rate of interest, explain **two** factors which influence the level of investment.

f Analyse how the increase in the savings ratio in 2008–09 will affect the value of the multiplier.

g Assess the likely effects of an increase in house prices on aggregate demand.

12 and 13 Aggregate supply/National income and macroeconomic equilibrium

1 Which of the following statements are correct?
   A The short-run aggregate supply curve shows how much output firms would be prepared to supply in the short run at any given overall price level
   B The aggregate supply curve can be derived by adding up the supply curves from individual markets in the economy
   C An important influence on the position of the aggregate demand curve is the availability and effectiveness of factors of production
   D There is no difference between short-run and long-run aggregate supply

2 Which of the following describes the change in macroeconomic equilibrium in the short run if there is an increase in aggregate demand?
   A An increase in the overall price level and an increase in real output
   B An increase in the overall price level and a decrease in real output
   C A decrease in the overall price level and an increase in real output
   D A decrease in the overall price level and a decrease in real output

3 Which of the following describes the change in macroeconomic equilibrium in the short run if there is a decrease in aggregate supply?

    A An increase in the overall price level and an increase in real output

    B An increase in the overall price level and a decrease in real output

    C A decrease in the overall price level and an increase in real output

    D A decrease in the overall price level and a decrease in real output

4 Figure 1 shows an economy in two different equilibrium positions, having moved from real output Y_1 and price level P_1 to real output Y_2 and price level P_2. Which of the following combinations of shifts in the curves could have led to this result?

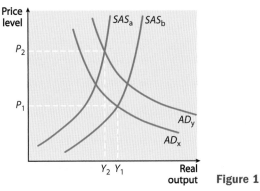

Figure 1

    A A rightward shift in short-run aggregate supply together with a rightward shift in aggregate demand

    B A rightward shift in short-run aggregate supply together with a leftward shift in aggregate demand

    C A leftward shift in short-run aggregate supply together with a rightward shift in aggregate demand

    D A leftward shift in short-run aggregate supply together with a leftward shift in aggregate demand

5 Aggregate supply

Since the 1980s, economic policy in many countries has focused on measures to increase aggregate supply. Despite the success of some of these measures, supply-side shocks such as increases in oil prices have often had the reverse effect. More recently, many governments have been trying to reduce their budget deficits by making steep cuts in public expenditure which, in the case of the UK, have fallen heavily on capital expenditure.

    A Explain the meaning of 'aggregate supply'.

    B With the aid of an aggregate demand and aggregate supply diagram, assess the likely effects on real output and the price level of a sharp increase in oil prices.

    C Analyse the effect of a decrease in public expenditure on real output and the price level. Refer to the multiplier in your answer.

    D Productivity has increased more rapidly in the USA than in the UK. Illustrating your answer with an aggregate demand and aggregate supply diagram, analyse the effect of this increase in US productivity.

14 Economic growth

1 Which of the following statements is true?
   A Low inflation impedes the effective operation of markets
   B Reducing unemployment increases the potential productive capacity of the economy
   C Disequilibrium on the balance of payments has similar effects on the macroeconomy regardless of whether there is a fixed or floating exchange rate system in operation
   D Economic growth is often regarded as the most crucial policy objectives for an economy

2 Output gap

Since 2008 the UK has had a negative output gap and this is not expected to close until after 2017. In the time between the beginning of 2009 and the end of 2012 there were 10 quarters of negative economic growth. Some environmentalists regard this as a benefit because rapid growth is often associated with environmental degradation.

In contrast, China has experienced rapid economic growth over the last decade, helped by a very high savings ratio and high rates of investment, including considerable amounts of foreign direct investment. This has contributed to a rapidly expanding manufacturing sector and export-led growth. However, there has been a sharp increase in income inequality.

Table 2

Country	2004	2005	2006	2007	2008	2009	2010	2011	2012
China	9.1	9.1	10.2	11.9	9.0	9.1	10.3	9.2	7.7
United Kingdom	3.2	1.9	2.8	3.1	0.7	−5.0	1.3	0.7	0.0

   a Illustrating your answer with a diagram, explain what is meant by an output gap.
   b Examine possible consequences of a negative output gap.
   c Explain what is meant by export-led growth.
   d Assess two factors which might enable a country to achieve a rapid rate of economic growth.
   e To what extent do the costs of economic growth outweigh the benefits?

15 Macroeconomic policy objectives

1 The UK's rate of inflation was 5.2% in September 2011 but by December 2012 it had fallen to 2.7% as measured by the consumer price index (CPI).
   a Why do the weights used in the CPI have to be changed each year?
   b Explain two consequences of a fall in the rate of inflation.

2 In February 2008, the claimant count measure of unemployment was 710,000 but by December 2012 it was 1.56 million. During the same period, ILO unemployment rose from 1.62 million to 2.49 million.
   a Explain how unemployment is measured using the claimant count method and the ILO method.
   b Explain two costs of the increase in unemployment.

3 Assess the possible impact on income distribution of a recession.

4 Assess the likely economic effects of an increase in real income on a country's current account of the balance of payments.

5 To what extent might economic growth conflict with three other economic objectives?

16 Macroeconomic policies

1 Analyse the likely effect of increasing public expenditure on interest rates and private sector investment. Refer to 'crowding out' in your response.

2 Explain how expansionary fiscal policy in the form of higher expenditure on infrastructure might have an impact on aggregate demand and aggregate supply. Illustrate your answer with an appropriate diagram.

3 To what extent might an increase in the size of public expenditure as a proportion of GDP be likely to increase the rate of economic growth?

4 Assess the effect of a reduction in interest rates and an increase in the quantity of money on unemployment and the rate of inflation.

5 Evaluate the effect of expansionary monetary policy on the value of the pound, real output and the rate of inflation.

6 Fiscal and monetary policy

Following the financial crisis in 2008, many governments and central banks used monetary and fiscal policy in order to prevent a depression. In the UK the Bank of England slashed the base interest rate to 0.5% and embarked on a policy of quantitative easing. Increased public expenditure and tax cuts resulted in an increase in the fiscal deficit. As a result of these policies and the perceived weakness of the UK economy, the value of the pound depreciated by about 25%. Some economists have suggested that new supply-side policies need to be adopted to improve long-term growth and living standards.

a Distinguish between fiscal and monetary policy.

b Explain what is meant by 'an increase in the fiscal deficit'.

c Illustrating your answer with an aggregate demand and aggregate supply diagram, evaluate the likely effect of an increase in the budget deficit on the level of real output and on the price level. Refer to the multiplier in your answer.

d Assess the effectiveness of supply-side policies as a means of decreasing the level of unemployment.

e Evaluate policies which a government might use to raise living standards.

Index

Page numbers in **bold** refer to **key term definitions**.